Snow Camping and Mountaineering

Snow Camping and Mountaineering

Edward A. Rossit

Illustrated by Charles P. Conley

Funk & Wagnalls   NEW YORK

To my father,

To Jeff, Erik, and Randy,

To Chuck and Eddie,

To Bobby and Kenny,

And, last but not least,

To unforgettable Nancy

Contents

Preface

When I think back to the cold weather camping I've done, two different nights come to my mind.

I remember clearly what was the coldest and most miserable night I ever spent outdoors. It was on a deer hunting trip many years ago in November.

I had no tent and I slept on the bare ground. I slept fully clothed except for my boots, which I had sense enough to remove. I had two thick and supposedly warm Hudson Bay woolen blankets, and I arranged them on opposite sides of myself so that each was folded once with two layers of blanket beneath me and two over me.

To cut the force of the cold wind, I slept on the ground in an open spot between shrubs and bushes which grew to a height of two or three feet. The ground was frozen earth interspersed with small rocks and pebbles, each seeming harder, colder, and more pointed than a diamond.

My campsite was near the top of a large hill which fell off on one side in rocky cliffs and which rolled more gradually into the valleys below on the other three sides. It was a wilderness, empty of people except for other occasional deer hunters, and consisted of open country with scrub pine and laurel and berry thickets alternating with thickly forested areas of birch, maple, oak, sycamore, tamarack, spruce, and balsam pine trees.

It had been beautiful country during the daytime, even in its frozen state. The hills had faded into the distant haze and a pale sun had shone through occasionally, followed by gray periods of cloudiness, at which times a very fine snow, almost like misted ice, had blown through the air.

But that night the cold stars shone brightly and, as I slowly froze in my blankets, I listened to the wind rattling the crisp brown leaves near me. The bushes did nothing to stop the wind, and it seemed my blankets could not stop it either, nor could all the clothes I was wearing.

I didn't really sleep until almost dawn, which comes late at that time of year, and when I finally dozed off, it was into a tense sleep in which the muscles of my body bunched in upon themselves in an effort to keep warm.

I was up and making a fire before the sun came up. I had eyes puffed from the cold and from lack of sleep, and I was so stiff that it was several hours later, after a warm breakfast and after considerable exercise, before I could move normally again.

How cold was it that night? It was 20 degrees above zero Fahrenheit, or 12 degrees below freezing. To an Eskimo this might have seemed warm, but to me it was just about as cold as I ever again wanted to get.

I remember another night, more recently, which I spent sleeping outdoors. I travelled down to Mount Shasta in northern California in March, 1967, to make a late winter climb on that beautiful mountain.

I put down my pack and put up my small two-man tent on a level spot in the snow at an elevation of 10,320 feet. After I set the tent, I crawled inside onto a neoprene-coated nylon floor which, although strong and waterproof, was about as thin as a human hair. I unrolled an ensolite pad, a quarter of an inch thick, and I unrolled my four-pound down sleeping bag onto the pad. After a hearty hot supper I took off all my clothes except for my cotton shorts and slid down into the bag. There, high on the mountain, I went to sleep on the snow. I was warm and cozy and slept like a baby, and I awoke rested and refreshed. It was altogether one of the most restful and comfortable nights I've spent outdoors.

How cold was it on that night? As measured on a good thermometer, it was 4 degrees above zero Fahrenheit, or 28 degrees below freezing. Not only that, it had been a stormy night with strong winds blowing the frigid air in tent-flapping gusts.

What had happened in the intervening years to make it possible for me to be cozy and comfortable even though the temperature was near zero?

Many things had happened. I had spent many nights outdoors during this period, and every time I went hunting, every time I went camping, every time I went out to climb a mountain, I learned a little more. In addition, as clothing and equipment wore out or grew old, I replaced these things with new and different clothing and new and different equipment. In short, I was gaining direct experience every time I went out into the cold woods and mountains and lived there. In addition, I met other mountaineers and other winter campers, and by observing how they dressed, what kind of equipment they had, and how they went about the business of surviving in winter conditions without benefit of solid roof and walls, I was able to absorb the benefit of their independent and cumulative experiences.

These were the things which made the difference—equipment and knowledge of how to use this equipment effectively. It is my hope that in the pages which follow I will be able to pass on useful information about these things. If I enable one man to avoid one night of frigid misery in the outdoors, I will have succeeded.

Edward A. Rossit

Seattle, Washington
September, 1969

Snow Camping and Mountaineering

1] The Nature of Cold Weather

THE CLIMATE of the earth varies from hot at the equator to freezing cold in the polar regions. The change in climate is gradual. At latitude 20 degrees it is not as cold as at 40 degrees, and at 40 degrees it is not as cold as at 60 degrees. The regions of the poles, at latitude 90 degrees, are approximately the coldest regions of earth.

However, there is an exception to this rule of gradual change. Elevation makes a difference. As we go up from sea level the climate changes from warm to cold, and this holds true even in tropical regions. The change in elevation makes much more of a difference than the change in latitude. You would have to travel hundreds of miles northward to encounter an average temperature reduction of 50 degrees Fahrenheit. But if you travel vertically—up the side of a mountain for example—you will find this 50-degree difference in a matter of several thousands of feet. In effect, gaining elevation will give you the same changes in climate as travelling northward, and will give it to you much more rapidly. This same chilling is experienced in airplanes flying at high elevations, and makes possible a warm or even hot day in the northern regions of the United States while snow lingers on mountaintops in California and in Mexico.

The rate of temperature change with increase in elevation can be determined by various complicated formulas which involve factors such as moisture content of the air, adiabatic lapse rate, barometric pressure, and others. The greater the moisture content of the air and the greater the barometric pressure, the less the temperature change will be with increased elevation. Conversely, the greatest drop in temperature, as elevation increases, takes place in dry air and with low barometric pressure. Unfortunately, for purposes of using these rules, low barometric pressures are frequently associated with highly moisturized air.

The following may be used as a general rule: Temperature drops 4 degrees Fahrenheit for each increase in elevation of 1,000 feet. Thus, going 10,000 feet up a mountain will produce an average temperature drop of 40 degrees. This holds true at all times of the year—both summer and winter.

Leaving a hot summer temperature of 90 degrees and going 10,000 feet up a mountain will bring you into a cool and refreshing 50 degrees climate. However, if you go up the same mountain when it is a cool 50 degrees at the bottom, in spring or fall, then the same gain in elevation of 10,000 feet will bring you into an arctic climate of 10 degrees, or 22 degrees below freezing.

To refine the rule of thumb a bit further, if there is very dry air, the temperature will drop one degree for every 180-foot rise in elevation. If the air is very moist, the temperature will drop one degree for every 360-foot rise in altitude.

From the foregoing it can be seen that if a person lives in relatively low areas, his only chance to do winter camping will be in the wintertime. However, if he has mountains near where he lives, he will have the opportunity of experiencing arctic climate conditions even in the summertime if he goes up into the mountains. For mountaineers, therefore, because of the essentially arctic conditions which prevail at high altitudes, the use of winter equipment and the knowledge of how to use this equipment is an absolute requirement.

Wind and Snow

The two elements common to cold weather with which the

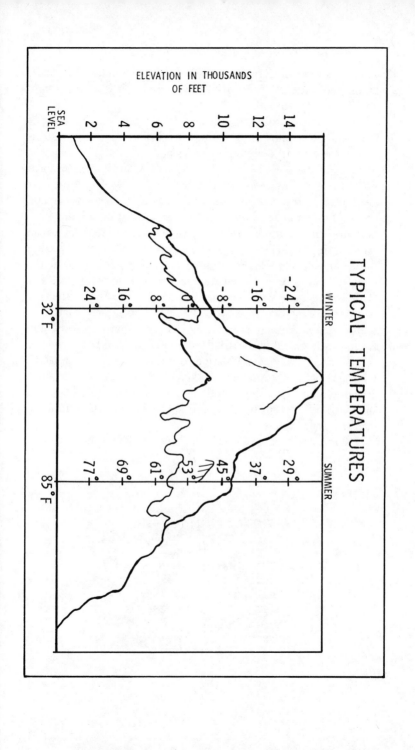

camper is most concerned are wind and precipitation. Precipitation may take the form of rain or snow. If it is cold enough, it will always be snow.

As a general rule for the winter camper, you "mind the wind and go in snow." Or, to put it another way, "the wind is your enemy and the snow is your friend."

Temperature alone is a physical condition. It can be measured on a thermometer and stated in degrees Fahrenheit or Centigrade. How you feel as a human being does not depend on the temperature alone, but on a combination of the temperature and wind conditions. At 30 degrees Fahrenheit, a man standing in a calm spot may feel quite warm if he is wearing sufficient clothing. But turn on a 30-mile-an-hour wind at the same temperature and even though the thermometer does not change, the man will become chilled. This cooling effect of wind (the same one that cools the engine in your car) can be quite severe. Among arctic travellers, northern Indians, and Eskimos, the wind is regarded as a hateful, spiteful force, and rightfully so. The combination of a very low temperature with a very high wind can quickly kill men and animals alike.

Snow, on the other hand, is your friend. Paradoxically, snow is like a warm blanket, and it can protect the outdoorsman from the killing wind.

Eskimos can easily stand the lowest of temperatures as

long as no wind blows. They go about their business of hunting, fishing, cooking, eating, sleeping, etc., spending a good part of their time outdoors. But no matter where they are or what they are doing, if an arctic blizzard begins to blow, they go into their igloos and remain there until the wind has stopped blowing.

If Eskimos are in the process of travelling when a storm begins, they will stop immediately and build igloos on the spot. Then, snug in their warm snow houses, they will let the frigid wind blow outside until the storm ends. They know full well that snow is their friend and wind is their enemy.

All arctic animals get out of the wind. Eskimo dogs curl themselves up into tight furry balls on the lee side of the igloo and let the drifting snow bury them completely, thus protecting themselves from the wind. Other arctic animals actually dig tunnels down into the snow to escape from the wind.

In the Swiss army, where much military deployment is done high in the snow-covered Alps, considerable training is devoted to digging caves into the snow on a mountainside so that troops can survive arctic winds high in the mountains. (In Chapter 9 of this book, digging snow caves is covered in detail.)

As a general rule, with the right kind of equipment, a man can camp and live comfortably outdoors no matter how cold it gets, providing he stays in one place. He can easily survive no matter how hard the wind blows, if he gets out of the wind and stays put. Also as a general rule, nobody should attempt travel or any kind of movement in frigid weather if there is a high wind blowing.

Cold wind is a killer! The movement of cold air can quickly weaken a strong man and reduce him to a confused, stumbling, uncoordinated, and helpless victim. When a person succumbs to cold wind, the term usually used is "died of exposure." It is amazing, frequently, how little time it takes to die of exposure. If the debilitating effects of strong, cold winds are applied to a man who is exhausted from physical exertion, then the time required to freeze him is even shorter, hence the greater need to stay put, and out of the wind to avoid adding the element of fatigue to an already dangerous situation.

Wind is always the enemy in any winter situation. Paradoxically, this is true even when the wind is warm. A prerequisite to keeping warm outdoors in snow and ice is dryness. If a man can stay dry, this will help considerably in keeping him warm. However, a strong and steady warm wind can turn a dry wintery landscape into a sloppy mush, full of low-lying ice-water ponds, slush fields, and areas of crashing snow and ice, where sodden snow clumps fall from high branches and heavy icicles thaw and let go of branches and cliffs and suddenly drop to the ground. Spring thaws are a dangerous time for this reason. Travel over glazed ice is slow and dangerous, and this condition frequently prevails in the spring as warm thaws alternate with freezing weather. This is the time to seek higher and drier ground.

Weather Variability

Mountain weather is erratic. On level ground and at lower elevations, the seasons follow one another in stately majesty, and such weather is predictable, even if only in general terms. The Fourth of July is generally hot and New Year's Day is generally freezing.

But up in the mountains a hot, calm period may be followed an hour later by a furious, freezing snowstorm. Even a change in position of a few yards may bring the climber out of a warm, gentle breeze into gusty cold winds blowing with hurricane force.

Thus, the mountaineer is especially vulnerable to weather changes—much more so than the camper at lower elevations. The mountaineer must accordingly be prepared for these changes and must have with him all the clothing and equipment necessary for comfort and survival under these varying conditions. The snow and ice camper who is outdoors in the winter has a somewhat easier time of it, as, for example, he is not likely to suddenly face freezing winds after having worked up a sweat in relatively warmer air.

Psychological Warmth

Weather is a combination of physical conditions such as wind, temperature, humidity, barometric pressure, all of which can be accurately measured with instruments. But as soon as man enters the picture, a new element is brought in, and this is the psychological reaction of man to his environment. A man psychologically prepared for wintry weather is already a man who is "warmer" than one who is not so prepared. If a man feels cold at 32 degrees Fahrenheit, then he is, in fact, cold. If another man feels warm at 22 degrees Fahrenheit, then he is, in fact, warm.

Some of this reaction may be caused by physiological conditions such as the feeling of well-being after a good night's sleep, or the extreme fatigue felt after much prolonged exertion. Other parts of this reaction may be purely psychosomatic in origin, such as feelings of loneliness, fear, insecurity, or inadequacy in a vast and grand but impersonal mountain panorama. Another human being may feel peace, contentment, and complete self-confidence in the same situation, or even fierce pride or exultation or euphoria as he stands on a high crag and surveys the landscape laid out below him.

This psychological reaction to the elements is at least as important as physical reaction to them, and man's physical reaction is determined just as much, if not more, by his mental attitude as by the clothes he is wearing.

This is probably why an experienced camper or an experienced mountaineer will inevitably be more comfortable in a given situation than someone new at the game. The old-timer will already have the peace of mind and confidence that come from sure knowledge of past successes in similar situations. Feeling secure in his situation, he will be capable of increased awareness of the beauty of nature all around him.

Thus, for a human being, keeping warm outdoors in

wintry conditions is not just a matter of clothing and equipment alone, although these things are important; it is also a
matter of concentrating the mind not on the temperature but
on the landscape in all its fascinating wintry varieties. Unques-
tionably, when considering the nature of cold weather, it is
also necessary to consider the attitude of the person who is out
in it, and no consideration is complete which omits this factor.

2] Clothing for Snow and Ice Camping

THE HUMAN BODY functions properly only within a very narrow range of temperatures. The average of these temperatures is 98.6 degrees Fahrenheit (37 degrees Centigrade). If body temperature departs more than a few degrees from this average, vital functions may become inpaired.

Fortunately, the human body has built-in mechanisms which assist in regulating this temperature. When we do physical labor, thus speeding up body processes, we produce heat as a by-product. If this heat were not immediately removed from the body, its temperature would rise quickly to fever levels, and higher.

Under these circumstances the body will exude liquids through pores in the skin. As these liquids evaporate, the heat consumed in the process of evaporation cools the skin. The amount of blood in circulation near the skin increases, and this lowers blood temperature. The cooled blood then circulates through the body where it again picks up more heat in much the same way as the cooled water in an automobile radiator recirculates back to the engine to become heated again. Thus heat is brought from the interior of the body to the surface where it is dissipated.

In a cold situation, natural muscular tensions cause the metabolic rate to increase. As the body functions at a more rapid rate, more heat is generated, and this warms the body.

Unfortunately, the range of temperatures through which the naked body can adjust is a narrow one. If the temperature goes much over 100 degrees Fahrenheit or much below 50 degrees, the human body may not be able to adjust quickly or adequately enough to prevent impairment of body functions.

This temperature range can be extended downward considerably, however, by the use of clothes as insulation.

The basic thing to keep in mind about clothing is that clothing acts as thermal insulation; that is, clothes serve to retain body heat in the immediate vicinity of the body. This fact is important to remember because no clothing, no matter how "warm" it is, can actually produce any heat at all. The body produces its own heat through body chemistry involving the release of calories obtained from food consumed.

Food and cooking for snow and ice camping are discussed in Chapter 7 of this book. Briefly, we can say here that heat is a form of energy and that the best sources of this energy are high-energy foods such as butter, oleomargarine, and fatty meats.

But assuming that the arctic weather camper has eaten correctly and well, and that his body is producing a satisfactory level of heat, his problem then is to keep warm by not allowing this heat to escape rapidly into the air. This brings us to the subject of insulation and conduction of heat.

From a physical standpoint, there is no such thing as cold. There is only heat or the absence of heat. Heat is a physical property. A refrigerator cools its contents not by injecting cold into itself, but by removing heat from itself. In the absence of any contravening factors, heat tends to dissipate itself; that is, heat tends to flow away from wherever it is concentrated.

Heat may be transferred in several ways. It may radiate away from its source, or it may be conducted away. When a substance conducts heat rapidly it is called a good conductor. If a substance conducts heat slowly, it is called a poor conductor, or an insulator.

For example, if you were to hold a copper rod and put one end in a fire, you would very soon have to let go of the other end, since copper is a good conductor of heat. If you didn't let go, you would burn your hand. Conversely, you could hold a stick of wood in a fire until one end burned without feeling any heat at all in the other end. This is so because wood is an insulator, a poor conductor of heat.

Obviously we would not prepare ourselves for winter camping by putting on a suit made of copper foil. Such a garment would quickly conduct body heat away from us and transfer it to the surrounding cold air. We would, instead, look for clothing which insulates.

It has been determined that one of the best practical ways of insulating heat is to surround the heat source with still air. Still air provides excellent insulation. But if air is given any space at all in which to move, it will do so and therefore will not remain "still." To prevent air movement, the insulator must be able to compartmentalize air into tiny separated units.

Warm air expands. When it expands it occupies more space than cold air, making warm air less dense than cold air. In any air space large enough for appreciable air movement, the heavier cold air will sink to the bottom of the space and the lighter warm air will rise to the top of the space. The warm air will then be able to give off heat where it is concentrated while the cold air will absorb heat in its own area. The cooled-off warm air will then contract, grow heavier, and descend again. The warmed-up cold air will expand, grow lighter, and rise again. This air moves then in what is called a convection current. A convection current of air will tend to distribute heat evenly in the space which it occupies.

But if such air spaces are made very small, the weight differential between warm and cold air becomes insignificant, and convection currents can be eliminated.

Any compartmentalization of air will have this effect. Therefore all cloth, with the small air spaces contained between the warp and the woof, tends to act as insulation. This insulation is provided by any single layer of fabric. In addition, if two or more layers of clothing are worn, additional still air or "dead" air is captured between the layers of clothing.

It follows from this that two layers of fabric will insulate better than one layer twice as thick. If two light sweaters, for example, are made of the same material as one heavier sweater, and if the combined weight of the two lighter sweaters is equal to the weight of the one heavier sweater, then the two light sweaters will provide better insulation than the one heavier sweater.

This applies to all clothing and may be reduced to the following general rule: *More layers of lighter clothing insulate better than fewer layers of heavier clothing.*

This rule can be misunderstood and misused, however, unless we keep in mind that it applies only to clothes made of the same materials and cut in the same way. For example, two cotton shirts each weighing a few ounces will not insulate as well as one long-sleeved woolen sweater weighing over a pound. In this case the heavier, thicker, long-sleeved sweater will obviously be able to do a better insulating job just because there is so much more of it.

Down Clothing

Another factor of great importance which must always be kept in mind when considering clothing for winter camping and for snow and ice mountaineering is that all clothing weighs something.

If the winter camper is a hunter or fisherman who will never be far from his car and who will not travel any great distance on foot, then weight does not become an important factor. The camper can weigh himself down with many heavy layers of clothing and wrap himself in several blankets and robes and stay warm in very cold air. However, if he is a mountaineer who will hike a great distance from his car, then weight will be a consideration in choosing his clothing, which is of at least the same importance as its warmth. In these circumstances, the weight of clothing will have to be held to a minimum consistent with having sufficient insulation to keep warm.

The most efficient insulation per unit of weight is down. Down is the soft breast feathers of birds, especially aquatic birds, and most especially of northern aquatic birds such as geese and ducks. Down from aquatic birds has the additional and desirable quality of being able to allow moisture to pass through itself while continuing to hold entrapped air.

The quality which makes down such an excellent insulator is called "loft." Loft is a springiness, so to speak, which causes the individual down fibers to push themselves away from each other. Put a heavy weight on a down pillow and it will be compressed. Remove the weight and the pillow will slowly rise to its former height, like a balloon being slowly inflated. Because down has this property of loft, garments insulated with down give great bulk with very little weight.

It is not the down itself which does the insulating, but the still air which the down is able to entrap because it has loft. Down gives a garment thickness because the loft will work to push apart the inner and outer fabrics of the garment, yet this thickness is obtained without appreciable weight because the down itself is so light. Many down garments will balloon out to a thickness of two inches, or more. This same thickness of wool would provide just as much insulation, but, of course, a two-inch-thick wool garment would be exceedingly heavy.

Down garments have proven their value time after time. The U.S. Army issues down garments and down sleeping bags for use in frigid weather. The U.S. Air Force also uses down equipment. Eighteen American scientists who lived for six months at the South Pole during the International Geophysical Year were equipped with down parkas and down pants. The temperatures they encountered averaged 70 degrees below zero Fahrenheit and sometimes sank to extremes of more than 100 degrees below zero. Down parkas, pants, sleeping bags, mittens, and underwear have been used on the arctic DEW line, on mountaineering expeditions to South America, and on numerous expeditions to the great Karakoram and Himalayan ranges, including all recent expeditions to Mount Everest. The more intense the cold, the more down becomes the only insulator capable of doing the job.

Cold-wet and Cold-dry Weather

For the snow camper and mountaineer, cold weather may be broadly categorized into two general types: cold-wet and cold-dry. Temperature which remains in the vicinity of 32 degrees Fahrenheit makes weather which is classified as cold-wet. Temperature which remains below 32 degrees makes weather which is classified as cold-dry. Obviously, since snow and ice melt at 32 degrees, this becomes the critical temperature.

But temperature does not remain constant during any given twenty-four-hour period. After sunrise, the day usually warms up and temperatures rise steadily until sunset, at which time the daytime temperature is usually at its highest. After sunset, temperature drops again, and continues to go down until dawn, or shortly after dawn. The diurnal temperature range will vary depending upon the locality, season, cloud cover, and other factors. Land which is near oceans tends to have oceanic climate. Such climate is moderated by the specific heat of the ocean mass, and temperatures tend not to go to extremes. Land which is at a greater distance from oceans has what is called continental climate. Such climate is characterized by wider temperature ranges and by hot days and cold nights.

The determination of whether the weather is cold-dry or cold-wet depends on the diurnal temperature range. The wider this range is, as in continental climate, the more likely that a part of the upper range of temperatures will rise above 32 degrees, and that cold-wet weather will be experienced. Taking the average temperature over a twenty-four-hour period will not help, because even if the average is well below 32 degrees, if there are several hours at above 32 degrees, cold-wet weather will nevertheless be experienced. For weather to be cold-dry, the average twenty-four-hour temperature would have to be considerably lower than 32 degrees since a temperature of 31 degrees, or lower, would be required at the warmest time of day.

Cold-wet weather is characterized by daytime thawing and by slush, mud, and running water. At night, cold-wet weather is characterized by hard freezes, ice crusting, and glazed ice.

Cold-dry weather is, just as its name indicates, cold and

dry, and it is characterized by frozen ground and powdered snow.

From the viewpoint of what kind of clothing to wear, it is relatively simpler to dress for cold-dry weather and to remain warm and comfortable in it than it is to dress for cold-wet weather.

Remaining warm in cold weather means remaining dry. If the outdoorsman puts on a pair of rubberized boots, these will prevent outside water from wetting his feet. Unfortunately, rubber is a poor insulator of heat. Therefore, walking in slush at a temperature of 32 degrees can be a colder experience than walking on dry snow at zero. But walking in slush with wet leather boots or wet felt boots may be no colder for the feet than walking in sub-zero temperatures in rubber boots.

Those items of clothing which are waterproof, such as rubberized boots, nylon coated with neoprene, vinyl plastic, etc., are poor insulators. Unfortunately, because of the absolute need to keep dry, we are forced to sacrifice better insulating materials to avoid ending up with wet insulating materials.

In this regard, the best insulator under cold-wet conditions is wool. Not only is wool a better insulator than any other material in a wet state, but wool also tends to dry out faster. Wet down will not insulate at all. Furthermore, wet down takes a long time to dry out, particularly in cold weather.

As a general rule, the outdoorsman should emphasize wool in all his clothes when going abroad in cold-wet weather, and he should wear mostly down clothes in cold-dry weather. In cold-dry weather, no rubberized outer garments are required at all. Indeed, because they are such poor insulators, they should be avoided in very cold-dry weather. In cold-wet conditions, the basic woolen wardrobe should be protected by outer garments which are water-repellent, or best of all, completely waterproof.

While considering waterproof outer garments, such as rain pants, waterproof parkas or ponchos, etc., it should be kept in mind that not all moisture comes from the outside environment. The human body perspires constantly, even in the coldest weather, and if this body moisture is not allowed to escape, clothing may become wet from within. Proper ventilation of clothing is important, and openings should be left through which moisture may escape to the outside.

Waterproof rain pants, for example, should never be tucked into rubber boots, but should be left hanging down so that the feet and legs may be ventilated. Waterproof sleeves of parkas, similarly, should not be tucked into waterproof gloves, but the wrists should be left ventilated. This applies also to overlaps of waterproof clothes at the waist and at the neck.

In cold-dry conditions, body moisture is usually able to pass through down or loose wool clothing and into the outer air without any trouble, and the problem of ridding the body of moisture is not a great one when such clothes are worn.

Although wool has excellent thermal insulation properties, both wet and dry, the care required of wool clothing sometimes is excessive. Wool socks, for example, have to be laundered in lukewarm water and then manually stretched while they are in the process of drying. If this extra care is not taken, the socks will shrink to the point where they cramp the toes when worn, thus impairing circulation and consequently making the toes colder. A wool sweater, if washed in hot water and then allowed to dry without being stretched, will shrink so much that it may be impossible to get it on again.

No shirttails!

These difficulties may be overcome by going from natural wool to some of the synthetic fibers. Orlon is one of the best now available. Orlon socks and orlon sweaters may be thrown into a washing machine into water of any temperature and washed. After washing, orlon requires no stretching or other special care. Orlon, therefore, is not only just as good as wool in many ways; in some ways it is even better. It certainly is easier to wash and dry orlon.

We can best summarize the subject of cold weather clothing by showing two lists: one for cold-wet weather and one for cold-dry (p. 20).

Shirttails

With regard to clothing, there are minor points to keep in mind in preparing for being out in the cold. One of my pet annoyances is wool shirts which pull out of my trousers when I bend over, leaving an exposed and drafty back. A great many shirts sold these days have the so-called "square tail." To me, all that a square tail means is that some shirt manufacturer made himself some extra profit by cheating me out of enough material to keep my rear warm and to keep the shirt from pulling out in the back.

Gloves

In severe cold conditions, gloves are more than a comfort and convenience. They are a vital necessity. Unfortunately, there are many chores around a campsite which cannot be conveniently performed except with bare fingers. These include striking matches, attending to toilet needs, fastening and unfastening straps on packs, tying and untying ropes, manipulating buttons and zippers, etc. Because gloves must be removed and then put on again so often, a danger exists that a glove may become forgotten or lost. To lose a vital necessity such as a glove may have serious consequences. In the case of mountaineers who remove a glove on a steep and windy glacier, the glove may slide away or be blown away, with tragic results. To prevent the loss of gloves, they should be physically attached somehow to the outer clothing, or to the mountaineer himself. One way to do this is to sew a nylon cord to the gloves and to pass this cord through the sleeves of the outer jacket. Thus, after the outer garment is put on, each

BODY ELEMENT	COLD-WET	COLD-DRY
torso	cotton-dacron, wool, or orlon underwear	wool or orlon underwear, or down underwear
feet	wool or orlon socks; rubberized or waterproof boots; shoe pacs (rubber bottoms and leather uppers) or leather climbing boots which have been waterproofed	wool or orlon socks; waterproofed leather boots or felt boots (mukluks); also insulated waterproof leather boots or fur-lined boots; also climbing double boots
legs	long wool trousers; outer rain pants of vinyl plastic or of neoprene-coated nylon	long wool trousers or down pants; outer wind pants of neoprene-coated nylon or of tightly woven cotton or cotton-dacron
upper body	wool or orlon shirts and sweaters; down vest; down jacket; waterproof parka (or one made of "Reevair" cloth)	wool or orlon shirts and sweaters; down vest; down jacket or down parka; "Reevair" parka or cotton parka
head	visored wool cap or waterproof hat or cap; sunglasses or sun goggles	visored wool cap with ear flaps or down hood; sunglasses or sun goggles
hands	inner wool gloves; outer leather and cotton shells or outer rubberized mittens	inner wool gloves; outer down mittens

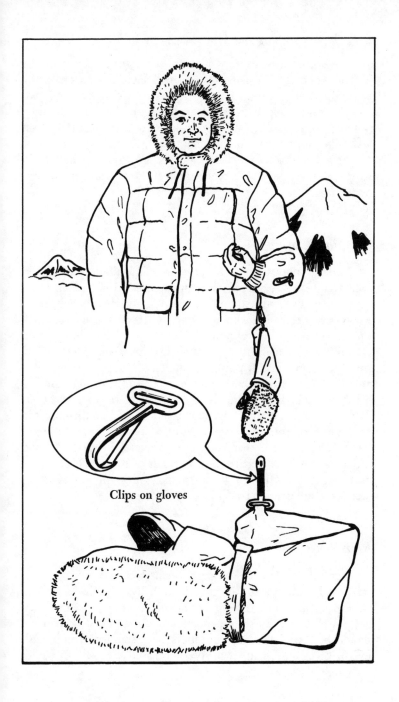

Clips on gloves

glove is secured by a line which runs up into the sleeve of the jacket. Another way is to sew a small snap link (such as the type found at the end of a dog leash) to each glove and two more to some part of the outer jacket. The glove may then be fastened to the jacket as soon as it is removed, securing it from loss. This system has the advantage of getting a glove out of the way temporarily when it is not needed. Gloves which hang from a line on the sleeve tend to interfere with manual operations.

Cleaning Clothing

Another minor point to keep in mind about clothing in cold weather is that such clothing, when and if washed (that is, not dry cleaned) should be thoroughly rinsed. Salt from perspiration will lodge in clothing and tend to absorb moisture. Soap and/or detergent which has not been rinsed from clothing will have the same moisture-absorbing effect. The rinse cycle in some washing machines, although adequate for normal needs, is too short for complete and thorough rinsing of clothes which must be worn outdoors in freezing weather. Socks and underwear in particular should be put through the washing machine for one additional cycle, using no soap whatever, to insure that they are adequately rinsed. All too often, "spongy" socks are not the result of too much perspiration at the feet, nor of leaky boots, but simply of wearing socks that still contain traces of soap or detergent.

Rain Pants

Many outdoorsmen prepare themselves for rain or wet snow only by preparing the upper half of their bodies. A waterproof parka or waterproof poncho are fine, as far as they go, but they usually do not go as far as the knees. Rain pants should be a part of every outdoorsman's standard equipment. Inexpensive rain pants can be purchased almost anywhere

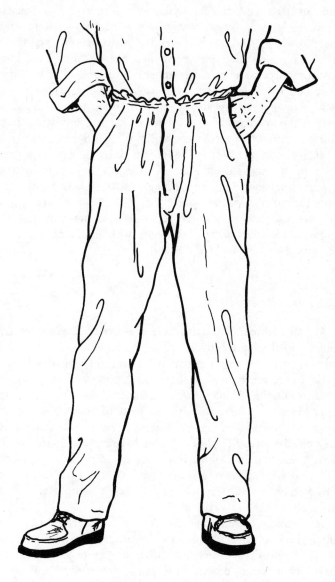

Rain pants

these days made of vinyl or polyethylene plastic. Such pants are made oversize and may be pulled on right over the trousers. They are held up by an elastic band at the waist. Rain pants insure dry legs, and, if the hiker is wearing rubberized boots, he will remain quite dry, even in a heavy downpour. Such vinyl or polyethylene rain pants are light, and after use, may be folded up into a very small package and returned to the pack. Rain pants may also be used as wind pants. Pulled on outside the regular trousers, they act to prevent wind from blowing through the trousers and cooling off the legs. More expensive rain pants may be obtained by purchasing pants made of neoprene-coated nylon. These are just as light as plastic rain pants, but far stronger and tougher. Plastic rain pants cannot be worn as wind pants if the temperature is very low because the plastic freezes and becomes brittle. In a strong, cold wind, plastic rain pants will simply rattle, crack, tear, and the pieces will blow away.

Boots

On the subject of boots, there are probably as many firm opinions as there are people. For the mountaineer, the choice is restricted to climbing boots with cleated and lugged soles and heels. There are a number of good brands available; among these are Raichle, Henke, Loewa, Danner, Bone Dry, Le Trappeur, Munari, Reiker, and others. Most of these boots, when properly waterproofed, are adequate for cold-wet conditions. For cold-dry weather, double boots have shown themselves to be of great worth. Double boots are made by Loewa, Hochland, and Cervin, among others, and consist of a laced boot with a smooth sole which is worn inside a second laced boot with a cleated and lugged sole.

In extreme cold, and in blowing powdered snow, the double boot is covered by a cloth (canvas or nylon) "overboot," which is really little more than one more layer of cloth, but which serves to close off the gap between pants and boots, acting like a legging, and which therefore *does* contribute to

Boots

Shoe pac

the warmth of the climber who wears this item. When over-
boots are worn, they are usually laced with a nylon cord.
Crampons, if required, are worn under (outside) the over-
boots, and laced in turn to them.

For the ski climber, climbing boots are available which
have cleated and lugged soles and heels, but which also have
projecting, square soles and grooved heels so that the boots
may be used as ski boots. Henke makes such a combination
climbing and skiing boot and the versatility of such a boot
makes it extremely useful to the climber-skier.

Whether the winter outdoorsman is a climber or not,
mountain boots should be seriously considered by him because
of their cleated and lugged soles and heels. Cold weather means
snow and ice. Snow and ice are usually slippery. The added
protection against slipping which cleated and lugged soles and
heels afford should be welcome on slippery level ground as
much as on slippery slopes.

For the non-climber, that is, for the cold weather hunter or
fisherman, who is faced with being outdoors in cold-wet conditions, the shoe pac is a good answer to foot protection. Shoe
pacs are boots with rubber bottoms and leather uppers. Excellent shoe pacs are available by mail order from L. L. Bean in

Freeport, Maine, and from Eddie Bauer in Seattle, Washington. When worn with warm socks, shoe pacs keep the feet warm and dry in a thawing condition where slush and even running water are encountered. Shoe pacs are now available with cleated and lugged soles and heels, and this feature makes them even more useful.

Winter boots and/or climbing boots should always be worn with two pairs of heavy socks. Because they will always be worn this way, they should be purchased only after trying them on while wearing two pairs of heavy socks.

No leather is waterproof. But wet feet can lead to frostbite. It is, therefore, necessary to treat leather to make it resist the passage of water. This is done by heating the leather boot and then rubbing in a waterproofing material. When the leather has been heated, the material soaks in more readily. Such waterproofing material should have either a wax or a silicon base. Fats, greases, and oils should be avoided. These substances, while they do waterproof leather, also tend to soften it, causing the boot to lose its shape. The heavy, stiffening piece of leather above the heel in particular should not be softened and allowed to sag gradually down over the heel itself; fats, oils, and greases may cause this to happen.

Trousers

Trousers may be made considerably more comfortable for cold weather use by sewing additional layers onto the seat. A horseshoe-shaped piece of material is used which covers not only the seat but extends down under the legs almost to the knees. Even one additional layer of wool material helps keep the bottom warm when sitting.

Ideally, for use in very cold weather and where it is expected that much sitting will be done, as in ice fishing or in glissading, three layers may be sewn on. If this is done, the first and third should be wool, and the intermediate layer should be neoprene-coated nylon so as to keep the bottom warm, but also dry. The layer closest to the trousers should be a thick,

Seat-of-pants patch

NYLON

WOOL

tweedy layer for maximum insulation. Next should come the neoprene-coated nylon for waterproofing. The third, or outside layer, should be a hard-finished wool gabardine with good wearing qualities. These seat thickeners should be large enough to cover the entire seat of the trousers adequately, and the thigh extensions should reach half-way up the sides on each side.

Although sewing these additions to your trousers will not make them look particularly stylish or fashionable, they will certainly be far more comfortable than trousers with only a single layer of fabric on the thighs and seat. Cold weather activity is usually very tiring, and it is natural to want to sit down when resting. Such rest cannot be very restful if it is accomplished with a growing awareness that the bottom is slowly freezing. Trousers with sufficient insulation on the seat make it possible to sit comfortably even on snow.

Hats

In cold dry weather many climbers and other outdoorsmen feel comfortable if they are wearing adequate clothing even if they do not wear a head covering of any sort. They may even insist that they do not need a hat. They are mistaken, however. Considerable heat loss is possible from the head area unless it is insulated. Even if the face, ears, head, and neck do not feel cold, they must necessarily radiate heat into the air. If no direct coldness is noticed in the head area, other evidence of heat loss may show itself, such as cold feet or general fatigue.

Heat loss from the area above the neck will be slowed down by wearing a hat. A visored cap with ear flaps will insulate the top of the head and the ears while the visor itself shields the eyes from glare. If, in addition to the hat, a turtle-neck sweater is worn and also the collar of the outer jacket is turned up, additional insulation will be provided. In very cold and windy weather a hooded parka should be worn, preferably with down insulation included in the hood. If this is worn over the visored cap, it affords excellent insulation in the head area.

FORAGE CAP

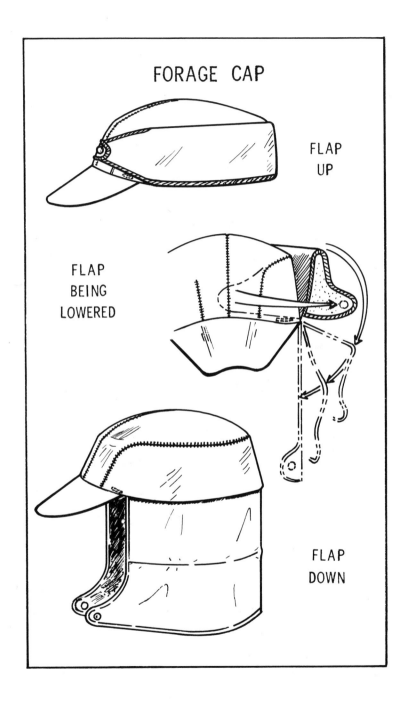

FLAP
UP

FLAP
BEING
LOWERED

FLAP
DOWN

The visor of the cap then prevents the front of the hood from slipping down over the eyes.

Bright Colors

It used to be that all outdoorsmen wore clothing which was colored khaki or olive drab (O.D.). Perhaps this was so because so much outdoor clothing was purchased in army surplus stores, where good quality materials were available at low prices. Perhaps it was because dull or drab colored clothing was less likely to show dirt. Perhaps hunters thought that they had to blend completely into their forest background before they would be able to get their deer.

My own preference has always been in the opposite direction. All my packs and knapsacks are a brilliant scarlet red. My favorite deer hunting shirt is made of bright red flannel cloth. My parka (made of "Reevair" cloth) is a brilliant orange. My visored cap is bright red. My tent is bright red with a bright yellow floor. I have painted my can openers, bottle openers, etc., with bright orange paint.

Why these bright colors? There are several reasons. Several states require red to be worn while deer hunting, and so it seemed practical to have one set of clothes and equipment for all occasions rather than a red set and another set of some other color. I am convinced deer are color blind. I have seen a deer look at me while I remained perfectly still, wearing bright red clothing, and then let his gaze wander from me. Yet my red clothes have served to warn other hunters who might see me that I am *not* a deer, but a fellow human being.

Next, from a practical viewpoint, bright colors are conspicuous, and highly visible at a great distance. From time to time, while descending from a mountain, I have spotted my red tent from very far away and so have been able to go down directly toward it rather than going out of my way and then dog-legging it back. Bright clothes also enable climbers and campers and hunters to see each other at a distance. Movements may be visually coordinated. At a great distance, a large orange parka becomes merely a tiny orange dot—a mere speck of color. At such a distance, however, another man would be invisible if he were not brightly colored.

Bright colors also make visibility easier where there is no movement. This is a safety feature, and can help make it easier to locate and rescue an injured or incapacitated outdoorsman. To search out and find the still figure of a man dressed in brown or in gray or in green will be far more difficult than finding the same man dressed in red, orange, or yellow. In the case of an injury involving bleeding, where even seconds may count, the use of bright colors may save a life.

Similarly, items of equipment which easily get misplaced or lost, such as can openers, bottle openers, flashlights, etc., are quickly located if they are painted orange or red, or, if they are objects which cannot conveniently be painted, if they are marked with bright-colored tapes.

In this respect, there are fabrics now available which are not only bright, but which are so highly reflective they seem to fluoresce. Fabrics with such brilliant coloration are excellent where high visibility is the only desirable factor to consider, such as clothing for mountain rescue teams, or for a helicopter pilot floating in a life raft. But where hunters are concerned it should be remembered that while a deer may be color blind, he is not blind altogether. Bright red may seem like just another shade of gray to a deer, but the deer will certainly notice any material which glistens almost like a mirror.

The last, but not least, reason for using bright colors out-of-doors is psychological. Good times can be had outdoors and bad times too. A mountaineer may be forced to spend the night in an emergency camp where he is cold, wet, tired, hungry, and generally in low spirits. He needs all the cheer he can get. Bright colors are cheerful colors, and sometimes every little bit of cheer helps.

3] Equipment

THE KIND of equipment that would be used for summer camping is not essentially different from the kind of equipment used for winter camping. What differences there are are differences in emphasis.

Equipment falls into three broad categories: shelter, transportation, and housekeeping. These categories apply whether you camp on the beach in the summertime or in the winter woods in snow.

Included under shelter are items such as the tent and sleeping bag.

Included under transportation are such things as the pack, or, under certain circumstances, a car, camper-truck, jeep, trailer, horses, or sled dogs.

Housekeeping includes toilet articles, items for cleaning and washing, cooking equipment, and food itself.

A fourth, optional, category would include items of recreational equipment or, in some cases, professional equipment. These items could be fishing rods and reels, etc., or rifles, shotguns, and ammunition. In the case of mountaineers, such equipment includes the ice axe, rope, crampons, Prusik slings, etc. Professional equipment might include surveying instruments, radios, cameras, chemical analysis equipment, or other equipment or instrumentation.

Any consideration of equipment invariably becomes in-

[33

volved with check lists. Over the years I have found that whenever I used a check list, I took along everything I needed. Whenever I trusted to memory or instinct alone, I invariably forgot one or more essential items.

In my own case, I have a very elaborate check list which contains more items than I could possibly use on any single trip. But by going over the list, item by item, I at least eliminate the possibility of overlooking something which will be useful, or even necessary. This check list is good for a week-end trip or for an expedition lasting one to two weeks. Any expedition which is expected to last for more than two weeks warrants a thorough planning job with all details worked out in advance on paper.

For the week-end trip, or for the short (not more than two weeks) expedition, I offer my own check list:

tent
tent poles
tent pegs
candles
lantern (battery or fuel)
sleeping bag
waterproof covering for sleep-
    ing bag
ensolite pad (or air mattress)
extra batteries
twine
tarpaulin
folding camp saw (or axe)
soap box
soap
washcloth (for washing self)
razor
blades
toilet paper
Kleenex
steel mirror
comb
insect repellent
Mum (deodorant)
Kaopectate

boots
wool socks (or orlon)
cotton underwear (or cotton-
    dacron)
wool underwear (or orlon)
down underwear
wool trousers
wool shirts (long tails) (or
    orlon)
wool sweaters (or orlon)
down vest
down jacket
down parka
cotton or wool visored cap
down hat or down hood
rainproof parka (or poncho)
rain pants
extra handkerchiefs
bathing suit
sunglasses
sun goggles
spectacles (if worn)
wool gloves
outer shell gloves
laundry bag

stove (Coleman, Primus, Optimus, etc.)
aluminum bottles for fuel
fuel (white gas, naphtha, etc.)
pots and lids
frying pan
detachable gripper handle (for pots and pans)
grill (small or folding)
hand trowel (in lieu of spade)
cotton gloves (for cooking)
menu
bottle opener
can opener
water bottles (metal or plastic)
water
wax plugs (fire starters)
extra matches
eating plate (plastic or melamine)
soup bowl (plastic or melamine)
knife, fork, and spoon
cup (plastic, thermal)
salt shaker
pepper shaker
salt
pepper
butter, fat, or lard (for frying) (in plastic jar)
paper towels
Brillo
washcloth (for washing dishes)
detergent (in plastic jar)
Thermos (unbreakable stainless steel)
plastic food jars
plastic food boxes
spatula (pancake turner)

needle and thread
playing cards
games (checkers, chess, Scrabble, etc.)
portable radio
magazines
books
ice axe
crampons
extra crampon laces (nylon)
60 feet of rope (nylon)
120 feet of rope (nylon)
Prusik slings (Manila)
sun cream
zinc ointment (Desitin)
climbing sketch (routes)
maps
compass
frame pack
summit pack (smaller cloth pack)
binoculars
first aid kit
camera
photographic equipment
extra film
photo lists (record of photos taken)
flashlight
pencil stubs
pocket knife
distress signal code lists
tobacco
waterproof matches
canteen
emergency food (canned)
sandwich boxes (plastic)
salt tablets
pickles or olives (in lieu of salt tablets)

From a reading of this check list, it is obvious that some of the items listed would not ordinarily be included in any expedition involving backpacking. It is also obvious that the use of some items would preclude the use of others, as for example, you would probably only bring along cotton underwear, wool underwear, OR down underwear, not all three; or, a mountaineer would bring along a 60-foot rope OR a 120-foot rope, but not both. But by having a check list, and by using the check list, you will at least be aware of the fact that you are leaving certain items behind. This is very different from simply forgetting to take something along which you will actually need.

Your choice of items will depend on the length and nature of your trip and, invariably, on your own experience and preferences.

In my own case, for example, I do not even own an axe. I find a saw much better for general camp use than an axe. An axe is heavy. When backpacking, where every ounce counts, lugging a heavy axe around seems completely senseless to me. Good, light, folding buck saws are now available in a variety of sizes and styles. Except for finger-thick twigs, I'll match my saw against anybody's axe in a speed contest through wood. Furthermore, if there is any possibility that there will be children around a camp, the use of an axe ought to be banned altogether. Even among adults, axes have been the cause of serious accidents including chopped toes and split shin bones, not to mention missing finger tips.

For extreme lightness, there is a serrated wire available with hand holds on each end. I have never used one of these wire saws, but they seem to be an excellent idea.

Knapsacks and packs should be purchased with wet weather in mind. Many fine packs are now available made of waterproof nylon, neoprene-coated fabrics, rubberized fabrics, or other waterproof material. Plain cotton, even heavy duck, is not waterproof. If you buy a pack made of waterproof material, you will be grateful on the very first rainy day you are out with it. It can be very discouraging to come through a rainy period completely dry because of good, weatherproof clothing, only to find the entire contents of the pack all wet at the end of the day.

The Ten Essentials

If you travel alone, you will, of course, have to carry all your equipment by yourself. If there are several members of an expedition, then some of the commonly-used equipment may be divided up among the several packs which will be used. If two campers are to share a two-man tent, then only one of them will have to carry the tent. If three mountaineers are to share one rope, then only one of them will have to carry the rope. To equalize weight among all the packs used, some items, especially items of food, can be redistributed into the lighter packs.

However, there are certain items of equipment which each and every member of the group should carry. In the event that one of the campers becomes separated from the others, he should have these items with him in his own pack. These items are known as the "ten essentials," and they should always be included in every trip by each member of the group. Here are the ten essentials:

1. Waterproof matches
2. Wax plugs (fire starters)
3. Extra sunglasses or sun goggles
4. Knife
5. Flashlight
6. Compass and map
7. First aid kit
8. Sun cream or zinc ointment (for mountaineers only)
9. Extra food
10. Extra clothing

How to make and how to use wax plugs are covered in the next chapter. Sunglasses or sun goggles may break or get lost. In glaring sun and on snow, a spare set should be available to prevent snow blindness. The flashlight should always have fresh batteries. The need for the other items among the ten essentials is obvious and self-explanatory.

4] Snow Camping

FIVE EUROPEAN prisoners who escaped from a Soviet prison camp in Siberia after World War II in the wintertime managed to walk not only across Siberia on foot but also across the Gobi Desert and across the Himalaya Mountains to reach safety in India. They did this with little more than the clothes they had on their backs.

I have read about Eskimos on Baffin Island, at more than 70 degrees north latitude, going outdoors from their igloos for brief spells naked from the waist up to tend to their dogs or to perform other chores in temperatures below zero Fahrenheit.

That inveterate world traveller Lowell Thomas has brought back photographs from Nepal showing barefooted Sherpas walking through the snow in the lower reaches of the Himalaya Mountains.

There is no doubt that man is capable of survival in winter conditions in the out-of-doors. He is capable of survival even in such cases as Patagonian Indians in the Tierra del Fuego, who have been observed going about their daily business while snow fell against their bare skins and melted there.

We are not so much concerned here with survival as such as we are with surviving in comfort, and, if at all possible, with a certain amount of luxury. Luxury is indeed possible. It is possible in the form of delicious meals, of cozy warmth, and in other forms.

[39

There are many similarities between camping in the summer and camping in the winter. But there are many differences too. One of the major differences is in the presence of moisture. An entirely dry summer camp is possible. An entirely dry winter camp is impossible. Indeed, the mere application of heat to snow or ice will immediately produce water. Wood, which can be found tinder dry in the summer, cannot be found except in a soaked condition in the wintertime. After autumn rains soak the landscape, they are followed by ever-colder weather. Since evaporation can only take place in the presence of heat, there is less and less chance for the wood to dry out until finally, after freezing weather has arrived, the moisture is locked into the wood in the form of ice. But put that frozen stick of wood onto a fire and the heat of the fire will soon thaw the ice and produce a soaking wet piece of wood. Keeping a fire going, however, is less of a problem than starting one at all.

Wax Plugs

Starting a fire with cold, wet wood usually requires the use of some sort of a fire starter. Gasoline or naphtha or other stove fuel may be used in an emergency. However, fuel is both heavy and precious when backpacking, and using it this way is really wasting it. In addition, using explosive fuels to start a fire is extremely dangerous.

Some winter campers and mountaineers use a candle to start a fire. But candles have their disadvantages. An entire candle, or at least a candle stub, must be sacrificed every time a new fire is started. This means bringing a bulky supply of candles along. Furthermore, candles are fragile, especially when they are cold, and the wrong kind of handling may crush some or all of them and make them all but useless.

There are some commercial fire starters on the market in the form of small blocks or tablets. Although I have used fuel tablets, I have never used the blocks and have had no experience with them. I have heard complimentary reports about

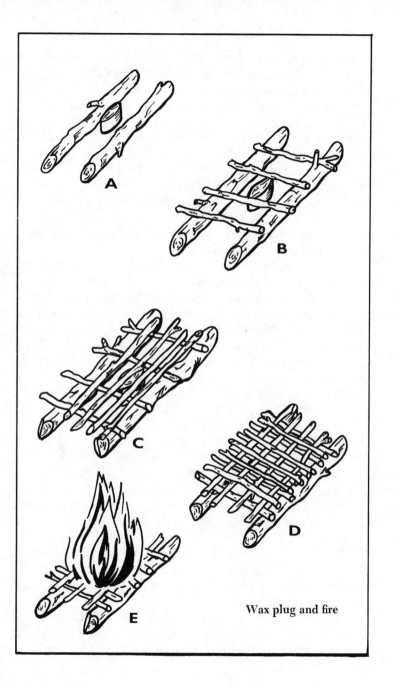

Wax plug and fire

them, however. I *have* used fuel tablets, and I don't care for them. My objection to the tablets is threefold: (1) They produce a bad smelling gas which I understand may be poisonous (and should, therefore, never be used in a confined space). (2) They are brittle, and crack easily. (3) They are not readily available for purchase and sometimes not available at all.

In my own case, I have used wax plugs as fire starters, and I have always made my own. This is how wax plugs are made: Obtain a roll of ordinary toilet tissue. A bright, colored paper is preferable to white because after the plugs are made you have colored wax plugs, which are less likely to be misplaced or lost. Yellow is a good color.

Roll the toilet paper loosely, occasionally reversing the direction of the roll until you have a roll approximately one inch in diameter. Melt wax in a pot. Ordinary paraffin, used for sealing preserved foods, serves very well for this purpose. Place the loosely rolled toilet paper into the melted paraffin and allow the paraffin to soak into the paper thoroughly. Using ice tongs or a pair of spoons, remove the roll of tissue from the hot wax and set it on a cool surface, preferably a porcelain surface such as a flat plate. When the wax has cooled slightly, press it flat. Liquid wax will run out of the ends of the roll when it is thus pressed. After pressing the roll flat, pour cold water over the entire roll of paper. The cold water solidifies the wax on the outside of the flattened roll. After this, place the flattened roll in your refrigerator for cooling, or immerse it in a pot of cold water.

Next, cut this waxed paper into lengths about one inch long, more or less. From four to six waxed plugs can be cut from one roll.

It is not necessary to flatten these wax plugs, as a rounded plug would start a fire just as well as a flat one. However, flattening them out makes them fit easier into pockets, and into odd corners of the pack.

A wax plug can be used as is. Or, several notches can be cut in it before using. Set the wax plug down where the fire is to be made. Place wet kindling and wet twigs around it and on it.

Light the wax plug (which obviously is waterproof), and after it has begun to burn, place additional wet wood directly over it. Start with finger-sized twigs, or thinner, and gradually increase the diameter of the wood added to the fire. The wax plug will burn long enough to start the wood burning. Using this method, it does not take long to get a good, roaring fire going, after which log-sized wood can be burned. The physical and psychological warmth of a fire is real, and in freezing weather it is comforting to know that you will have no trouble at all in getting a good fire started.

Tent

There are probably as many preferences for tents as there are campers. Any tent will do as long as you are satisfied with it.

Certain features of tents are very desirable and other features are liabilities. When camping, you will probably be making a mental list of these features, and you will have them in mind when you buy your next tent. (Tents are like boats in that the owner always swears by the one he presently owns, but he always has something a bit different in mind for his next one.)

If you have not yet bought your first tent, or if your present tent is getting pretty worn, here are some things to think about when you shop for your next one.

Tent Floor

Every tent should have a floor. This is true even of tents for summer camping. For snow camping, a floor is an absolute must. Not only should the tent have a floor, but that floor should be absolutely waterproof. A so-called "water-repellent" material will not do. Waterproof floors are best made of neoprene-coated nylon, or other similar superior materials which not only are light, strong, and long-wearing, but which, in addition, remain soft and pliable even in very low temperatures. When camping directly on snow, the waterproof floor will keep you dry even if you cook meals inside the tent. If you camp on frozen earth, body heat and stove heat will thaw the earth and release water, but the waterproof floor will keep you dry.

Tent Pegs

I have two complete sets of tent pegs for my small, two-man tent. One set consists of long but light aluminum pegs for use in snow. These are usually driven into the snow with the heel of the boot. The long length is needed because the soft snow does not make a good anchor for these pegs, particularly if any wind is blowing. Such pegs should be ten or twelve inches long, formed of heavy aluminum sheet into semicircular forms, the circle having a diameter of about one and one-half inches. If such pegs have a flange at the top to hold the tent line, they have more than enough strength to do their job. Such stakes, needless to say, should never be hammered into the earth, frozen or not, as this kind of treatment would quickly ruin them.

A second set of stakes should be carried for use off the snow, on cold or frozen earth. Large steel nails, or spikes, are excellent for this purpose. Using a small rock, these nails are driven into the ground and the tent secured to them.

If a campsite is to be made in a rocky area such as that found in the upper reaches of alpine zones on mountainsides, then the tent cannot be staked down unless the camper brings along a pneumatic hammer for drilling holes in the rock. Since it is not very likely that this equipment will be found in your campsite, nor in mine, the tent cannot be staked down. In such circumstances, the tent lines should be tied to heavy rocks, or wrapped around them, and other rocks piled around each anchor rock.

Just because this kind of a situation may be frequently encountered, it is desirable to have long lines attached to the tent for staking purposes. The extra length is frequently an asset and a blessing. When the extra length is not needed, excess rope can be left lying on the ground.

Tent Configuration

In an effort to save weight for backpackers, many small tents are made today which taper down in height from front to rear, and which taper in on the sides from wide at the head to narrow at the feet. Such tents do not eliminate any consequential amount of weight, but they do eliminate a large amount of comfort and convenience. If two people jam themselves into two mummy-type sleeping bags in a tapered tent, they will not be able to move, except for an occasional twitch of the nose, for the entire night. If they encounter rain the next day, and are forced to remain in their confining little tent, they will quickly develop claustrophobia. Such a tent is little more than a cloth coffin in size, and little if any shifting of the body is possible.

I have always felt that the foot of a tent should be just as high as the head of the tent, and just as wide. The largest tent made for winter camping is not really large, and certainly not what could be called spacious. The few extra ounces that an adequately sized tent weighs is well worth the effort it takes to carry it along. After all, your tent is your home when you are away from your other home, and when you settle down into a camp, you want as much of a home as you can get.

In addition, if you are one of those who can't sleep in a mummy-type sleeping bag, as I am, then you must have a rectangular sleeping bag. And if you have a rectangular sleeping bag, so that you will be able to move your feet around, then you are forced by geometry to have a rectangular floor in your tent.

Tents are more necessary at certain times than at others. In the summer, tents are most useful in assuring the camper a dry night's sleep in the event that it rains and in the event that no other shelter is available. I have gone on summer backpacking trips for the greater part of a week in Olympic National Park and in Mount Rainier National Park and not even taken a tent along. I have lain in my sleeping bag and watched a deer wander through camp at night, and I have gazed at the bright stars overhead from my supine position on the ground. Indeed, if the weather is good, a tent can give you a feeling of confinement in the warm summer weather, and rain, or hordes of insects, are the only excuses for using a tent in the warmer months.

But in the winter a tent is always a necessity. Even if there is no snow, a tent can help to give you a warmer night's sleep by cutting down or eliminating the force of the wind. Camping on snow should always be done in a tent if it is at all possible to do this.

In winter mountaineering and in high mountaineering in the summer, on snow and ice, a tent assumes special importance as protection during blizzards. In a snowstorm, the safest thing to do is remain in the tent until the weather becomes clear and mild again. Since the kind of tent used in this situation will invariably be small, and since the temperature will invariably be below freezing, the only way to spend time while a blizzard rages is in the tent in the sleeping bag. The long hours can be used in sleeping, in the preparation of meals, and in general lounging around and reading. A good, light, soft-covered book should always be brought along on a winter climbing expedition just for this reason.

Personal toilet needs may be handled in a number of ways, depending on the situation. If you will use your tent for any amount of snow camping, you should install a relief flap in the floor, if the tent does not already have one. This should be about half-way from front to rear in the center of the tent, so that if two men use the tent, the flap is convenient to either one of them. The flap should consist of a cut opening in the floor on three sides of a square, so that the floor may be lifted up, exposing the snow below the tent. A back-up square flap, of the same material if possible, should be bonded to the floor on one end only, and larger in size than the square below, so that the upper flap overlaps the lower flap and hinges on the opposite side. The lower flap should be about six inches square, and the upper, or overlapping flap should be about twelve inches square. Some tents have a relief opening in the floor put in by the manufacturer, and no further alteration is necessary. Such an opening may be in the form of a sewn-in open-end tube, or in the form of a zippered floor flap.

At the time when the tent is pitched, and while the snow is still relatively soft and uncompacted underneath the tent, both flaps are opened to expose the snow under the floor. The shaft of the ice axe is used to make a deep hole in the snow directly in the center of the opening. By moving the ice axe in a circular motion, the size of the hole can be enlarged near the top. The hole should be driven down as deeply as the snow will allow, or until the ice axe is down to its full length. With most ice axes, this will make a hole in the snow about three feet deep, about an inch in diameter at the bottom and about two or three inches in diameter at the top, just below the flap. Once this hole has been used, it cannot be enlarged, since the wet snow will tend to freeze solid.

To relieve himself, the camper simply kneels near the opening and opens both flaps.

The relief opening should be used only to pass water, and only at night when the camper is undressed and in his sleeping bag. Daytime relief, while fully dressed, should be accomplished at a distance from the tent, and all bowel movements, day or night, should be done away from the tent, no matter how inconvenient it seems at the time.

The need to answer natural calls in severe blizzard conditions may expose the climber or camper to frostbite, or may result in severe exposure or chilling. Also, there may be a tendency to become lax in the practice of sanitary habits. This must be consciously prevented by using special care. To avoid inconvenience, the camper should make an effort to tend to all his toilet needs while he is still dressed, the last thing before going to bed. It is a terrible dilemma to be awakened in the middle of the night by a powerful call of nature, while warm and cozy and dry within the sleeping bag, not to mention drowsy, and hear the frigid blizzard raging just outside the tent. A strong-willed man's powerful resolve can quickly turn to jelly in such a circumstance.

Tent Accessories

Fresh, fine, wind-blown snow has a way of getting into even the smallest openings in the tent and forming little drifts on the floor near the openings. In the warmer environment inside the tent, this snow may melt and cause a great deal of inconvenience. In addition, if the tent flap is opened while the wind is blowing, so that the camper may enter or leave the tent, large quantities of snow may enter the tent in just a little while.

To overcome this inconvenience, winterized tents are made in which the conventional zippered flap is eliminated, and a cloth tunnel is substituted for it. The cloth tunnel may be rolled in or folded in, and tied in an open position when there is no wind, or when the camper is entering and leaving the tent frequently. In a blizzard condition, the tunnel is unrolled and extended out, and the camper enters or leaves the tent through the tunnel. This keeps the wind from blowing directly into the tent. At night, when sleeping, the tunnel is closed shut and tied in the closed position with a cord.

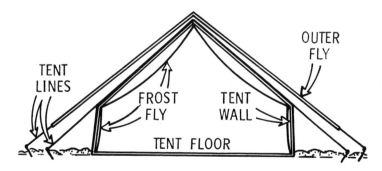

Tent outer fly and tent frost fly

Two cloth tunnels may be joined together to connect two tents so that campers may go from one tent to another without exposing themselves to the outside snow.

Even in the coldest weather campers perspire, and this adds moisture to the air inside the tent. Breathing also adds moisture to the air. Cooking inside the tent may add large amounts of water vapor to the air. When this moisturized air touches the walls of the tent it immediately condenses and freezes into a fine hoarfrost. It does not take long to turn the inside wall of a tent into an ice palace if conditions are right. Touch the wall of the tent, and you can get a fine spray of ice particles down the back of your neck! A strong wind may flap the tent enough to dislodge the frost onto camper, sleeping bag, or tent floor.

Unfortunately, there is no easy way to get rid of this frozen moisture. If it happens at night, while you sleep, there is a possibility that the frost may be dissipated during the daytime from solar heat absorption in the tent. If the day promises to be sunny, leave the tent alone, and when you return in the evening there is a good chance the frost will be all gone, and the tent warm and dry. After all, a tent is usually well ventilated even if it is all zippered shut, and moisture can easily pass through any cloth wall as long as it is not water-proof. In this respect, summer camping high on a mountain, in snow and ice, is different from winter camping.

In the winter, at high elevation or low, the days will be short and the nights will be long. Sunshine is not dependable, and does not last long. In these conditions, it is best to be ready to remove the frost from inside the tent physically. This is done by installing a vapor fly or a frost fly inside the tent.

A frost fly should have the same configuration as the tent, and should fit inside it. It is held against the outer wall of the tent by means of tie tabs along the ridge and down in the corners. The installation of an inner frost fly has the effect of making an ordinary tent into a double tent. In addition to serving its purpose as a vapor barrier, the frost fly makes a tent more resistant to the cooling effect of wind, and, therefore, a warmer tent.

A frost fly is most effective at night, because it is during the night that the camper spends his time in the tent. When he awakens in the morning and finds the inner walls of his tent completely white with frost, he simply unties the tabs on the frost fly, takes the entire fly out of the tent, and beats it like a carpet. Beating the frost fly, or even flapping it vigorously in the outside air, will dislodge the frost from it. The fly, thus cleaned, can then be returned to the tent and re-tied.

In addition to an inner fly to trap frost, a tent may also have an outer fly, to shed rain or sleet. The need for an outer fly can be eliminated by having the tent itself made of completely waterproof material. However, a waterproof tent is not as efficient as one which is not waterproof. This is so because a waterproof tent not only prevents water from coming in, it also prevents water from going out. A tent made of cotton, cotton-dacron, or nylon is better because these kinds of materials "breathe"; that is, they allow moisture to escape constantly through the fabric. As we have seen, a considerable amount of moisture may be generated from within the tent.

Unfortunately, if water can pass out, which is desirable, it can also pass in, which is very undesirable. Rain or sleet can quickly soak a tent fabric. Touch this fabric with your finger, with your head, or with your back, and you will immediately cause a drip to begin at the place where the fabric was touched. This dripping water can quickly wet the floor or soak a sleeping bag. You can stop the drip by drawing a line with your finger on the inside of the tent fabric from the point where it is dripping down to the floor. This converts the drip into a trickle along the line you have drawn, and the water will then run down to your waterproof floor and collect there, again soaking your sleeping bag, or other gear.

In heavy rain or sleet, an outer rain fly is a blessing because the rain fly sheds water and keeps the tent itself dry. In extreme cold situations, a rain fly is not necessary. But if there is any chance at all that you will encounter rain or sleet, you should definitely have and use a rain fly. A rain fly should be made of completely waterproof fabric such as neoprene-coated nylon, rubberized cotton, or reinforced vinyl. It should be large enough to do the job for which it is intended, and should generously overlap the tent in all directions so as to protect the tent even in driving rain. A rain fly is well worth the expense it costs to buy one and the effort it costs to carry the extra weight.

Tent Color

Tents are manufactured in almost every color of the spectrum. The choice of a color is more than a matter of aesthetics or personal taste. Colors are functional. Olive drab or green tents are useful in the army because they serve to conceal the location of the tent from observation by the enemy. In arctic combat, a white tent would have the same effect, since it would blend in with the snow.

However, unless they are poachers, hunters have no reason for concealing their tent. It just makes it harder to find the tent when returning from the hunt. Mountaineers not only do not want to conceal their tent, they want a tent which is highly visible so that it may be easily seen at a great distance. Ease of visibility calls for bright colors such as red or orange, and these are excellent colors for tent fabric for winter camping. If it were a question of high visibility only, the best tent colors would indeed be bright scarlet or brilliant orange.

However, another factor has to be considered. This is solar heat absorption by the tent. The color of a tent may make it warmer or colder depending on how much sunshine there is, and on how much solar heat is absorbed. A silver fabric, such as that worn by astronauts on the outer layer of their space suits, will act like a mirror and reflect light and heat. A white tent fabric, or a light colored one will, to a lesser extent, reflect a good amount of light and heat. Very dark colors, on the other hand, and particularly jet black, will absorb light and heat.

Ideally then, if only heat absorption were considered, the best color for a tent fabric would be black, and a black tent would be the warmest tent in the winter in sunshine.

But black is not an ideal color for other reasons. For one thing, a black tent would not be easily visible at a distance, except possibly on a completely white snowscape. At a great distance, the shape and outline of a tent cannot be defined. It is merely a speck. A black dot might be lost among other black dots in the distance. An orange dot or a red dot is unmistakable.

In addition, sitting inside of a black tent in the middle of the day might seem like being there at midnight. The light would be poor if there were light at all. This would force the camper to throw the tent flaps wide open so that he could see, and with tent flaps wide open, heat would go out while light came in, thus defeating the main purpose of having a black tent.

Another factor must also be considered. Living in a black tent day after day may be psychologically depressing. The sun shining through brightly colored tents, such as red, yellow, or orange, lights up the inside of the tent with a warm and cheerful glow. The constant gloom of a darkened tent might prove to be irritating as well as depressing. This is a psychological factor, however, and different campers may react differently. Some might even find it soothing and relaxing.

Perhaps the ideal winter tent should sport Halloween colors. A tent sewn together with orange and black panels, or broad orange and black stripes would combine high visibility with high solar absorption, and also let light in. I have never seen such a tent, but would be curious to know how it would work out. It sounds like it might offer promise.

Tenting

My own tent has four lines tied into it. These are red nylon parachute cord. One of the lines is tied to the peak of the tent at each end. The other two lines are tied to pull-tabs on the sides, at the center of the walls. These cords are tied on permanently, and I have not removed them since the first day they were attached.

I know that some campers detach all cords each time they take a tent down, but I have never understood why they do this. It is very easy to simply toss all the cords onto the flat tent just before it is rolled up, and to enclose them inside the tent roll. Also, a cord which is permanently attached to the tent will never get lost.

I don't remember measuring the length of these lines, although I must have done this once, but I do know that my tent lines are quite long, about twelve feet perhaps or longer. The longer your tent lines are, the better.

If you have short tent lines on the ends, the force of the line will be upward, and this may facilitate pulling a tent peg up out of the earth, or snow. A long tent line puts most of the force vector at right angles to the peg rather than along its longitudinal axis.

If your tent has pull-tabs on the sides, as mine has, the use of a short rope would merely pull the wall down along its own oblique line. A long line, on the other hand, pulls the wall outward, which is the reason the pull-tabs are there in the first place. This gives you much more room in the tent.

Incidentally, if you use a frost liner in your tent, you should make sure it ties on the inside at the point where the pull-tabs are on the side. Unless this is done, there is no point in having pull-tabs at all, since although the tent proper will be pulled out, the frost liner will sag down and get in the way.

Another reason for having long tent lines is that in cold weather camping directly on the ground (that is, not on snow), the earth may be frozen and it is impossible to drive down pegs. When this is the case, it is sometimes possible with long tent lines to reach near-by trees or other growth and tie into them. On a rocky mountainside, or on barren ground, the tent lines may be placed under large rocks or boulders, or wrapped around them and tied. Large rocks make excellent anchors, even in very high winds.

Usually a tent is used only at night, as a bedroom, and then is unoccupied during the daytime. When the tent is left for the day's activities, it should always be zippered shut no matter how good the weather promises to be. For one thing, the weather may break its promise. A tent left open, so that it may air out, will not keep out the driving rain or falling snow which did not look like it would come. In addition, if you are camping in the spring or fall and insects are still around, they may hide in your open tent.

Even a tightly closed tent "breathes" if it is not made of waterproof fabric, and your tent will ventilate itself during the course of the day quite thoroughly even when closed, so zipper it up and you can be gone all day knowing it will be cozy and dry when you return.

Mattresses and Pads

One of my climbing partners always carries an inflatable air mattress for use under his sleeping bag.

I always carry a rolled-up ensolite pad. I think my friend is foolish to carry along that heavy air mattress.

He thinks I am foolish to carry a bulky ensolite pad which is only a quarter of an inch thick when unrolled, and allows every twig and pebble to be felt right through it.

We have discussed mattresses versus pads from time to time and have never agreed.

We have both shared the triumphs and the disappointments which accompany mountain climbing over the years, and speak from personal experience when we speak.

Let me present both sides of this case and let you, the reader, be the judge. But, be warned. I am prejudiced in favor of my ensolite pad, and I may be less partial than I would like to be. But here is your comparison.

An inflatable rubber mattress is bulky and heavy after it is deflated. There is no denying the weight penalty a mattress imposes. An ensolite pad, on the other hand, is light as a feather. An ensolite pad, a quarter of an inch thick, two and a half feet wide, and six feet long weighs next to nothing. Unfortunately, an ensolite pad is bulky. No matter how tightly it is rolled, it remains a large bundle, and occupies a lot of space in the pack. For lightness, ensolite beats the air mattress. For bulk, the air mattress and the ensolite pad are about even. If anything, the air mattress may even be slightly less bulky than an ensolite pad.

From the viewpoint of care, an ensolite pad is superior to an air mattress. If a sharp twig punctures some point in the pad, it will not in any way affect any other part of the pad. A punctured air mattress will not work at all. On the other hand, most air mattresses are made of tough materials, and will be less likely to be damaged than an ensolite pad. An ensolite pad which has been in use for several seasons begins to look very ragged.

From the viewpoint of comfort, both mattress and pad have advantages and disadvantages. It is true that an ensolite pad is very thin, and that objects underneath the pad can be felt right through it. But on the other hand, the pad does have considerable resilience, and does help considerably to make its user more comfortable. The advantage of an air mattress is that it lifts you up completely off the ground, and no pebble will ever dig into your hip or back while you ride on that cushion of air. Yet, for many people, sleeping on an air mattress is like sleeping on a rubber ball, and they cannot get used to the bounce and rebound which every turn while sleeping invariably produces.

My friend and I have slept side by side in the same tent in temperatures just below zero, with twenty-five feet of snow between us and the ground beneath the tent, he on his air mattress and I on my ensolite pad, and we both have been cozy and warm in this extreme cold. I can only presume that the air mattress and the ensolite pad both provide good and adequate insulation under the sleeping bag, and I don't know of any way to prove one warmer than the other.

The price of an air mattress is about the same as the price of an ensolite pad, and no advantage accrues to either one from a price viewpoint.

There is the comparison. Take your choice. And, no

matter what my friend says, I hope, for your own sake, that you will choose the ensolite pad. Too much impartiality can make a person wishy-washy.

Both ensolite pads and air mattresses can be obtained in full-length, or in half-lengths, or long enough to cushion the hips while leaving the legs uncushioned. Needless to say, if you will be out in the wintertime you should get full-length comfort for yourself. It is not comfortable trying to spend the entire night with your chin tucked between your knees because the bottom half of your sleeping bag is like an icebox.

I have discussed only air mattresses and ensolite pads. However, other pads are available, made of materials other than ensolite.

An inexpensive pad is made of bonded sheets of polyethylene, bonded in such a way that the pad consists of uniform-sized air capsules. I have never used one of these sheets and can't talk about it from personal experience. However, I have the impression that the air bubbles are not sturdy, but may be popped between the thumb and forefinger. If this is true, then the air bubbles will certainly pop if you step or kneel on this kind of a pad. Even the weight of your hips on the pad may rupture the air capsules. If these bubbles are not sturdy and dependable, you may not be able to depend on the pad for the warmth and comfort the air bubbles should provide.

Another type of mattress or pad is one made of poly-urethane foam and enclosed in a fabric cover, usually cotton on the upper surface and a waterproofed nylon on the lower surface. The ones I have seen have a thickness of an inch and a half. I have never used these sleeping pads either, and so can't talk about them from personal experience. These pads seem like adequate and comfortable items of equipment. They are very bulky, however, and fairly heavy—almost as heavy as rubberized air mattresses. For sleeping inside a station wagon, this might be a useful and comfortable pad. The thing that makes me wonder about them is why the lower part of the pad has a waterproof covering. If this material soaks up water like a sponge then this is a major disadvantage. Ensolite, at least, in addition to affording lightweight and comfortable insulation, is one more waterproof layer you can get between yourself and the ground. If polyurethane foam is not waterproof (and I don't know whether it is or not) then it will not be very useful.

All in all, I believe that ensolite pads, cut to the proper width and length, are the ideal insulation and padding for use underneath sleeping bags in the wintertime. The proper size is about twenty-eight inches by seventy-eight inches. The pads are always a quarter of an inch thick. When rolled up, they weigh very little. When unrolled, they provide marvelous insulation in the most frigid weather. One pad should be enough for temperatures around zero degrees Fahrenheit. If you expect temperatures much below zero, simply use two ensolite pads, one on top of the other. This double insulation and double padding should be adequate for the coldest possible weather anywhere on earth.

If you go out camping much in the wintertime, or, in the summer, up on mountains where the snow is, you will always be able to spot an old, experienced hand by the look of his ensolite sleeping pad. It will be old and worn and torn in spots and ragged on the edges, and creased with fold marks. But if you offer to buy it from him, he will not sell it to you. It's his personal bed, and he's used to it. He could buy a new pad if he wanted to, but he figures there's still plenty of use left in the old one. In fact, there are mountaineers who claim that an ensolite sleeping pad really isn't properly seasoned until you've used it for the third year.

One word of caution about ensolite pads: When the pad is not in use, it should not be left tightly compressed in the pack. Take it out and roll it up loosely and put it on a shelf in the closet.

Sleeping Bags and Sleeping

Winter campers and high climbers look forward to sleeping every night with great anticipation. Not only is this a time of rest for the weary hunter and the exhausted climber, it is also the warmest time of the expedition. Using today's well-made sleeping bags with their down insulation, the camper knows he will be warm, dry, and cozy, and after dinner he does not wait long to experience the delicious glow of warmth that suffuses the body once it has been zippered into the sleeping bag. Here at last, it is possible to relax the body, to let it go completely limp, and still remain wonderfully warm. Here in the sleeping bag it is possible to wiggle the bare toes in luxurious warmth, rid at last of those cold and heavy boots. Under the grim conditions of snow camping, what more can a man ask for?

Sleeping Bag Shapes

Although sleeping bags come in a variety of sizes, weights, shapes, and materials, there are basically only two configurations: the mummy bag and the rectangular bag.

The mummy bag is the lighter of the two, and pound for pound, it is the warmer. Theoretically, the mummy bag should be the ideal choice of the backpacker. For many experienced mountaineers, it is the only bag worth considering. Bundled up in his fluffy down, with only his mouth and nose exposed to the cold air, the mountaineer is like an insect in a cocoon.

However, this is only part of the story. Blessed indeed is he who can zipper himself into a mummy bag and spend a comfortable night sleeping in it. There are many snow campers who regard a mummy bag as one fiendish step worse than a strait jacket. Designed to contain a human body, mummy bags give that body no extra space for moving, turning, spreading the legs, spreading the arms, etc., and it is easy to become quickly overcome by a sense of overwhelming confinement and restriction within the bag. Since many of these movements are natural in sleep, sleeping inside a mummy bag is, at best, unnatural. At worst, it is frustrating and maddening, and one is tempted to kick a hole through the bottom or through the side just to be able to move the legs with some freedom.

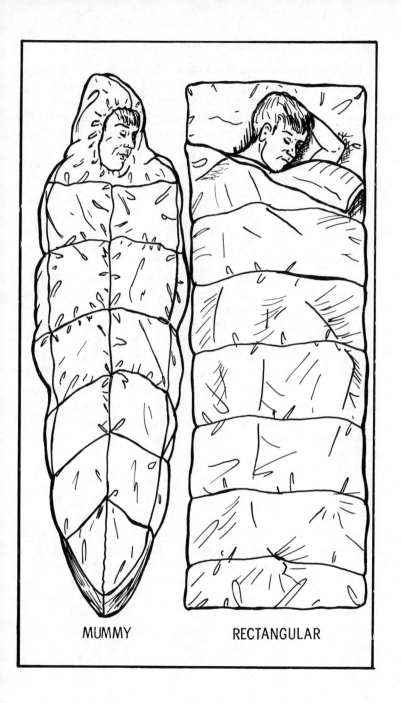

MUMMY   RECTANGULAR

A rectangular bag, although it may weigh a few ounces more, and take up just a bit more space than a mummy bag, provides the snow camper with complete freedom of movement. Sleeping in a rectangular sleeping bag is no different than sleeping in bed. You can turn, move, and change position without any effort whatever.

If you are an occasional climber, and if weight counts very much, and if you will sleep at very high elevations in very cold weather, then a mummy bag may be an acceptable item of equipment.

If you will use your sleeping bag a lot, and if you want to sleep in total comfort, then the only bag to get is a large rectangular bag.

I have always been willing, when backpacking, to pay the penalty of carrying the slight amount of extra weight that comes with taking along a full-sized tent (not one that tapers), a full-sized ensolite pad (not a three-quarter length), and a full-sized sleeping bag (not a mummy bag). Camp is your home away from home. It lacks most of the comforts, conveniences, and luxuries of home just because it is a camp. Why make it worse? If you are very tired in the woods, or up on a bleak ledge on a mountain, and it is freezing cold, it is not asking for too much to be able to sleep in completely relaxed comfort, and only full-sized accommodations can provide this maximum comfort.

Robes, Blankets, etc.

Perhaps a word about sleeping in something other than a down-insulated sleeping bag might be in order here.

First, sleeping bags may contain insulating material other than down, such as dacron, wool, cotton, or other fibers. None of these materials even comes close to down as an adequate insulating material. Only down, and only good quality down, will keep you really warm in freezing weather. There is no substitute for down, and you have no other choice. For frigid weather camping, a mummy-type bag should have three pounds of down and a rectangular bag four pounds of down as a minimum.

Second, you may consider sleeping with protection other than a down bag. Better forget it. I have tried sleeping on a length of carpeting cut especially for camping, and with the warmest, most expensive wool blankets. These things just don't work as well as a sleeping bag. I have never tried sleeping with animal robes, such as buffalo robes, sheepskins with fleece, goat hides, or others. I have talked with people who have tried some of these robes, and although they claimed these things were warm, I was under the impression they had not tried them in really cold weather, outdoors, on snow.

And even if blankets or robes could provide adequate warmth, which they cannot, they would certainly be too heavy and bulky to consider taking along on a backpacking trip.

Sleeping Bag Care

Down will provide thermal insulation as long as it is kept fluffy, clean, and dry. Greases and oils will compact the down and decrease its efficiency. When eating in the tent, care should be taken with fatty items like butter to prevent them from spattering or dripping or falling on the down bag.

Salt should be kept away from the bag too, as salt attracts and holds moisture. Salt may get onto the bag from perspiration. If you are too warm in the bag, slide the zipper down and open the bag up and let some fresh air in from time to time. Avoid using a winter sleeping bag in the summer, when it will be too hot for the bag anyway.

When sleeping in very cold weather, keep the face outside the bag. If you breathe inside the bag, you will quickly moisturize the air and make the bag damp. I know it is a great temptation on a very cold night when you first get into the bag to slide in deep. Your breath is warm, and it helps to warm the bag faster. But too much moisture will soon result in a damp and clammy bag, and in a cold one.

Normally, the down can handle body moisture on a cold night. You will not perspire excessively and such body moisture as gets into the bag will pass through the down (this is one of the excellent qualities of down) and out of the bag. But just to be sure you don't trap moisture in the bag when you leave it in the morning, it is best to unzip the side and throw the bag open, allowing moist air to escape as much as possible before the bag cools off, which it will do soon after you have left it.

Sleeping in the Car

A tent camper in the wintertime, after waking up in the morning and seeing the inside walls of his tent all covered with white hoarfrost, may feel that the cotton walls of his tent do not "breathe" very much. Actually a great deal of the moisture he has released during the course of the night is already out of the tent. What he sees is only that fraction which remained behind. If the same camper really wants to see how much moisture he can put out between his perspiring and his exhaling, he should sleep one night in the back of his station wagon, as I have done.

The steel walls and the glass windows of a car are *really* waterproof. Moisture released during the course of one night's sleep remains, almost in its entirety, inside the car. If the weather is freezing, then all moisture, as soon as it touches glass or steel or any other part of the interior of the car, will condense and freeze. The amount of ice which can build up in just one night in a car has to be seen to be believed. It is impressively thick, and it covers every square inch of the interior of the car.

Even if the windows are left partially open, for ventilation, the frost build-up is fearsome.

For the above reasons, I would emphatically recommend that you do not try this method of winter camping.

Furthermore, the opinion held by a few people who haven't tried it, that sleeping in the car will be a warmer experience than sleeping outside in a tent, is just wrong. True, the car may offer protection from the wind, but then so does a tent. On the other hand, the metal frame and chassis of a car, being made of steel, will quickly conduct all heat away, steel being a very poor thermal insulator. The net result is that the camper ends up sleeping in what amounts to an oversized ice-box, and one that needs defrosting at that.

Sleeping in a camper-truck or in a trailer is something else. A trailer or a camper will ice up too. But these shelters are often manufactured with insulation in the walls, and this can make the inside of a trailer quite a bit warmer than the inside of an automobile. In addition, there is usually more air volume in a trailer or camper than in a car, and the use of a space heater is feasible. If the temperature within the shelter is maintained above 32 degrees Fahrenheit, there will be no frost at all.

Emergency Shelters

The use of igloos and snow caves is covered in this book in Chapter 9. It is best for the winter camper to keep a watchful eye on the weather and not get caught in a blizzard. But the camper may be far from civilization and unable to do anything but sit the blizzard out. Mountain weather is very unpredictable, and a full-blown blizzard may develop very suddenly. In a blizzard condition, or in a very severe cold spell, it is good to keep in mind that the wind is your enemy and the snow is your friend. Try to get down into the snow and out of the wind.

If you are in a wooded area, it may be possible to get behind the large, exposed root of an uprooted tree. Hollow tree trunks or hollowed root areas in tree stumps can sometimes be found. Sometimes it is possible to find a small, but thickly clumped, growth of evergreens which not only can protect you from the wind, but also from the falling snow.

In a mountain situation, it may be possible to find several large boulders close together and to use these for a shelter. If there is any wood around, some of this may be used to build a lean-to, and to close the space between two boulders. Such boulders may be quite large in some places, and rise in height above the height of a man.

In blizzard situations on a glacier, shelter may sometimes be found in a moat. A moat is the gap between solid rock and the glacier itself, caused by heat absorption of sunshine in the rock. Out on the glacier itself, away from rock or dirt, a mountaineer can keep warm by digging a cave into the uphill slope of the glacier and by using a part of the snow removed to build a wall near the mouth of his cave. Once in the cave, he sleeps or sits there until the blizzard has blown over.

Napping

Cold weather activity is almost always very strenuous. The body is compelled to consume many calories just to keep warm and continuous activity consumes even more calories. This tends to make cold weather activity very tiring. How often one rests is a matter of individual metabolism and individual preference.

Generally, more rest is needed in frigid weather than in the summertime. This is acquired naturally, to a certain extent, because nights are long in the winter, and days are short, and the winter camper sleeps longer at night.

But in cold weather, and while engaged in strenuous activity, even the longer sleep obtained at night is not enough sometimes to ward off fatigue.

The best way to handle a fatigued condition is to take naps. Frequent short naps can be very helpful. Don't worry about freezing. If you are generally well-rested, and if you take a nap, you will not freeze to death in your sleep. As soon as you cool off, you will wake up shivering, and you can resume your activity refreshed.

In deer hunting or other hunting in cold weather, it is sometimes necessary to take a shooting position somewhere, and to remain still and wait for a deer to cross a given field of fire. In such a situation, if slumber comes to you, don't fight it. Give in and go to sleep. No matter how comfortable your position is, it will grow uncomfortable after a while and this will wake you up. If you don't wake up because of this, you will get cold, and the cold will wake you up. Don't worry about a deer getting away while you sleep. The chances are that a deer is less likely to get away if you sleep than if you are awake. If you remain awake, you will inevitably move, either to smoke, to scratch yourself somewhere, to shift your position, or for some reason. This movement will result in noise which a deer may hear, or the deer may be able to directly see your movement from a distance before you see the deer.

If you are sleeping, on the other hand, you will not move nor will you make any noise. Surprisingly, in the quiet of the woods, especially if you consider yourself normally to be a heavy sleeper, you will instantly hear a deer if one passes by, and your eyes will fly open. Once you are tuned in to the silence of the forest, even the sound of a falling leaf hitting the ground can sound like a crash. If your sleeping position is one

where you have your rifle at the ready, you will then be able to get your deer quickly. The nap which you just completed will then be a double blessing in the strenuous work required to get your deer back to camp.

Taking naps is a very natural way to rest. Unfortunately, napping is gradually disappearing from the routine of so-called "civilized" living and you may not know how to take short cat naps. Imagine, for example, taking a fifteen-minute nap on the job. You wouldn't dare do this! But learning to nap is easy and pleasant. Napping rests the heart, lowers the blood pressure, and sharpens the wits and the senses. All animals in a natural state take naps. In this case, we can all profit from learning from the animals.

Boots at Night

Getting dressed on a freezing cold morning is not the most pleasurable occupation in the world. The interior of the sleeping bag is warm, cozy, and dry. Just to get out of it and into the freezing air can be a major effort. But sooner or later you do get out and you do get dressed, and the activity of dressing generates enough heat to make you warm inside of your cold clothing. Warm, that is, until it is time to put your boots on. If the boots are frozen solid and have as much "give" as if they were made of steel instead of leather, much of the joy of winter camping fades just below your ankles.

Boots are a special item of clothing, and boots require special care. Boots are the only item of clothing which are in constant, all-day contact with the snow, or the frozen earth. There is no way in the world to keep boots absolutely dry. If they don't pick up moisture on the outside, which they unavoidably do, they will pick up moisture on the inside from perspiring feet. In freezing weather you may think that your feet do not perspire, but they do. Whether from without or from within, all moisture in the boot consists of water. Lower water to below 32 degrees Fahrenheit in temperature, and you get ice.

If you leave your boots where they will be exposed to freezing temperatures during the night, they will be literally frozen stiff when you go to put them on in the morning. *This must not be allowed to happen.* In the first place, it is very difficult, and sometimes impossible, to put on a pair of boots which are frozen stiff. Next, even if you do succeed, you may well wind up getting frostbitten feet.

Since the only warm place in the tent at night is inside your sleeping bag, this is where the boots should be if they are to be kept from freezing. Muddy or wet boots should never, of course, be allowed directly inside your sleeping bag. But if the boots are wrapped in something, such as sheets of newspaper, a waterproof jacket or poncho, or even placed inside of a waterproof plastic bag, the boots can then be taken inside the sleeping bag and kept from freezing during the course of a cold night.

Some campers prefer not to take the boots into the bag until an hour or two before they themselves come out. But I think it is better if you put the boots into the sleeping bag just as soon as you yourself get in. Heavy boots have a lot of mass, and trying to warm a pair of them in a short while in the morning is like trying to thaw a block of ice of the same weight in the same time interval. Kept in the sleeping bag all night long, the boots are an inconvenience when you first get into the bag, but by morning, they will be far from frozen. Indeed, they may be quite warm.

This business of giving respectful care to your boots is a serious one. Allowing boots to freeze solid is a serious thing. If you can get frozen boots on at all, you can quickly get frozen feet and lose your toes. And it is possible, if the boots freeze into a squeezed configuration, that they can't be put on at all. If you are deep in the wilderness, or high on a mountain, you have the choice of thawing the boots out or of walking barefoot through the snow and ice, a grim prospect indeed.

In an emergency, if the boots have become frozen overnight, a possible course of action is to light your stove and thaw the boots out over the heat from the stove. In doing this, you take the chance that you may overcook your boots and burn them. Even if you don't burn the leather visibly, there is a possibility you may overheat some area of the boot and cause the leather to crack later on when you are wearing the boots. Using fuel to heat boots is a waste of fuel, and this should not be done as a routine thing every morning. If there are several campers together in a group, and one of them can get out and start a fire, the fire may be used for boot-thawing purposes, thus saving fuel. The danger of burning boots must always be kept in mind, however. Also, if there is much snow around, and if boots are heated by a stove or over a fire, the hot boots will melt any snow they come in contact with, and this will result in wet boots and eventual cold feet again.

5] Glacier Mountaineering

MANY PEOPLE who have never climbed mountains have mistaken ideas about what mountain climbing is all about. They visualize sheer cliffs and they think about men clinging to steep rock walls like flies on the wall of a room. One slip, and down goes the climber thousands of feet to his sudden doom. Or they picture pitons, nailed into solid rock, and tight ropes with climbers being hauled up on ropes, one by the other.

This is not how it really is.

A considerable amount of mountain climbing is not climbing at all. It is uphill hiking, either on trails or on open ground. On most occasions when the hands are used as well as the feet, it is for short stretches, after which the climber is able to stand up again and walk, or sit down on a flat rock and rest.

Very little climbing is done up the face of sheer cliffs, and this is certainly not typical mountaineering. In fact, many climbers who have practiced the sport for years just simply do not go in for human-fly type of activities. Like the general public, they look on people who do as "some kind of a nut."

Not only is climbing dangerous where pitons and ropes are used for direct aid, it is almost always hard work and boring work. To a large extent, it is not at all sporting, since such a human-fly is not testing himself against the mountain but testing his equipment. The more equipment he has, and the more technological this equipment is, the better are his chances of getting up the mountain. This is not really sport unless you include landing at the summit in a helicopter as sport also. Nor is it "fun," unless you include climbing up a ladder in the category of fun.

Many good mountaineers refuse to use direct aids in climbing. Their attitude is that if they can't climb the mountain with their hands and feet, they shouldn't climb the mountain at all, certainly not by nailing rope ladders up the mountainside.

I, myself, am one of the believers in the "natural" school of climbing. I believe that uphill hiking and simple scrambling (hand and foot climbing) are healthful and exhilarating exercise. It is possible to climb most mountains this way, without using any pitons, expansion bolts, snap-links, rock hammers, or any other artificial aids. And when you do climb a mountain naturally, you don't leave a lot of expensive and unsightly equipment behind to disfigure the mountain for those who come after you have gone.

None of the information given in this book will be applicable to "steeple jack" types of operations. All of it is applicable to safe and sane mountaineering.

As far as high climbing is concerned, that is, climbing at the elevations where glaciers exist, a good deal of "rock engineering" is already eliminated because snow and ice cannot exist for long on sheer cliffs. Snow and ice slopes may lie at rather steep angles, but they do not stand vertically.

The Nature of Glaciers

Geographically, glacier climbing is possible in every part of the world where mountains are high enough to sustain glaciers. There are glaciers on mountains in the tropics, some of them quite close to the equator.

A glacier is born and grows where the amount of snowfall exceeds the amount of summer melt-off. The snow falls during the winter (and on some mountain heights all year long). The snow melts, softens, becomes compacted during the warmer summer season. If the entire snowfall disappears during the

summer, there is no glacier. If some portion of the snow remains by the following winter, then the snows of the next
season are added to the snow remaining from previous seasons
and we have what is called glacial snow. Any permanent snow
on a mountain is glacial snow. However, since some snow lies
at near horizontal angles, and, therefore, does not slide slowly
downhill, such snow is called a "snowfield" and not a glacier.
The qualifying features of glaciers are not only that they must
be permanent, that is, exist during all twelve months of the
year, but in addition, they must lie at an angle steep enough
for gravitational force to slide the snow in a downhill direction. Thus a glacier takes on the characteristics of a river while
a snowfield may be said to resemble a lake.

The comparison of a glacier to a river is a very good one,
for a glacier is really a river composed of compacted snow
rather than liquid water. Its flow downhill is exceedingly slow
and varies with the temperature and the angle of the slope on
which it lies.

Where rivers flow slowly and majestically in level river
beds, glaciers flow even more slowly and more majestically
where the glacial bed is nearly horizontal.

Where rivers encounter sharper drops in elevation of the
river bed, the water tumbles and churns in the form of rapids.
Where glaciers encounter sharper drops in elevation in the
glacial bed, the glacier tumbles and churns, but much, much
slower than a river. As portions of the glacier begin to move
faster than other portions, the glacier slowly splits apart and
forms what are called crevasses. (A "crevasse," with the accent on the last syllable, is a "crevice" in the glacier, with the
accent on the first syllable of crevice.) If the change in slope
under the glacier is abrupt, the glacier at that point may have a
very crevassed and jumbled appearance, similar to rapids in a
river.

Where a river bed is even steeper than in rapids, the water
tumbles headlong down the rocks, and this is called a cascade.
If the water falls freely, this is called a waterfall.

Similarly, where the glacial bed plunges steeply downhill,

the glacier becomes a maze of crevasses crisscrossing each other in a very jumbled and chaotic mass. Where a glacier encounters a cliff, parts of it move out and are suspended in air. They then fracture and fall to the ground below. Such a high glacier, which terminates at a cliff, is called a hanging glacier.

The glacial environment, as is to be expected, is generally a cold one. But this does not mean that it is always cold on a glacier. Indeed, during the summer months it may be warm, or even hot, on a glacier. It is often possible to strip down to a bathing suit and to stretch out prone on some blankets on the snow and acquire a sun tan, just as one would do on a beach. On such warm or hot days, considerable melting may take place and tons of water trickle down into the snow itself while additional tons of water run off in streams down the mountainside. During the summer, the glacier loses mass and it may even shrink in size. It is a time of compaction of the snow. The surface snow is melted each day, and such water as remains is right in the snow. Fuffy snow disappears and is replaced by granular snow which really consists of ice granules rather than

Boat with huge glacier in background

snow granules. This is why, even though a glacier is described as being made of ice, it looks and feels like snow. Only in a few areas does enough water melt to form pools in the snow which can then freeze into solid ice, and the greatest part of a glacier is not composed of solid ice but rather of granular ice.

Granular ice generally has a white appearance, like snow, while those portions of the glacier which have melted and then frozen into solid ice generally have a bluish or greenish coloration. A glacier is usually white or near-white at its upper end, and looks like snow. Part of the way down, the color changes gradually, and the glacier takes on a slight grayish tinge. At the lower terminus of the glacier, called the "snout," the glacier may be very dirty, and quite dark in color. If the ridges on each side of a glacier are gradual, not much debris will avalanche down onto the glacier, and its color will remain white right down to the snout. On the other hand, if the lower portion of the glacier lies between two precipitous and close-in ridges, so much avalanching will occur that the glacier becomes covered with rocks, dirt, and dust, and the glacier will be so dark and dirty that it is very difficult to tell where the glacier ends and where bare ground begins.

Glaciers vary in size from small to large. Some of the larger glaciers are mighty masses of ice indeed. The accumulated snow and ice may be hundreds or even thousands of feet deep. The weight of so much ice must be stupendous. In the state of Washington, on Mount Rainier, Emmons Glacier is over two miles wide at its widest point, and about five miles long from summit to snout. Winthrop Glacier, which branches off from Emmons Glacier at Steamboat Prow and points straight to the north, is about a mile wide and over three miles long.

Mendenhall Glacier, near Juneau, Alaska, is too vast and too tremendous to try to describe. Its ineffable grandeur must be seen to be appreciated. It terminates in the fiords off the Gulf of Alaska, and when large ships go by, they are dwarfed by the titanic mass of the ice.

One glacier in Alaska, Malaspina Glacier, is larger than the entire state of Rhode Island! It lies just off Yakutat Bay, on the Gulf of Alaska. Indeed, the Alaskan coast between Anchorage

Boat next to iceberg

and Seward on the north and Juneau on the south, is almost one continuous mass of glaciers.

As large as some of these glaciers may seem to be, they are dwarfed, in turn, by the super-glaciers of Greenland, whose masses, lengths, thicknesses, and widths have not been totally explored yet. The glaciers of Greenland show us that we have not yet emerged completely from the Pleistocene Epoch, the ice age. Some parts of the ice covering Greenland are over 8,000 feet thick, or over a mile and a half thick! The largest glacier in Greenland is the Humboldt Glacier. When little pieces of this glacier break off and "calve," the results are the huge floating islands we call icebergs, which, huge as they

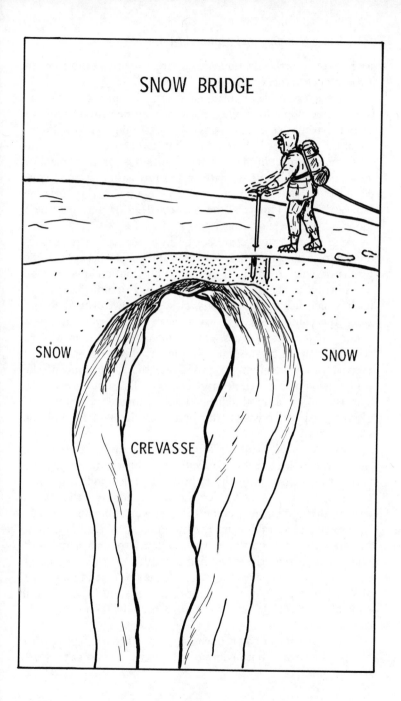

SNOW BRIDGE

SNOW

SNOW

CREVASSE

seem, are nevertheless nine times larger because most of an iceberg floats underwater.

All glaciers, large or small, have certain common characteristics. They slope downhill. The slope may be gentle or it may be quite steep. Because all parts of a glacier do not flow downhill at the same speed, there is jumbling and crevassing.

Crevasses may be gaping wide openings, or they may be very narrow and covered with fresh snow and, therefore, concealed from view. They may be a mile long or they may be ten yards long. They may be ten feet deep or they may be a thousand feet deep, or deeper.

As a general rule, crevasses lie in a line which is perpendicular to a line pointing downhill. This is so because as the glacier moves downhill, if the downhill motion quickens on one portion of the glacier, it will pull away from that part of itself which lies uphill, and this cleavage line will tend to run along the contour line. However, even though most crevasses occur along contour lines, all of them do not. It is well to remember that a crevasse may run in any direction, sometimes, even if rarely, straight up and down the slope. One of the prime dangers in moving on glaciers is falling into a crevasse, and the more a mountaineer knows about the nature of glaciers and of crevasses, the better off he will be and the safer.

Open crevasses can almost always be easily seen before they are reached. This is particularly true when approaching them from below. Sometimes, however, the uphill edge of a crevasse is high enough over the lower edge so that when coming downhill, approaching the crevasse from above, it may be hidden and invisible until the last minute. What may appear to be a change in the slope may develop into a sheer drop-off when you arrive there. Sliding downhill, or glissading, or skooming, must always be done with the thought in mind that all changes in grade must be approached cautiously, and in full control of the slide, so that a stop can always be made in time.

All crevasses are not open. A heavy snowfall may drift enough snow over both edges of a crevasse, or lips, as they are

BERGSCHRUND

SNOW

SNOW

ROCK
AND
DIRT

GLACIER

MOAT

sometimes called, to cover the opening completely. Covered crevasses are particularly dangerous in the winter and early spring because there are so many of them at that time. A climber walking over the fresh snow may suddenly drop out of sight if he happens to be walking over a crevasse.

Later in the season, in summer and in fall, after considerable surface melting has taken place, almost all crevasses are open to view, and this makes glacier travel much safer.

On mountains, glaciers begin at or near the summit. The usual upper limit of a glacier is in what is called a bowl, or cirque, or amphitheater. Above the bowl, the walls of the mountain are usually too steep to hold a glacier. Snow may cling to these steeper slopes above the glacier, but there is usually a distinct break where the glacier starts in the form of a crevasse called a "bergschrund," or simply a "schrund." A bergschrund is the cleavage between the stationary snowfield above, and the moving glacier below. A bergschrund, like any other crevasse, has snow or ice on both sides, but unlike other crevasses, which have both sides of the split at approximately the same level, the uphill side of a bergschrund is distinctly higher than the downhill side. While a bergschrund is a crevasse, it is a special kind of crevasse. Another type of opening exists in glaciers which is not a crevasse. This is what is called a "moat." Sometimes a bergschrund may slant sideways and downhill, and it may gradually become a moat.

A moat is the fissure which develops between the side or edge of a glacier and the rock or dirt of the ridge where the glacier ends. A moat is caused when warm sunshine is reflected from the white snow but absorbed by the dark rocks or dirt. As the rocks and dirt absorb sunshine and heat up, this heat melts the glacier which lies next to it and touches it. The melted ice then allows sunshine to shine deeper into the fissure and this causes the melting to take place deeper. In time a rather deep fissure, or trench, or moat, develops all along the line where the glacier's sides touch solid rock. The moat, on each side of the glacier, may extend all the way down to the bottom of the glacier, at the snout.

Those portions of bare rock which extend up through the

snow are called buttresses or ridges or cleavers, since they "cleave" up through the snow. The sides of ridges or cleavers, where they meet the glacial snow, are the places where moats are located.

To sum up, the glacier is flanked on each side by a moat. The moats run uphill parallel to the glacier and blend in gradually with the bergschrund, which runs crosshill. A moat has snow on one side and bare rock or dirt on the other. A crevasse has snow or ice on both sides. A bergschrund is a special form of crevasse, with the uphill lip higher than the downhill lip. Glaciers lie between ridges.

Although all glaciers originate at or near the summit of a mountain, the elevation at which they terminate depends on the latitude where the mountain is located, and on the type of climate which exists there.

Along the coast of Alaska, glaciers continue to exist all the way down to sea level. As we move down the coast of Canada and encounter milder weather, glaciers terminate before reaching sea level. In the state of Washington, most glaciers have their lower terminus, or snout, or foot, at about 6,000 feet above sea level. This may vary, however, and Blue Glacier, for example, located on Mount Olympus, extends downward to below the 4,000-foot level. Over two hundred inches of annual precipitation on Mount Olympus account for this massive and persistent glacier. Going further south into Oregon and California, the lower level of glaciers increases to 10,000 feet and higher. In effect, what this means is that if the mountain itself is not that high, no glacier can exist. Many good and high mountains to the south do not have any snow or ice on them in the summer for this reason. To encounter snow and ice, such mountains must be climbed in the winter, or in spring.

Climbing on Snow Slopes

The Rest Step

At whatever elevation the climber encounters snow, he walks out from the bare rock and onto the snow. If it is a snowfield, and not a glacier, he does not have to rope up yet, but may continue as an individual.

If the climber is wearing boots with cleated and lugged soles and heels, this should provide enough security against slipping on gentle slopes, and he continues to walk uphill on the snow just as he did on the rocks at a lower elevation. At first, as a matter of fact, patches of snow may alternate with patches of bare rock, and the climber proceeds upward over either one of them as he meets them.

Eventually the bare rock becomes scarce and disappears, and the climber continues uphill on continuous snow.

One of the most basic steps in climbing, whether on rock or on snow, is the rest step. Since only proceeding up the mountain, and not stopping to rest, will bring you higher and higher and since marching uphill can become very tiring, a way of resting without stopping has to be used. This is the rest step. The rest step ingeniously (or fiendishly, if you prefer) provides the climber with rest without allowing him to sit down, or even to stop at all, while he is getting that rest.

Rest stepping is done as follows: As the climber advances his uphill foot and places it on the ground, he allows his weight to remain on his downhill foot. He then stands there and rests for a period of time. Next, he advances the downhill foot and this now becomes his uphill foot. As he does this, he shifts his weight to his other foot, which is now downhill, and he rests again for a period of time. In the rest step, the weight is always on the downhill foot.

The duration of the period of rest with each step is not left up to chance, but is timed. Too short a rest would not really be a rest. Too long a rest, and the climber would not move on uphill in time to get to the top, or, he might cease moving uphill at all.

The timing of the rest step is measured in breaths, usually in exhalations. The climber advances one step; he leaves his weight on his downhill foot; he inhales and exhales five times, let us say, and then, after his fifth breath, he takes another step. Five more breaths, and he takes one more step.

Holding to a fixed number of breaths not only allows rest

with each step, but it tells the climber when he has stood still long enough and when he should move on up again.

Just as much as it is a physical maneuver to obtain rest, the rest step is a psychological maneuver to keep the climber moving up the slope. Without a device such as the rest step, an exhausted climber might fling himself to the ground to rest in a sitting or prone position. Once in the sitting or prone position, considerably greater effort is required to get moving again than is needed to take one more step while still erect.

The number of breaths to be taken between steps depends on the steepness of the slope and the condition of the climber. It may also depend on the elevation, since at elevations over 10,000 feet, more breathing is necessary to get the same amount of oxygen. At elevations approaching 15,000 feet and higher, breathing enough oxygen is a constant problem, and the type of unconscious, ordinary breathing which people do at sea level will not do to give the body the oxygen that it needs.

On moderate slopes with an occasional steep pitch, five breaths per step may be more than enough to rest the climber. On steep slopes, at high elevations, and in very cold weather, the number of breaths counted for each step may go as high as twenty, or thirty, or more.

Deciding on how many breaths to take between steps is not just a hit or miss matter. The rest step does actually give the climber rest, and it does actually give him a chance to catch his breath. If you are puffing hard and go into a rest step at, let us say, three breaths per step, and if you continue to be winded after proceeding a while this way, then obviously three breaths per step is not enough. Double the number of breaths to six and continue rest stepping uphill at six breaths per step. If you still continue to puff hard, take even more breaths per step.

Conversely, if you are breathing hard after moving up a short but steep pitch and you go into a rest step and count ten breaths per step, and you find that you have already caught your breath after one or two steps, then ten breaths per step are too many. Either cut down the number of breaths to a smaller number, or stop rest stepping altogether. When you stop rest stepping, you simply proceed uphill without paying any further attention to how many breaths you take per step.

Rest stepping is an excellent technique, and it works. All it amounts to is coordination between stepping uphill, which causes you to consume oxygen, and breathing, which gives you the oxygen you need. In ordinary activity, in warm weather, and at sea level, it is never necessary to coordinate your breathing to your activity. At high elevations, and while performing the strenuous work of lifting the weight of your body and your pack, this coordination is often necessary.

The Kick Step

The kick step may be used at the same time as the rest step, or it may be used independently.

As the mountaineer advances uphill through the snow, sooner or later he comes to slopes which are steep enough to slip on. Even with cleated and lugged soles and heels on his boots, he may not be able to obtain sufficient purchase on the surface of the snow to prevent him from sliding back down.

The use of crampons would give him secure footing on such a slope. But putting crampons on and taking them off again is a lot of bother, and the climber should not put crampons on unless he is reasonably sure he can leave them on. If he is still in terrain where patches of snow alternate with patches of bare rock, he should not put crampons on and take them off continuously, nor should he put crampons on and leave them on while he walks over bare rock. Using crampons on any surface other than snow or ice can cause the crampons to wear out quickly, or may cause the prongs on the crampons to be bent out of shape.

In this circumstance, the climber uses what is called the kick step. In the kick step, the climber advances his uphill foot but then instead of simply putting it down on the slope, he swings his foot forward and kicks once or twice into the snow. This kicking into the snow makes a small, flat platform where the forward half of the boot may be placed. With the foot on this small but level platform, he advances his next foot, and again he kicks a hole in the snow where he can place his other foot. What the kick step does is convert a steep and slippery snow slope into a series of flat and secure foot holds.

The kick step may be used with or without crampons, whenever a steep slope is encountered. Several climbers who are travelling together as a group may proceed up a steep snow slope using the kick step while they are roped together, or they may proceed unroped, depending on the terrain and on other conditions. Where several climbers travel together, the first man kicks holes in the snow for his feet and the climbers who follow after him use the holes made by the first climber. If each succeeding climber also uses the kick step, he enlarges the hole somewhat, and by the time the last climber in the group goes up, the foot platforms may be quite large and easy to use.

The kick step is a standard technique used by all mountain climbers, and one which they learn early in their training. It is almost effortless, is a simple step to use, and a very great convenience on slippery snow slopes.

Unfortunately, many other climbers do not know what a simple thing it is to go up a steep snow slope, and they expend a great amount of effort clawing and fighting their way through the snow, freezing their hands in the process, or they take circuitous routes over less favorable terrain just to avoid moving out over the snow.

A hunter, for example, may be faced with a snow slope above which may be a good spot for a look at the terrain ahead and for a shot. To move off to either flank may put him in thick underbrush where movement must necessarily be noisy, or it may not be possible to move off to either flank because of steeper terrain on the flanks. All he has to do is sling his rifle over his shoulder so that he may have his hands free for balancing, and kick step his way directly up the snow slope. Kicking the snow does make some noise, but is not very loud and the slope itself would direct such noise away from the direction in which he is moving. Also, if there is any amount

Man kick-stepping up a slope

of wind blowing, this can help to carry the noise away, or to blend it in with noises made by the wind itself.

Safety must always be kept in mind in all mountaineering operations. Even though kick stepping provides a reasonably secure way of travelling up a steep snow slope, the possibility remains that a climber may slip. When travelling in a group, climbers should keep their distance from each other so that if one man slips he does not slip directly into the next man, and so on, until all the climbers are back down at the bottom of the slope in a sputtering pile of fresh snow. Also, for this reason, kick stepping should not be done directly uphill if more than one climber will be on the slope at the same time. Instead, the route should angle off to one side or the other so that the climbers do not find themselves vertically one above the other. If a short but steep snow slope is encountered, one climber may kick step his way straight up the slope while the others rest and wait below. After the first climber is off the slope and on more level ground above, the next climber can then move up the steep pitch, and each of the succeeding climbers can do so when their turns come.

Crampons

Sooner or later, as the climber travels uphill, snow and bare rock stop alternating with each other, and the climber moves on snow only. Whatever rock there is beneath him is under the snow. Or he leaves a snowfield and moves out onto a glacier. In some situations, especially in the summertime, he may travel on rock and dirt all the way to the glacier, and the boundary between rock and glacier is distinct and obvious.

Before venturing out on the glacier, there are two things the climber must do if he has not done them already. He must put on his crampons and he must rope up. A climber should never venture out onto a glacier alone, as this may put his life in danger. And he must not go out onto the glacier with others unless they are all tied in on a rope. The characteristics and the uses of ropes will be discussed shortly. But first, crampons.

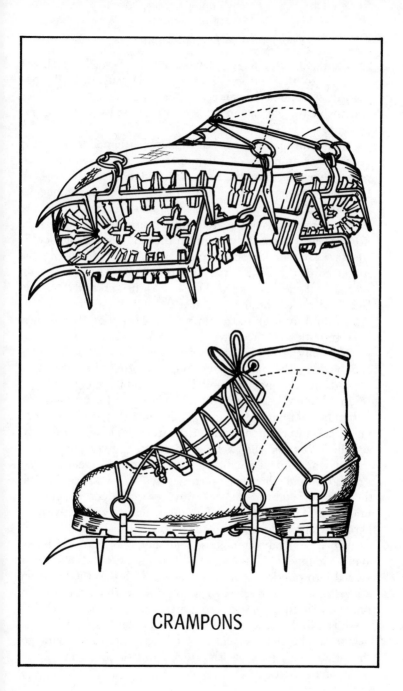

CRAMPONS

Crampons are hinged devices made of steel which are attached to the bottom of the boot. When attached, they provide steel points which crunch down into the snow and ice and enable the climber to walk with increased security against slipping.

Crampons may be attached to climbing boots or any other boots either by means of canvas or leather straps with buckles, or by lacing them to the boot with nylon cords. It has been my own experience, and that of others, that straps and buckles are hard to handle with frozen fingers. Straps and buckles are cumbersome and awkward to handle even when the fingers are not frozen. A better way to attach the crampons to the boot is to use a six-foot length of nylon parachute cord. Using the nylon cord, the cord is passed through the harness rings on each side of the crampon at the toe. It is then crossed, like shoe laces and passed through the next set of harness rings, and so on, all the way back to the rings at the heel. The cord is then tied into a bow at the instep, just as you would tie a shoelace.

Not only are nylon cords much easier to use than straps and buckles, they are lighter too, and often they are more dependable, since buckles sometimes slip and loosen.

In addition, crampons cost less when you buy them without straps and buckles. It used to be once that you could not buy a pair of crampons without the straps and buckles already attached. You had the choice then of waiting for the buckles to go, which they eventually did do, and then cutting the straps off and throwing them away; or, you could cut the straps off and throw them away as soon as you bought the crampons. These days, you can buy crampons with or without harness straps, and so you have a choice.

When you buy crampons, you should bring your boots along. Crampons should fit snugly to the boot without being forced into position. The fit should be such that the crampon clings to the boot because of its snug fit, without being laced on. The shorter, hinged end goes under the heel. Usually, there is a heel hold-in, in the form of a steel wire which goes behind the heel in a semicircle from one heel ring around to the other. This prevents the boot from slipping out of the crampon to the rear.

Descending in powder snow

Crampons come with various combinations of tines or prongs or points. Ten-point and twelve-point crampons are the most popular. I, myself, use twelve-point Grivel crampons and have had very satisfactory service from them. These crampons are very light, yet they are made of very tough steel. I have abused these crampons by walking alternately on snow and on scree, and I have even occasionally walked on rock with them for short spells. They have held up very well and nothing has broken. Indeed, when I examine them closely, I can't even see any wear.

I get a new pair of red nylon one-eighth-inch laces for my crampons every winter, and I always carry one extra pair of nylon laces in my pack. The nylon has held up very well and, so far, I have not had my laces break. At the end of the season, before throwing away the old laces, I have examined them critically. Although the laces are quite dirty and greasy (from boot waterproofing), I have not seen any real signs of wear. Nevertheless, in the matter of crampons, it is better to be safe than sorry. When you first buy your nylon laces, burn each end so that it will melt together. This will prevent unraveling.

Crampons, when laced on to the boot, give the climber a very great amount of security. You pick your feet up and put them down, and you feel the points crunch down into the snow. You cannot slide your foot forward or back, try as you may. With crampons you can walk up or down very steep snow slopes with no danger at all of slipping. Twelve-point crampons are especially effective in "self-arrest" which will be explained later, and they are excellent for use when proceeding up steep slopes using the kick step. The two forward prongs add a great deal of security to standing in a kick step foothole.

Snowshoes

In the summer and in the fall, the heat of the sun melts surface snow and compacts it. All snow consists of ice crystals, but new-fallen snow is powdery or fluffy in character as it lies on the ground, and there is considerable air space between individual snowflakes. Such powder, or fluff, blows and drifts easily, and is very soft. After several thaws, this same snow melts down into itself and refreezes. Air is released and the snow becomes granular and heavy, and is capable of supporting considerable weight. This kind of snow is sometimes called "rice" snow or "barley" snow because of its resemblance to these cereals. It is easy to walk on compacted snow with only the boots, or, if the slope is steep, with boots and crampons.

Travel in the winter is not so easy. Powder and fluff may lie in deep drifts, and this kind of snow, being uncompacted, cannot support much weight. Even without a pack, the weight of a man concentrated in the area of his foot is so great that his foot plunges down into the snow and sinks to solid ground below, or down to a compact layer of snow. Needless to say, it can be very tiring to attempt to walk any great distance in deep fluff. Great effort is required to lift the foot and leg with each step, and the effort must be directed not only upward against gravity, but forward against the drifted snow.

If we say that the area of the bottom of the boot is about 50 square inches, more or less, and if we say that a man weighs 200 pounds (because this is also a good, round number), then by simple arithmetic we can calculate that such a man with such a boot will exert a pressure of 4 pounds per square inch on the snow. This is more pressure than soft snow can resist, and so down goes our 200-pound traveller into the snow.

Obviously, if this same man could exert less pressure on the snow, he might not sink so deep. Obviously also, he cannot

reduce his weight by a half or even a quarter. But if he can increase the area on the snow over which he exerts this pressure, this will reduce the pressure per square inch. This is the principle upon which snowshoes work, and if the primitive American Indians did not understand mathematics and physics, they nevertheless intuitively understood why snowshoes should work, and they made and used snowshoes as one of their own unique inventions.

Going again to good, round numbers, a bear paw snowshoe has an area of about 300 square inches. A trail model snowshoe has an area of about 600 square inches. If we take our same 200-pound man and put him on bear paws, he will now exert a pressure of .67 pounds per square inch. On trail model snowshoes he will exert a pressure of .33 pounds per square inch, or about 5 ounces. These pressures are considerably less than the 4 pounds per square inch which he exerts on the surface of the snow with only his boots. Usually, this difference is enough to prevent a man from sinking into the snow, and allows him to walk on the surface of it without floundering.

Snowshoes actually work. That is, they make it possible to travel in the winter time over new-fallen snow. However, this is about all that can be said in favor of snowshoes. They are heavy and they are awkward to use. Walking any distance with snowshoes is very fatiguing.

Snowshoes may be used in winter mountaineering to travel uphill, and they have been used this way. But usually, their use has been so tiring that it is difficult not to conclude that the climber would have been better off without them. In walking with snowshoes, the legs must be kept apart so that you do not step on one snowshoe with the other one. After walking a while in this fashion, somewhat like a pregnant duck, the thigh muscles begin to shriek in agony. In walking on snowshoes, the foot is not lifted up clear of the ground, but is brought up just enough to enable the walker to slide or shuffle the foot forward. Since snowshoes do sink somewhat into the snow, it is not only necessary to step forward with each step, but also, to a certain extent, upward, back up to the level of the snow. Because of this, the user of snowshoes finds himself always seeming to walk uphill, even when he is walking on level ground.

Skis

Archeologists have uncovered some very ancient skis in Scandinavia, and it is certain that cross-country skiing has been done in that area of the world, at least, for over two thousand years. Since wooden skis are not a particularly durable type of equipment, it is possible that skiing was practiced as a means of travel over the snow for far longer a period of time than that in which skis can be traced back to.

A ski is really a specialized form of snowshoe. Rather than concentrating on an enlarged area in the vicinity of the foot, this enlarged area is spread forward and to the rear along a narrow axis. This makes skis more awkward to use than snowshoes in certain respects, such as turning, especially turning to the rear, but it also gives skis certain advantages over snowshoes. Among these are the fact that you can walk on skis with the feet and thighs close together, which is less fatiguing than walking on snowshoes, and also the great advantage of being able to slide downhill with a minimum of effort.

Skis can be used in mountaineering when the snow is deep and powdery and when the snow is compacted, with almost equal ease. When going uphill, skins must be attached to the bottoms of the skis. The skins are detached for downhill runs, which, needless to say, require far less effort than walking down on your feet, or on snowshoes.

The types of skis, ski bindings and ski boots used in cross-country travel in the wintertime and in high mountaineering are different from the fancy skis used at ski resorts for riding uphill and racing downhill. More is said about skis and ski travel in the next chapter.

Characteristics of Rope

Climbing rope comes in various sizes, colors, and materials.

Once upon a time, not so very long ago, all climbing rope was made of Manila hemp. The era of the Manila rope is now gone forever, and all mountaineering ropes are now made of nylon.

Nylon is superior to Manila hemp in three ways. First, nylon is much stronger than Manila. Next, nylon has far more elasticity than Manila. Third, Manila deteriorates over a period of time, whether it is used or not, and its strength gradually diminishes. Nylon, on the other hand, seems to undergo a slight loss of strength after which its strength remains unchanged. Nylon's usefulness, therefore, is enhanced by its durability.

In addition to the material from which it is made, another factor which will materially affect the elasticity and durability of a rope is the way the rope is constructed.

Tests have been made which demonstrated that when ropes are stretched to the breaking point, the rope breaks first where the greatest amount of abrasion and wear have already separated individual rope fibers. In standard lay rope, the fibers are twisted in such a manner that all fibers in the rope are sometimes within the interior of the rope and sometimes on the outer surface. This means that in a standard twisted rope, all fibers within the rope are subject to abrasion because all fibers perform the double duty of contributing to the strength of the rope and also protecting the outside of the rope.

It was just a matter of simple logic, after determining this, to realize that if a rope could be made in two parts, an inner part and an outer part, this would make a superior rope. The Germans and the Swiss have done this and produced ropes which consist of an inner core of parallel nylon strands which give the rope its body and its strength, and an outer sheath of woven nylon to protect the inner strands from abrasion. Not only is this kind of rope superior to twisted strand rope in regard to durability and safety, but it has the additional advantage of being very elastic, having an elasticity of about 80 per cent at its rupture point. It is elasticity in a rope which eases a falling climber to a stop instead of jerking him to a dead halt, perhaps with a broken rib or two caused by the "hit" of the rope. Because of this elastic feature, the European ropes are called "dynamic." And as if all these advantages were not enough, the European rope, with its parallel strands of nylon, has the additional advantage of not twisting and kinking as much as twisted strand ropes.

All things considered, it appears that the best climbing rope is European parallel nylon strand, nylon sheathed rope. This kind of rope costs more than twisted strand nylon rope, but it is well worth it. Out on the glacier, where your life may depend on a good rope, it will be a small comfort to you as you plunge to the bottom of a deep crevasse to realize that your rope, which just broke, was cheaper than other rope. Current information indicates that nylon rope may be used for many seasons with no decrease in its strength, and may be used with confidence until it shows signs of wear. This is not how it used to be in the days of climbing with Manila rope. In those days every climber got a brand new rope at the beginning of every season, and sometimes a climber might buy another new rope towards the end of the season, just to be safe.

Being able to use nylon rope for many seasons before dis-carding it makes the use of such rope more economical since the cost of the rope may be amortized over the longer period rope toward the end of the season, just to be safe.

Climbing rope, as all other mountaineering equipment, should be purchased in the brightest color possible, to get the highest visibility. The best color for rope is bright, mountain-eering orange. This color affords the highest visibility over the widest range of conditions. Bright orange stands out equally well on rock or on snow, and is easiest to see at dawn and at dusk. Red is also a good color for climbing rope.

Rope comes in several diameters. I have always believed in using the largest standard diameter available. When using nylon, smaller diameters will give you considerable tensile strength, but the smaller diameters are painful to hold in the hand if there is much tension on them, and they are painful when digging into the bones and flesh of the chest, if you happen to end up suspended from the rope. The larger diam-eters give even more strength, and they are more com-fortable.

If you buy European rope, buy Mammut (Swiss made) or Edelrid (German made) or some comparable rope in a thickness of 11 millimeters. This is a standard size. I would recommend avoiding the 9 millimeter rope.

Similarly, if you buy American nylon rope (twisted strand), buy the 7/16 inch rope and not the 3/8 inch rope.

I would not recommend buying Manila rope at all. It smells, it kinks, it dries slowly, and it is nowhere near as strong as nylon.

The tensile strength of nylon rope is about 5,000 pounds in the 7/16 inch and 11 millimeter diameters.

The most convenient length of rope to buy is 60 feet. This is ideal for a party of two climbers. If you will always climb in a party of three, buy a 120-foot length, or use two 60-foot lengths. Shorter lengths are better than long lengths because they kink less and are easier to handle. Also, if longer lengths are needed, it is always easy to tie two ropes together.

Use of the Rope

Contrary to popular belief, a rope is never used to pull a climber up a mountain. There is one reason, and one reason only, why a rope is used when travelling on a glacier, and that reason is safety.

On a glacier a climber may slip on a steep slope or he may drop into a crevasse.

Slipping on a steep slope is usually not dangerous unless there is a rock outcropping below to crash into, or unless the steep slope becomes even steeper and becomes a drop-off. However, it is inconvenient and discouraging, after slowly and painstakingly gaining elevation at much labor, to lose it abruptly in a long slide. The use of the rope, by confining such slides to the length of the rope, prevents the need to regain lost elevation and thus prevents unnecessary fatigue. Fatigue can be dangerous, and so the rope helps to make a climb safer by helping to avoid unnecessary fatigue.

But the greatest danger on a glacier is not slipping down a

steep slope. On the contrary, a slip down a slope usually presents little or no danger to the mountaineer. In fact, sliding down is one of the ways he may descend from the mountain. The greatest danger on a glacier comes from falling into a crevasse.

Wide, gaping crevasses are easy to see, and there is no problem in avoiding these. But sometimes crevasses are covered by snow, and concealed from sight. The unsuspecting climber may be standing directly over a deep crevasse and not know it. A shift in weight, perhaps caused by taking one more step, may cause the snow beneath his feet to collapse, and down he goes through the hole which he himself just made.

If such a climber is roped up to another climber, and if the two climbers were a full rope length apart so that the rope between them did not contain any slack, then the fellow who drops down into the crevasse cannot fall very far before the rope is pulling tight on the other climber. If the second climber then goes into a "self-arrest" position (which will be explained shortly), he can not only prevent himself from being dragged into the crevasse, he can also hold the full weight of the other climber on the rope. The climber who has fallen into the crevasse can then use his Prusik slings and climb back out again. (The use of Prusik slings will also be explained shortly.) Thus, because the climbers are roped up, what could have been a tragedy turns into a minor mishap.

Needless to say, since some crevasses are very deep, if an unroped climber were to fall into a crevasse, he could be killed from the fall, or seriously injured if he survived.

Climbers do not knowingly walk over concealed crevasses, but try to avoid them at all times by walking around them. Concealed crevasses can sometimes be partially seen as a trench-like depression in the snow, which continues in a line from an open and visible crevasse. If a crevasse is suspected, the climber plays it safe by detouring around the suspicious area. The ice axe is useful in this regard in that it can be used as a probe. If the ice axe hits solid snow, it is safe to continue one more step. If the ice axe plunges easily down into the snow for the full length of the shaft, better back up and go some other way.

There are occasions when an area is so crevassed that it may be necessary to cross a crevasse by walking over a snow bridge. A snow bridge is a span of compacted snow and ice over a crevasse. Some snow bridges are so light and fragile that it is obvious they cannot be crossed. Some are so huge and massive and thick that an automobile could safely traverse them. And some snow bridges are question marks. If there is any reasonable doubt about whether a snow bridge can support the weight of a man, that snow bridge should not be used.

But no snow bridge should be trusted completely, and the climbers should cross the bridge one at a time and at a full rope's length from each other. If doubt about safety exists, each climber should be belayed by means of an ice axe belay while crossing the bridge. Ice axe belays will be explained later in this chapter.

The first thing a climber does when he ropes up is tie the rope around himself. This is done in the following manner: The rope is taken and passed three times around the waist. There will now be two ends to the rope; we call them the long end and the short end. The long end goes to the next climber. The short end should be about a foot long. The climber takes the long end in his left hand, close to his body, and he makes a simple loop. After he has done this, the long end leaves his waist, turns once and passes under itself, and continues on to the next climber. The short end of the rope is then woven into the loop by passing it over, under, and over again. The long end is then pulled tight outside of the loop and this forms a knot. This knot is known as the bowline (pronounced bo'len) and is the standard knot used for tying into a rope. Usually, after tying the knot, there will be too much slack in the three coils around the waist. Rope should then be worked a little at a time through the knot to bring the knot in close to the body and eliminate this slack. The rope around the waist should not be tight, but it should be snug. If there is much loose rope left in the short end after tying the knot, this can be tied into the body coils in a series of half hitches.

If two men tie into a rope, one of them ties in at each end,

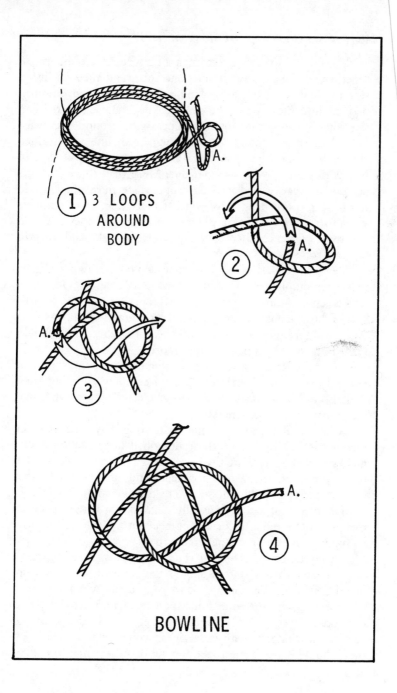

① 3 LOOPS AROUND BODY

② A.

③ A.

④ A.

BOWLINE

as described above. If three men or more are to be roped together, one man may tie into one rope, and then tie into a second rope separately. If a long rope is used, then one man may tie into the rope at the center. This is done by doubling the rope, passing the doubled rope twice around the waist instead of three times, and then tying a bowline as described above. In tying a bowline this way, the doubled rope is used just as though it were a single rope. More than three climbers are not ordinarily tied into one rope, since most climbers do not have 180-foot lengths of rope. If more than three climbers want to rope up into one party, two or more ropes are used and some of the climbers will have to tie into the ends of two separate ropes.

Very large parties on one rope should be avoided. The maximum on one rope should be five or six people. (One rope, in this sense, means people connected together by rope regardless of how many actual separate ropes are used.) If six or seven or more climbers intend to travel together, they should make two separate rope parties, or more.

Normally, at the time when the climbers rope up, they will not only tie themselves into the main climbing rope but they will also tie their Prusik slings onto the main rope so that they are prepared for emergencies.

New developments in mountaineering have resulted in techniques different from those described here, but the techniques described here are the basic ones. The newer techniques require new specialized equipment, and are covered later under the subject of "harnesses and belts and clamps."

The center of a rope is usually marked as a convenience so that it can be quickly located if necessary. This is done by wrapping some colored tape around the rope.

The question of when to rope up, that is, at what point after the climb has started should the rope be used, has no definite answer. The best time to rope up is when you feel more secure with the rope. For experienced climbers this point may come later than for beginners. Certainly if the climbing party is working its way on a zigzag course among crevasses they should have been roped up before they met the first crevasse. It is always better to be safe than sorry. More than that, it is better to be safe than fearful. The rope not only provides safety, it offers peace of mind. Climbs should offer excitement, but they should not inspire fear or terror. Using the rope makes the climb more relaxing and more enjoyable.

Now and then I have been in the situation where fear came to me as I had to negotiate a particularly tricky or slippery area. But I only felt that fear with my buddy crowding close behind me, the rope held in coils in his hand. After I asked for a belay, and he backed off to a secure position and belayed me, I noticed that I was able to handle the same situation with confidence and dispatch. The slope had not become less steep or less slippery, and whatever danger of slipping existed before I was belayed continued to exist after I had a belay on me. The thing that made the difference was the knowledge that the rope was there. It was the rope that could turn my fear into confidence.

Moving along a glacier while tied into a rope has its inconveniences. The rope is heavy. It fixes the distance between climbers. If the first man on the rope moves faster than the second man, the rope will become taut. This will tend to drag the second man along faster than what would be his normal gait. It will press him to move faster than he would perhaps like to, and this will tire him out. This will also tire out the first man on the rope because he will not only be moving his own weight up the mountain, but in addition he will have to exert extra energy to overcome the extra pull on the rope. On the other hand, if the second climber tends to move faster than the first man, thus closing the distance between them, he will have to pick up slack rope and hold it in coils in his hand. If he does not do this, the rope will trail behind him in a loop, or get under his feet and in his way. And everybody who uses a rope and realizes he may dangle suspended from it, will be very careful never to walk on or step on his rope.

The only correct way to travel on a glacier is at full rope's length between climbers. The rope should not be so tight that it is suspended over the snow. This would quickly tire everybody out. The rope should trail in the snow between climbers, but it should be stretched out in a fairly straight line, or, at most, a long and graceful arc, with no loose rope or excess slack anywhere.

In regard to this, climbers should be aware of the configuration of the rope as it trails in the snow. Sometimes it is necessary, when weaving in between crevasses, to travel in a semicircle. If the lay of the crevasses forces this kind of route, the second man on the line should wait in a secure position, take in the slack rope, and prepare for an ice axe belay. A rope stretched out in a big semicircle only means one thing: there is too much slack in the rope. Even if this means the second man should back up, he should do this to keep slack to a minimum.

The most dangerous practice of all is for two or more climbers to bunch up, and to gather up slack rope and carry it in coils in their hands. Carrying coils of rope on a glacier is inexcusable.

If two climbers are walking close together with a large amount of coiled or slack rope between them, and if one of them suddenly falls into a crevasse, he will fall freely until all the slack is gone, gathering speed and momentum all the way. If any coils of rope lie on the snow or are held in anybody's hand, they will be yanked away immediately. The tremendous jerk which follows, when the slack is all gone, will probably yank the next climber into the same crevasse. If, by some fortunate happenstance, the climber above could remain in a secure position and not be jerked loose, the "hit" of the rope would surely be bone crushing to the man below as his plummeting fall came to an abrupt halt, and it would be no less bone crushing to the man above who had to absorb and stop so much kinetic energy all at once.

Allowing for loops and coils and knots, if two men are roped together with a sixty-foot rope, there are less than fifty feet of loose rope extending between them.

It is possible, if two climbers are walking close together and dragging or carrying slack rope, for one of them to suddenly fall into a crevasse only forty feet deep. In this case, neither one of them will feel the jerk of the rope because before the full fifty feet of rope can be brought into play, the man who fell will have hit the bottom. Since a forty-foot fall can kill a man just as dead as a four-hundred-foot fall, the fifty feet of slack will not have helped one bit. Slack rope is not good. Coiled rope, held in the hand and carried, is useless. Climbers should always stay a full rope length away from each other while walking, no matter how inconvenient this is.

If you are right-handed, it is a good idea when walking to move the knot at your waist over to your left side somewhat. This will help to prevent the rope from getting underfoot, allowing the rope to trail forward or back on your left side. If the rope must be handled, this can be done with the left hand, leaving the right hand free to handle the ice axe. If you are looking forward to posterity, you should never allow the rope to drop down from your waist and pass to the rear between your legs.

An effort should be made to maintain the full rope distance between climbers at all times. This means that even if you stop to rest, rest apart from each other, with no slack rope between members of the party. If you sit down on the snow to rest, make a mental note of the climber or climbers you are tied into, and how, if they fell, this would pull on the rope, and rest in such a position that you are able to go into action with the least time and effort lost.

Occasionally, it may be necessary to assemble into a close group, to converse without shouting, to share food from another pack, or for some other legitimate reason. If close assembly is necessary, every climber should be especially watchful for clues which might indicate a crevasse, and ice axe probes should be made continuously in the snow until the group is together. In this case, you have no choice but to gather up the loose rope in coils and carry it in your left hand (if you are right-handed and holding your ice axe in your right hand).

Remember to secure everything with a cord before letting go of it whenever stopping to rest on steep snow slopes. If you remove your pack, drive your ice axe deep into the snow first, and throw one loop of the shoulder strap of the pack around the ice axe. If anything starts to slide downhill, the chances are it will go faster and faster and you will probably never see it again. Hold your canteen in your hand to drink, or put it back in your pack. Don't lay it down on the snow. Don't take off a glove and lay it down on the snow. Snap it onto something, or put it in your pocket. If the wind blows your glove away, you may pay for your mistake with frostbitten fingers.

The most important thing to prevent from sliding downhill is yourself. If you sit down to rest, after you have driven your ice axe into the snow, be sure to take a length of your rope and throw a couple of loops around the ice axe. This is enough to secure you. A knot is not necessary. If you slip and if the rope keeps slipping around the shaft of the axe, you will succeed in dragging another member of your party up to the axe, and he will stop you when he gets to it.

When resting, take the coil of slack rope and use it for a seat. Cold as the rope is, it is nevertheless much warmer to sit on than the snow and ice around you. One final word of caution about the rope when sitting around and resting on a glacier. The rope may seem to run in every direction and to get in the way of everything. This fact combined with the fact that you and everybody else will be wearing crampons should make you very careful not to step on the rope with your crampons. Some of the right-angled edges of the prongs may be sharp enough to cut the rope, or the points of the prongs may dig into the rope and damage the fibers. Be careful so that this does not happen.

Characteristics of the Ice Axe

The term "ice axe" is not a good one. The tool that is called an ice axe has many uses, and its use as an axe for chopping ice is only one use out of many. Also, the ice axe is used much more for doing other things than it is for chopping ice. As a matter of fact, a climber may go on many climbs and use his ice axe constantly on all of these climbs, and never once use it to chop ice. A better name, perhaps, for this excellent and versatile tool would be "pike." But every mountaineer knows the term ice axe and is familiar with it, even though he knows it is poorly conceived, and so we will continue calling this thing an ice axe in this book.

Most ice axes are about three feet long, more or less. They come in sizes, in increments of a half inch. The length is not too important and I have climbed with borrowed ice axes, rented ice axes, and my own ice axes which have varied in length anywhere between thirty-four inches and thirty-eight inches. They have all felt comfortable to me, and I have only noticed the difference in length when comparing with another ice axe.

The length of an ice axe should be such that the hand is able to hold the axe comfortably while the arm has a very slight bend at the elbow.

The wooden portion of the axe is called the shaft. This should be made of ash or hickory or other straight-grained, strong and durable wood. Ash is excellent for both strength and lightness. Ice axes weigh about two pounds. If your axe is a few ounces heavier than this, don't worry about it. If your axe weighs less than two pounds, so much the better.

The bottom end of the ice axe has a tapered metal sleeve. This is to prevent the bottom end from splintering from the constant wear it gets. This sleeve is called the ferrule.

Bare wood is exposed in the opening at the bottom of the ferrule. A steel point or spike is driven up into this wood, and the point of the spike is left exposed at the tip. The spike may be square or rounded, or it may be shaped like an arrowhead. I think the long square or rounded points (about three inches long) are somewhat dangerous, and I prefer the broader and shorter (about two inches long) arrowhead spike, but this is more a matter of taste than anything else.

The upper metal portion of the axe is called the head. The long, narrow part of the head is the pick, and the shorter, broad portion of the head is the adze. The part of the axe where the head joins the shaft is called the neck or the throat.

The adze may have a pronounced downward sweep, or it may extend almost straight back from the pick. Also, the adze may have a pronounced curve, or it may be almost flat.

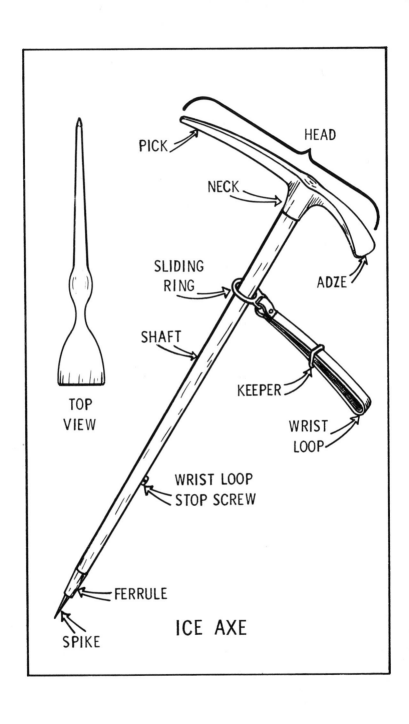

PICK

HEAD

NECK

SLIDING
RING

ADZE

SHAFT

TOP
VIEW

KEEPER

WRIST
LOOP

WRIST LOOP
STOP SCREW

FERRULE

SPIKE

ICE AXE

A steel ring with a slot is introduced onto the shaft of the ice axe from the ferruled (spiked) end, and slid upward on the shaft. A stop screw is then screwed into the shaft about a foot from the spiked end to prevent the ring from sliding off again. A wrist band or wrist loop is attached to the slot in the ring. The loop is made of cotton webbing or nylon or other material and is about one-half of an inch to three-fourths of an inch wide.

Most climbers, when they first buy their ice axe, get some friction tape or mystic tape and tape the shaft from the center of the ferrule to about half-way to the stop screw. This is a part of the shaft that receives a considerable amount of abrasion, and the tape is put on to protect the wood from wear and tear. The tape itself, or what is left of it, can be removed and replaced every few years with new tape.

Many mountaineers, in addition, use other tape in various combinations of colors at other locations along the shaft to enable them to identify their ice axes at a glance. Ice axes tend to all look alike if stacked together in a pile, and a quick means of identification is convenient.

Also, some climbers paint their axes, or parts of them, with orange or red or yellow paint so that the axe will be more highly visible at a distance.

To my knowledge, all ice axes are made in Europe (and lately, a few in Japan), but none in the United States, except perhaps for the assembly, occasionally, of a wooden American shaft to an imported metal head.

Fritsch is a Swiss brand. Grivel is Italian. Ralling is Austrian. Simond is French. Each of these brands is excellent, and all of the ice axes made by them are first-class tools. The axe I own now, and wouldn't be without, is a Fritsch Himalaya. Although I have only owned this axe since May, 1966, (it is early 1969 as I write this), the axe is battered and scarred and scratched enough to look like it is a hundred years old. Despite its appearance, the axe has many years of good service left in it, however, and considering all the adventures we have shared together, I wouldn't sell my axe for a hundred dollars. A man can grow very attached to his ice axe.

Using the Ice Axe

Most of the time the ice axe is used as a cane, or walking stick. The mountaineer strides along on level ground or he walks slowly uphill and while he does this he holds the head of the axe in his right hand and carries it along, touching the ground with every second step he takes.

When walking this way with the axe, the pick is pointed to the rear and slightly outward, away from the body. The palm of the right hand rests on the flat upper surface of the adze. The thumb is curled naturally under the left edge of the adze and the other four fingers hold the adze on the other side. If the snow is fairly level the wrist loop is brought up over the adze and the keeper slide is slid up to tighten the loop and hold it at the narrow portion of the adze where the adze blends into the pick. The width of the adze prevents the loop from slipping off over the adze itself. The mountaineer walks along and he swings the ice axe easily forward in a natural motion, just as he would swing a cane. Indeed, if the snow is level, he may pick up the axe by the shaft and carry it in an horizontal position. The head may be carried to the front or to the rear, but the pick is always pointed downward.

If the snow will remain level for a considerable period of time, the hiker may stop carrying the axe altogether, and strap it to his pack.

When the snow slope grows steeper, out comes the axe from the pack again, and it remains in his hand.

On steep snow slopes when climbers are roped together, the climber puts his wrist through the wrist loop and slides the keeper up snugly so that the wrist band will not be loose. Holding the axe by the adze, he continues forward and upward, still using the axe like a cane. With the wrist loop attached, he can't drop his axe by accident.

Once the climbing party arrives in the vicinity of crevasses, real or suspected, the cane turns into a probe. A quick thrust of the spiked end into the snow should tell immediately what is below the visible surface. If the spike hits solid snow, it will not penetrate deeply. If the spike sinks deeply into the

ADZE

PICK

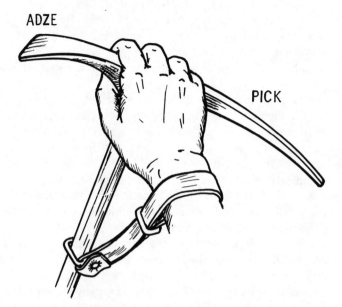

HOLDING AN ICE AXE

snow without meeting resistance, it means a hidden crevasse
has been discovered. The climber can then stop his advance and
probe in a semicircle to the front. If all his probes show thin
snow ahead, it is best to take a step or two back before probing
any more. The climber should especially not probe behind
him. If he has already advanced out onto a concealed crevasse,
such probing to the front, to the side, and to the rear may do
more than establish the fact that he is walking on air. Such
probing in a complete circle may result in the climber's
manufacture of a manhole cover made of snow with himself
standing in the center of it. One probe too many, and he may
drop down into the crevasse still standing on the circle of
snow which he himself carved out.

When playing among crevasses, discretion is always the
best part of valor.

It is not necessary to probe constantly when moving on a glacier, as many parts of a glacier are quite solid. But when the snow looks suspicious the ice axe should be jabbed ahead as often as it is necessary to feel secure.

In addition to its use as a probe, the ice axe is also used as a prop.

The safest stance for a climber on a steep slope is a vertical one. If the climber leans in toward the slope, he increases the downhill vector of force which his boots exert on the snow and decreases the vector exerted vertically down. The closer he leans into the hill, the more likely he is to slip and slide. Unfortunately, there is a natural tendency to lean into the slope, as though ready to grab the snow with the hands. The ice axe is used as a prop to hold the climber away from the slope and in a completely vertical position.

If the snow slopes uphill to the left, the climber holds his ice axe at the adze in his normal grip. He then holds the shaft in his left hand, down near the ferrule, with the shaft of the ice axe crossing in front of his body diagonally down to the left. The spike is then pushed into the rising snow on the left side and the axe is used to help keep him in an upright position. As he proceeds, the climber will from time to time feel the urge to lean into the slope. Using his axe, he pushes himself away and he remains vertical.

If the slope rises to the climber's right, he reverses his grip, and holds the head of the ice axe in his left hand and holds the ferrule end in his right hand.

Because of the need to use the ice axe as a prop on either side, it is necessary when learning self-arrest to learn to do this with the axe held in either hand.

Normally, a climber will find that if he acts naturally and follows his instincts, he will act safely when he is up on a mountain. Fear is natural in the presence of danger. The instinct to grab with the hands is also natural. This instinct is of value when on a steep but bushy hill, or where tree roots are exposed, or even on a steep rocky surface, but the instinct to lean into a steep snow slope to grab a handful of snow is dangerous and provides a false sense of security. The only

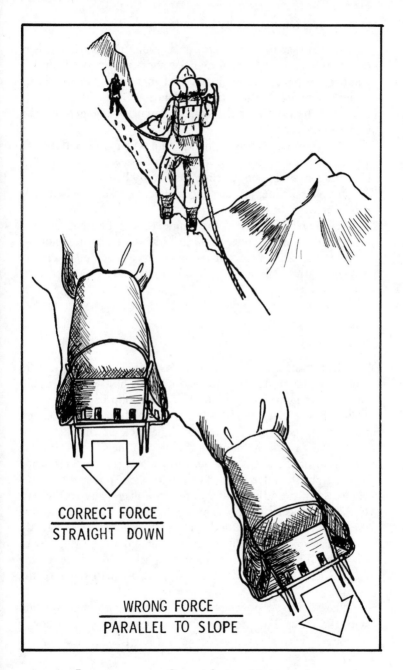

CORRECT FORCE
STRAIGHT DOWN

WRONG FORCE
PARALLEL TO SLOPE

Ice axe as a prop. Correct foot position on a slope

explanation that occurs to me for a wrong instinct like this is that nothing in man's evolutionary ancestry prepared him to climb on slippery snow slopes, and in a case like this he is without any valid instinctive guidance. Worse than that, his instinct to be parallel to the slope is downright dangerous if he is out on snow or ice.

Although the ice axe is a handy tool when used as a cane, as a probe, and as a prop, its most effective use is as a tool to stop himself from sliding once a slide has already begun.

Stopping a slide, or arresting a slide, is called "self-arrest." It is done with the ice axe.

Learning self-arrest is the single most important thing a high-climbing mountaineer can do. If he does not know how to arrest a fall, a climber is in constant danger, sometimes grave danger. If the climber does know how to arrest a fall, he is really quite safe.

Self-Arrest

The self-arrest position is as follows: The mountaineer is in a prone position, flat on his belly, with his head pointed uphill and his feet pointed downhill. The wrist loop of his ice axe is around his right wrist, and he has a tight grip on the ice axe on the narrow portion of the adze. The pick of the ice axe is pushed down into the snow all the way to the shaft of the axe. The head of the axe is held just above and just to the outside of the right shoulder. The shaft of the axe is under the mountaineer's body, and it crosses under him diagonally to the left. His left fist has a tight hold on the lower end of the shaft, near the ferrule. The ferrule and spike extend out past his left hip somewhat so that he will not poke himself in the thigh with the spike. The legs are spread apart slightly, and the toes of the boots and the toes of the crampons are used to dig into the snow.

The self-arrest position is a position of maximum friction with the snow. The prone body provides friction because it is in contact with the snow for its full length. The toes of the

SELF-ARREST

boot and the forward-leaning prongs of the crampons provide additional friction as they dig into the snow. The greatest friction, however, and the prime arresting force in self-arrest, comes from the point of the pick of the ice axe. This is thrust down into the snow as deeply as possible, and held in a deep position.

Since it is the ice axe which primarily stops the fall, it is important to hang onto the ice axe with both hands, and with as strong a grip as possible. If the mountaineer stops the ice axe from sliding by thrusting it into the snow but then lets go of the ice axe, he will experience the wan pleasure of watching his ice axe recede uphill into the distance while he himself shoots downhill at an ever-accelerating rate. This is one reason why it is important to keep the wrist loop attached snugly to the wrist.

Normally, it is possible to go into a self-arrest position as soon as a fall starts; that is, before the mountaineer has developed any speed sliding downhill. The faster the self-arrest position is reached, the easier it is to stop falling, because there is less speed to overcome. A mountaineer should not hesitate, therefore, in getting into a self-arrest position the moment he feels himself falling. Speed and momentum develop quickly once a fall has begun, and every bit of this speed and momentum must be overcome.

If, for any reason, the climber finds himself shooting downhill at a good speed before he can act, he should not thrust the pick forcefully into the snow in a plunging motion. The shock of too sudden a stop may strain his ability to hold on to the axe. In this case, the point of the pick is pushed into the snow in a slow but steady application of braking power until the mountaineer slows down enough to stop gradually. This is not to say that the stop should be delayed overly long. It is merely that the pick should not be plunged deeply into the snow all at once in a stabbing motion while sliding at high speed.

The self-arrest position just described is the one used by a right-handed person who is holding the head of the ice axe in his right hand at the time when he goes into the self-arrest position. The position can be reversed, and done left-handed.

Self-arrest should be practiced both right-handed and left-handed until it can be done easily and effortlessly either way. When done left-handed, the adze is gripped in the left hand and held just above and just outside of the left shoulder. The shaft of the ice axe crosses under the prone body diagonally to the right, and the shaft is held near the ferrule in the right hand near the right hip, just away from the body.

Whenever the climber feels himself falling or slipping, he immediately goes into the self-arrest position. In addition, and at the same time, he shouts the word "falling" as loud as he can.

Whenever any member of the climbing party hears the word "falling," he immediately goes into the self-arrest position too. He does this *immediately* and without waiting or turning around to see who has fallen. As he goes into self-arrest, he waits for a jerk on his rope, and he digs in so that he can resist the yank on the rope when it does come.

Most of the time, when a climber falls, he is able to stop himself from sliding very far by going into the self-arrest position. Whether or not he jerks anybody else off balance depends on the position of the climbers relative to the slope and relative to each other. If they are stretched out crosshill, along a contour line, and if there is any slack at all in the rope, the chances are that a falling climber will be able to arrest his fall before he tightens the rope to the next climber. This may be true even if the climbers are stretched out uphill and downhill, and it will generally be true if the climber who falls is the one furthest uphill.

Often, however, it will be just a very brief period of time from when one climber falls until the rope is pulling hard on one or more other climbers. This is the reason for shouting "falling." It gives all the other climbers an extra fraction of a second for getting into the self-arrest position.

If the falling climber is directly downhill from the man he is tied into, and if the snow and ice are slippery and steep, the pull of the rope on the climber above will be strong and sudden. If the higher man succeeds in getting into a self-arrest position before the climber who is shooting downhill, he will have to dig in as hard as he can with his ice axe and with his toes because he will not only have to hold himself into the snow, he will also have to stop the man who is sliding. If this happens, the falling climber will be brought to a halt before he can himself gather enough wits together to go into self-arrest. The rope will stop him.

If climbers are stretched out crosshill, the pull of the rope from a falling climber is never great, since the pull is not directly downhill, but in a vector off along the contour line, to the side. Even if a man continues to slide for a time from a crosshill position, the pull on the rope to the next climber will never jerk hard, but will merely increase gradually as the sliding climber swings from crosshill to downhill. Usually, because of the gradually increasing aid he gets from the rope, such a climber will be able to arrest himself long before he is directly downhill from the climber above.

In normal climbing on fairly steep snow or ice, one member of the party or another may occasionally slip and fall. When this happens, the man who is falling shouts the warning, "falling," and goes into self-arrest. If he forgets to give the warning and another member of the party sees him falling, that man then shouts "falling," and all the members of the party go into self-arrest. After the slide has been stopped, everybody rises. After dusting off the snow from their clothes, they proceed on to wherever they are going.

The self-arrest position is a very secure position, and it is possible for one man in self-arrest to stop a whole rope party from falling.

Because self-arrest is so easy and so effective, high mountaineering has become a potentially very safe sport. Situations which once used to be dangerous are rendered safe if all members of a climbing party have ice axes and rope and use them properly.

When learning self-arrest and practicing it, the climber starts first with a slide in the sitting position, facing downhill.

Self-arrest from sitting position

Self-arrest from a backward slide

He gives himself a push and down he goes, sliding on the seat of his pants. Holding the head of his ice axe in his right hand and the ferrule in his left, he rolls to his right and plunges the pick into the snow near his right shoulder. He rolls over onto his belly and he digs his toes into the snow. Almost instantly he has stopped.

It is possible when going into self-arrest to swing either way, but it is best to swing to the right, and roll into the ice axe. The danger, when rolling left, is that the spike of the axe may dig in abruptly and be wrenched uphill while the climber tumbles and twists, and the head of the ice axe swings downhill, along with the head and shoulders of the climber.

After practicing self-arrest from a sitting position, facing downhill, the climber next practices going into self-arrest from a supine position. He lies down on his back, feet downhill, head uphill, and gives himself a push. Down the slope he goes. To arrest himself, he merely rolls to his right (always into the head of the axe), digs his pick into the snow, spreads his legs slightly, and digs into the snow with his toes. As soon as he is in the prone position with his axe dug in, he stops. It does not take much practice going into self-arrest from a sitting position or from flat on the back before the climber realizes that he can stop himself easily.

But there is no way of guaranteeing that a slide will always begin feet first, and so, stopping from other positions must be learned and practiced too.

The next position to be practiced is going into self-arrest while sliding headfirst down the hill, flat on the back. The climber lies down on his back, feet uphill, and kicks himself off into a slide. To stop, he rolls to his right (always into the side where the head of the ice axe is held), and he sticks the pick into the snow. At the same time he kicks his feet over to the side. The friction from the ice axe will slow down the upper portion of his body and allow his legs to continue down until his feet are lower than his head. Digging hard with the pick he then brings himself to a stop. If the feet are not completely downhill by the time he has stopped sliding, he can then maneuver them down in a series of kicks. The feet must end up downhill, or it is difficult to stand up from the self-arrest position. Care must be taken when practicing self-arrest while sliding headfirst down the hill that the head and face are held away from the axe. Since the axe is further downhill than the climber's head, and since the axe slows down before the climber's head does, the climber must make a conscious effort to pass the axe on one side, and not slide down directly into it. While prompt self-arrest is desirable, it should not be so prompt that it results in a gashed cheek or gashed forehead from sliding into the protruding adze of the axe.

The final sliding position practiced in learning self-arrest is arrest from a slide while sitting down and facing uphill, that is, arrest while sliding downhill backward, in a sitting position.

The climber stands and faces uphill. Then he squats down. Next he drops his rear end onto the snow and at the same time kicks himself off backward. Off he goes, shooting down the hill. This is not a very convenient or dignified stance, but many a slip might happen in just this way, and so arrest must be practiced this way too.

The arrest from this position is almost the same as when arresting a slide going headfirst down the hill flat on the back. The climber swings to his right (into the head of the axe), and thrusts his pick into the snow. At the same time he raises the ferrule end of his axe somewhat and swings his feet off to the left. Then he rolls over onto his stomach, swings his feet downhill, or kicks them downhill, and ends up in the final self-arrest position.

Practicing self-arrest is strenuous work. If the practice is done on a warm day on a snow slope on a mountainside, the combination of body heat generated by physical exertion and solar heat, both working on the snow which the climber will constantly have on his clothes, will sooner or later make him soaking wet.

If you go out specifically to learn and to practice self-arrest, it is a good idea to bring along an extra set of dry clothes to change into after you have finished all your slides.

Self-arrest should first be practiced on gentle slopes and then later on steep and slippery slopes. As a matter of safety, the practice should be done on a snow slope which has a flattened run-out at the bottom so that if the climber fails to arrest himself, he will nevertheless come to a safe halt.

With practice comes confidence. After the climber has arrested his falls many times from all possible falling positions, he will gradually come to realize that slipping and falling can happen easily and that it is just as easy to arrest a fall. Also, with practice a new affection will grow for the ice axe, for it is this tool that makes self-arrest possible. After a time, the climber handles his ice axe easily and naturally, and though his treatment of the ice axe may seem casual to an inexperienced eye, the climber will somehow always have the ice axe ready if self-arrest should suddenly become necessary.

The Ice Axe Belay

In addition to its use as a cane, as a probing device, as a prop to hold oneself erect, and as a tool for achieving self-arrest, the ice axe is also used as an anchor in belaying.

The ice axe belay is a fast and convenient way of belaying a climber while out on a glacier. Often, because of the terrain, it is the only belay possible.

First, what is a belay? A belay is a method of making a climber secure by giving him only enough rope to move ahead while at the same time having the other end of the rope ready to "lock in" on some friction point. A belay is used at critical points in a climb where the possibility of a fall is greater than usual, or where the consequences of a fall would be serious. A belay might be used in negotiating a very short but very steep and slippery ice slope, for example. Or it might be used when a climber is crossing a snow bridge. Once the danger point is passed, the belay is discontinued.

If a climber were crossing a snow bridge and the snow bridge suddenly collapsed beneath his feet, the climber would instantly fall. With an acceleration of thirty-two feet per second, the weight of a falling man would exert a powerful and sudden yank on the rope. No climber could hope to hold such a rope in his hand and expect that he could stop the man from falling. If he had strength enough to maintain his grip on the rope, he would himself be yanked off his feet and into the crevasse. But more likely, the rope would be jerked from his hands, and then, after it ran its full length into the crevasse, the second man would himself be yanked into the crevasse when the tight rope grabbed him by the loops around his waist.

The powerful and sudden pull of the rope could be resisted by the second climber if he were in a self-arrest position. But if he anchored himself this way, the full length of the rope would play out before he could hold the falling climber, and this would not be satisfactory. If the second climber assumed a self-arrest stance far enough away from the snow bridge or other potential danger point, so that the slack in the rope could all be taken up, then obviously the first climber could not proceed any further because he would be at the end of a fixed length of rope.

Belaying is a method of giving an advancing climber enough rope to proceed forward while at the same time not allowing any slack rope.

In rock climbing, a hip belay can be used. In a hip belay, the belaying climber sits down in a secure position. He jams his feet against secure rock footholds, and he passes rope out to the advancing climber around his hip or waist. Should the advancing climber slip or fall, he braces himself and holds on to the rope. The friction of the rope around his body plus the grip on the rope from his gloved hands is enough to hold the rope and secure the slipping climber. The fact that the belaying climber is braced in a sitting position enables him to resist the force of the pulling rope without being yanked out of position.

Unfortunately there are not many occasions where a hip belay can be used when out on a glacier. Most snow and ice terrain provides no secure position from which a climber can make a body belay. This is the beauty of an ice axe belay. It can be used anywhere on snow.

The ice axe belay is simple, easy to set up, and it provides an absolutely secure belay.

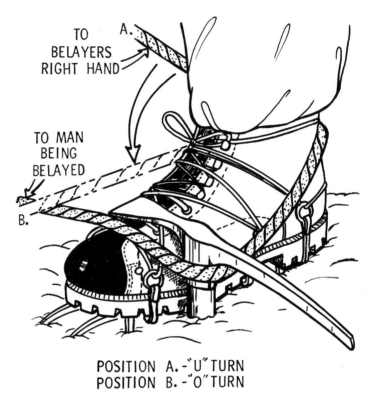

TO
BELAYERS
RIGHT HAND

TO MAN
BEING
BELAYED

A.

B.

POSITION A. -"U" TURN
POSITION B. -"O" TURN

Ice axe belay

First of all, the belayer drives his ice axe down into the snow for its full length, or almost to the head of the axe. The axe should be in an absolutely vertical position, tilting neither uphill or downhill. The axe is driven down in such a manner that the pick of the axe points away from where the potential pull of the rope will come. Usually, this means the pick will point uphill and the adze downhill, but this is not always so. If the point of potential danger is a crevasse lip, or a snow bridge, the pick should point away from them.

The belayer then takes up a position downhill from the

axe, or between the axe and the man being belayed if this is some position other than downhill. Standing at 90 degrees to the direction of the rope, the belayer puts his uphill boot directly next to the axe, to help hold the axe in position by providing a brace for it. With a few kicks of his downhill boot, he makes a flat platform in the snow for that boot so that he can stand in a secure position. For a right-handed person, it is usually easiest to stand with the hill sloping upward on his left side and downward (or toward the snow bridge) on his right.

The rope comes from the person being belayed and passes over the uphill toe of the belayer's boot. The rope then goes around the shaft of the ice axe, under the pick, and passes around the heel of the uphill boot. The rope is held in the right hand of the belayer and allowed to slip through his fingers as the belayed climber advances across the snow bridge or proceeds wherever he is going. The belayer, at the same time bends over and holds the head of the ice axe down with his left hand.

As long as the advancing climber is proceeding safely, the belayer holds the rope out, somewhat away from his heel, so that the rope can play out freely, with a minimum of friction. No slack whatever should be allowed, merely a freely-running rope.

If the advancing climber should slip or fall, the belayer immediately brings the rope well around his heel and partially around his ankle over the toe of his boot to get added friction, and he immediately tightens his grip on the rope. The pull of the rope will bring his boot tightly up against the ice axe. The friction of the rope going over the toe of the boot, around the shaft of the ice axe, and then around the heel and ankle, combined with the grip of the fist on the rope, will be enough to hold the falling climber. At this point, the belayer can, if it seems desirable, bring the rope up and pass it under the pick to obtain additional friction if it appears he will have to hold on for any length of time. If the climber has slipped into a crevasse, the belayer will have to anchor the rope until the fallen climber can be brought out. If the person being belayed has merely slipped on a steep slope, the belayer will be able to release the belay as soon as the belayed climber has stopped sliding and risen to his feet.

In the event that it does become necessary to pass the rope under the pick in order to hold the anchor for a longer time, the belayer should remember to pull sideward on the rope and not upward. If he is pushing down with one hand on the head of the ice axe, and pulling up against it with the rope in his other hand, he will soon tire himself out in this one-man tug of war. If the hand holding the rope wins, he will yank the ice axe up out of the snow and destroy his belay. He may also destroy his fellow climber in the process.

The form of ice axe belay just described brings the rope around the uphill boot and ice axe of the belayer in a "U" turn. When a fall or slide occurs, the rope is brought around further and the "U" turn is closed into an "O" turn, or complete loop. This provides enough friction to do the job if the rope is not slippery from a greasy boot smeared excessively with snow-proofing, and if the rope is not icy (wet and frozen).

In the event that the rope is frozen and slippery, a variation of the above is used to get added friction. This variation is in the form of an "S" turn.

Using the "S" turn, the rope comes from the person being belayed and passes over the uphill (usually left) boot of the belayer, over the toe of the boot. The rope continues up, passes once around the shaft of the ice axe (always under the pick), then over the instep of the boot, then uphill again behind the heel of the boot. When using an "S" turn in an ice axe belay, the arms are reversed from the way they are used in the "U" turn. Using the "S" turn, the right hand holds down the head of the axe while the left hand plays out the rope.

Although using an "S" turn provides a considerable amount of friction, and makes a sure stoppage of running rope even surer, this method has its disadvantages too. For one thing, a belay should not be such that excessive friction prevents the rope from running freely. The advancing climber should be able to advance without making any special effort to drag rope along behind him. Unless the rope is very slippery, the use of the "S" turn will have this very effect. Also, when using the "S" turn, the belayer is forced to take a position in which he almost has his back to the person being belayed. To view the advancing climber, the belayer has to twist his head and neck almost 180 degrees. Since a belayer should at all times be watching the person he is belaying, being forced to do this awkwardly is a distinct disadvantage.

Variations of the ice axe belay may be used, depending on circumstances and conditions.

One variation is for the belayer to take up a position above (uphill from) the ice axe, rather than below it. Sometimes this is the most convenient way to belay on a very steep slope. Doing it this way, if the belayer keeps the uphill slope on his left, he plants his right boot, which is the downhill boot, on the downhill side of the ice axe and right next to it. He then kneels in the snow with his left knee above the ice axe. The rope is handled the same way as when taking a stance below the axe.

Step Chopping

We have mentioned that the ice axe is used as a cane, as a probing tool, as a prop to insure a vertical stance while on a steep snow slope, as a device for achieving self-arrest, and as an anchor point for belaying. We now come to the use for which the ice axe is named, and this is step chopping.

On moderately steep slopes it is possible to move up by kick stepping. However, if the degree of steepness of the slope becomes too great, it becomes inconvenient or impossible to proceed further by means of kicking steps. This is where it becomes necessary to chop steps with the ice axe.

In step chopping, the wrist sling is retained around the wrist, but the hand slides down the length of the shaft and holds the axe between the stop screw and the ferrule. The right hand brings the head of the axe down at the point where the next foothold is to be chopped. In doing this, it is not necessary to swing with great force, as if chopping a log with a regular axe. The use of excessive force may drive the climber off balance. Also, the snow yields to the axe with considerably less resistance than that encountered in a wooden log.

In normally compacted snow, the adze is used for chopping and also for scooping loose snow from the hole. If the snow is very hard, the pick end should be used once or twice first, then the adze to get rid of the loosened snow. Sometimes, in an area which has repeatedly thawed and frozen, hard ice will be encountered on the surface and perhaps for some depth. The point of the pick should be used for chopping in glazed ice. The adze is then used as a scooper.

If the snow is very hard, a deep step is not necessary. All that will be required in this case is a flat and level platform for the toe of the boot and crampon. Or, the forward part of the hole may be made just a bit deeper than the opening. If the snow is somewhat looser, the foothold should be made deep enough to insert the entire boot, or the greatest part of it.

If the snow is very steep, it will also be necessary to cut some snow away from directly above the hole so that as you step up into the hole, there is a place made for your shin. This is necessary so you can stand upright after you step up to the hole. When step chopping on a very steep slope, it is often convenient to slide the hand up somewhat higher on the shaft, and hold the axe a bit closer to the head. This makes it easier to maneuver the axe and still retain your balance.

If the slope is steep enough to make balance precarious, hand holds should be chopped as well as foot holds. This should only be done for a short but sheer stretch of snow. A high, sheer wall of snow should be bypassed if possible.

If there is any possibility that you will descend by the same route you are using going up, and if the snow wall is too sheer to glissade down from, you should chop your foot holds closer together than you need them for the ascent. The closely-spaced steps will be needed on the way down.

From the viewpoint of safety, step chopping is a dangerous procedure. Not only is it done in a steep and slippery environment, but it is also done while holding the ice axe in such a way that normal self-arrest cannot be accomplished. It is true that if the climber feels himself starting to slip he can take a last, desperate swing with his pick into the slope. But even if this holds him, he will be suspended essentially from the ice axe by one hand in what by no means can be called a secure position.

For this reason, step chopping should be done slowly, deliberately, without haste, and as carefully as possible. A high, steep snow wall, more than one rope length in distance, should be avoided if possible by bypassing it. Two climbers, one vertically above the other, ascending by means of step chopping makes the situation doubly dangerous.

In Among Crevasses

Steep snow or ice slopes, even very steep ones, are not as terrifying as they may appear from a distance. A climber cannot really fall on such a slope. At most, he will slide. And a slide can be arrested. But if a climber falls into a crevasse, then he really falls, and this is definitely dangerous.

Nevertheless, it is frequently necessary in the mountain environment to be out among crevasses. It is therefore essential to become familiar with the surface features of a crevassed area.

Crevasses tend to lie parallel to each other in any given area, or in lines which are extensions of the lines made by other crevasses. In travelling among crevasses, the direction of the rope should be kept at 90 degrees to the line of the crevasses. While this is excellent in theory, it is sometimes very difficult to do in practice. This is because it is necessary to zigzag around the ends of crevasses, and the dog-legs taken in these zigzag routes tend to be parallel to the crevasses in the area.

We have already discussed snow bridges, and the care which must be exercised in crossing them. The two dangers involved in crossing snow bridges are: (1) that the mountaineer may slip off to one side or the other; (2) that the bridge itself may collapse.

A snow bridge is one which spans a crevasse from one side

90°

LINE OF
CREVASSE

LINE OF TRAVEL

Crossing a crevasse

to the other and which is not solid. It is a bridge which has air beneath it.

Sometimes, however, there may be solid snow across a crevasse which does not have air or space beneath it. Even though such a bridge probably will not collapse, the climber may nevertheless slip off it to one side or the other, and down into the crevasse. Such snow crossings cannot properly be called snow bridges. I call them "Z" bridges or "I" bridges, depending on their configuration.

If two crevasses extend past each other and then one of them pulls slowly away from the other one, the solid snow connection between them gradually is pulled out into a "Z" shape. If one of the crevasses moves laterally from the other one as well as away, the "Z" bridge will gradually become straightened out, and the crossing between the two crevasses will be at about a right angle to the line of the crevasses. This is an "I" bridge. As already mentioned, these are not true bridges, since they do not arch out over empty air, but extend all the way down to the bottom of the crevasse. Nevertheless, if a climber slips off such a crevasse crossing, his fall will be straight down into the crevasse.

The edges of a crevasse are called the lips. In early spring, the lips tend to overhang the walls of the crevasse. As summer melting takes place, the overhangs disappear, and the lip of the crevasse is the upper edge of a vertical wall.

Where two masses of snow move away from each other, a crevasse is formed. Where two masses of snow move toward each other, the snow is compressed and forced up into a tower which rises above the surrounding snow. Such a snow tower is called a serac. In a very jumbled portion of a glacier, seracs and crevasses may be close to one another. Where the glacier is very jumbled, it is often the case that where crevasses do occur, they are narrow and shallow. Sometimes they are so shallow it is possible to cross the crevasse by climbing down into it and climbing out on the other side.

The Prusik Sling

A climber who has fallen into a crevasse may emerge in one

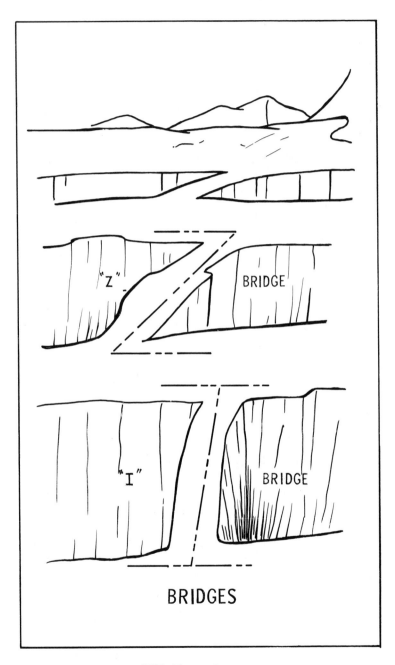

BRIDGES

"Z" bridge and "I" bridge

of several ways. Sometimes it is possible to climb right out. If he is hanging from the rope and if there are enough people present in the climbing party, they may be able to pull him out. If there are only two climbers in the party, then it is obvious that the person anchoring the rope cannot assist in the rescue since he will have to continue holding the rope where he is. In this case, the mountaineer who is down in the crevasse has to climb out by himself. He does this using Prusik slings.

Prusik slings are made from Manila rope one-quarter of an inch or five-sixteenths of an inch in diameter. The sling has a loop tied at each end of it. The loop at one end should be large enough to hold a cramponed boot with ease. The loop at the other end can be smaller. These loops are tied with a bowline. Once tied, they need never be untied again. The length of the Prusik sling should be such that if you insert your foot in the large loop and hold the rope taut, the upper loop will be at about the height of your chin or nose. Every climber should have two Prusik slings, and they should be made specifically for his height. Since once the two loops are made, they are not untied again, and since Manila rope has a tendency to fray at the ends, it is a good idea, after the knots are tied, to put a few stitches through the knot with nylon thread to hold the rope in place, and then to cover the knots with tape to keep them from coming apart and to keep the rope from unraveling.

The Prusik Knot

A Prusik knot is made when the Manila Prusik sling is tied into the larger nylon rope which is the main climbing rope. The Prusik knot is tied in the following manner: The smaller (upper) loop of the Prusik sling is placed under the nylon climbing rope. The other end of the Prusik sling, which contains the larger foot loop, is then passed over the nylon rope and through the small loop. The foot end of the sling then passes under the nylon rope, around it, over it again, and through the same loop a second time. The sling is then pulled tight and this tightens the Prusik knot.

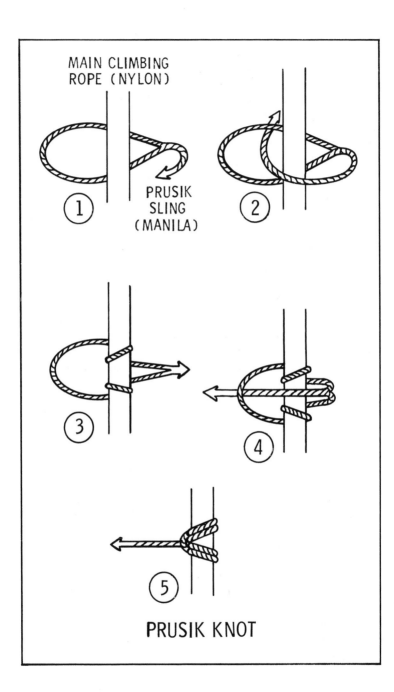

MAIN CLIMBING
ROPE (NYLON)

PRUSIK
SLING
(MANILA)

① ② ③ ④ ⑤

PRUSIK KNOT

What is so unique about a Prusik knot? It has a slip, no-slip quality. If you hold the nylon rope in one hand and the Prusik sling in the other, and try to pull the Prusik knot along the nylon rope, you will find that it will not slide. In fact, the harder you pull, the tighter it grips the nylon rope. On the other hand, if you release the Prusik sling so that there will not be any tension on the nylon rope, you will find that it is easy to slide the Prusik knot up or down the nylon rope. This is the very quality of the Prusik knot that makes it so useful. Give it slack and it is easy to slide. Put tension on it, and it acquires such a grip that it cannot be slid at all. The greater the tension, the tighter its grip.

One reason Prusik slings are not made with nylon rope or nylon cord is that nylon stretches under tension. If the Prusik knot were tied with a nylon rope, it could stretch and tighten the knot when pressure was applied. This would make the knot so tight it would be difficult to loosen it again. A Prusik knot must be just as easy to loosen as it is to tighten, and Manila rope is the best rope for doing this. Some very tightly woven nylon ropes with a very hard lay may be used to make Prusik knots, but it is best not to fool around, and to stick with Manila.

Each climber ties two Prusik slings into his nylon climbing rope, one for each foot. He ties the Prusik knot about a foot away from where the nylon rope is knotted around his waist. After tying the two Prusik knots, he takes the slings and passes them through the rope which is around his waist from above to below. He then gathers up the loose ends of the slings and he puts them into his side pockets, one on each side.

How to Prusik

If a mountaineer slips and falls into a crevasse, he will find himself hanging from his main climbing rope. The shock of the fall will usually do two things. First, it will move the rope from around his waist up to his chest and under his armpits. Next it will tighten the rope around his chest so much that it will be difficult to breathe.

The mountaineer must now act fast. Reaching into each of his side pockets, he pulls out the foot loops of his Prusik slings, and allows them to hang down. Next he inserts his cramponed boots into the slings, each boot into its own sling. Next he slides the Prusik knots up the rope, away from his body.

As soon as the Prusik knot on one side or the other has been slid to the point where there is tension on it, it will grip the nylon rope. The climber can now stand in the Prusik sling instead of hanging from the nylon rope. As soon as he is able to stand in the sling, the pressure of the tight loops around his chest will be loosened, and he will be able to breathe normally again.

There are two Prusik slings on the main rope, one for each foot. The climber now raises his lower foot. This puts slack on the Prusik knot which is holding the sling for that foot. Without tension on it, the knot can be slid a bit further up the nylon rope. The climber then "steps down" into that sling by pushing down on it with his foot. As soon as he does this, the Prusik knot tightens and grips the nylon rope. Since the sling is now higher on the nylon rope than it was before, this means that the climber actually "stepped up" when he put tension on the sling.

If the climber now releases tension on his other sling by bending his knee and raising his foot on that side, he will in turn be able to slide the Prusik knot on *that* side a bit higher. When he again steps down hard into this sling, it too will be in a higher position than it was before, and so he will actually be stepping up when he puts his weight on that foot.

By alternately raising first one foot and then sliding the Prusik knot for that foot upward and then repeating this same procedure with the other foot, the climber will raise himself along his nylon rope, going higher and higher up the rope as he slides one sling up and then the other. He can continue this process until he has climbed right up to the lip of the crevasse. At this point all that is left to do is climb out of the crevasse altogether. Using Prusik slings is very similar to using a rope ladder except that with Prusik slings the climber, instead of climbing into higher rungs of a ladder, simply raises the rungs themselves by sliding them up the main nylon climbing rope.

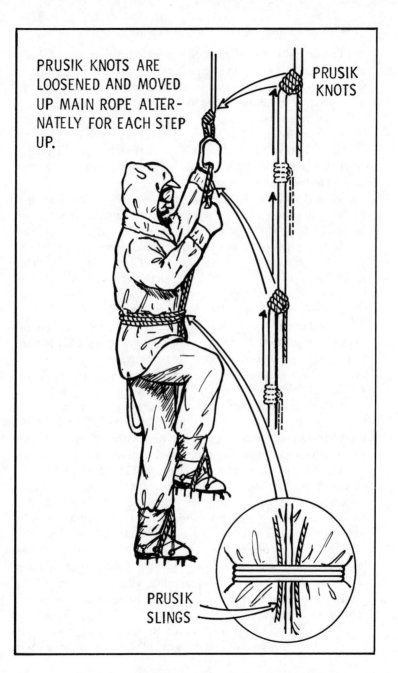

PRUSIK KNOTS ARE LOOSENED AND MOVED UP MAIN ROPE ALTERNATELY FOR EACH STEP UP.

PRUSIK KNOTS

PRUSIK SLINGS

Prusikking up a rope

The invention of Prusik slings is a brilliant one, all the more brilliant in its simplicity, and all mountaineers everywhere owe a debt of gratitude to Mr. Prusik, whoever he was. The system is glorious and ingenious and it really works.

Knowing how prusikking works in a general way, and having actually prusikked, are two different things. Nobody should go out on a glacier and tie into a rope with other people until he has practiced prusikking and knows how to do it from actual experience.

A good way to practice is to tie your nylon climbing rope to the limb of a tree about twenty-five or thirty feet from the ground, letting the rope hang down to the ground. Tie into the nylon rope with both your Prusik slings. Then prusik your way from the ground up to the limb and back down again. Not only is this invaluable experience, but it will also let you know if your Prusik slings are too short, too long, or just right.

Prusikking not only requires dexterity, it requires a good physical condition. The man who would save his own life by prusikking up out of a crevasse must be physically able to do this. Without a certain basic minimum amount of strength and stamina, prusikking becomes difficult, perhaps impossible.

If a climber falls through a snow bridge at a distance which is ten feet from the wall of the crevasse, and if he is being belayed and there is no slack in the rope, then he will swing in an arc which has a ten-foot radius and slam into the wall of the crevasse ten feet from the top. This will knock the wind out of any man. The fact that the crevasse wall consists of snow which will cushion the impact somewhat does not alter the fact that he will hit it with a good deal of force. Snow down in a crevasse is not drift snow or powder by any means. Once the wind is knocked out of the man, he may have trouble getting his wind back, since the rope will now be tight around his chest. In a dazed condition, the climber will be hard put just to get his feet into his Prusik slings, so that he can relieve the rope pressure on his chest.

Some climbers who have fallen into crevasses have been completely uninjured, and have been able to assist in their own rescue. Some have been able to prusik up the rope without any assistance at all from above. Others have been dazed by the fall, or suffered worse injuries, such as being struck or stabbed by some part of the ice axe. For this reason, it is best to keep parties travelling on a glacier to a minimum of three men. If one man falls into a crevasse, one man will be occupied full-time holding the rope. The third man can then move about and assist in the rescue.

Theoretically, two-man parties are feasible out on a glacier, but two-man parties should be limited to two experienced mountaineers who are in excellent physical condition. This is not the place for weaklings, fatties, sissies, or softies, and it is not the place for unskilled and inexperienced beginners. Even if a two-man team is tough and resourceful, such a two-man team should not travel in the winter on a glacier, at a time when crevasses are mostly covered over and concealed. They should limit themselves to summer climbing when crevasses are mostly open and visible. Adding a third member to the team makes it much safer for any season of the year.

Chimneying

All crevasses are not great, gaping canyons in the glacier. Many are quite narrow. When crevasses are very large, they are very obvious, and very easy to avoid.

Consequently, the chances are that if a climber falls into a crevasse, it may well be a small and narrow one. If he has not already hit the bottom when he fell, he may be hanging very close to the bottom. In this case, rather than prusik up the rope, it may be better to call to the man above and tell him to slacken the rope and let him be lowered to the bottom of the crevasse. He will then be able to walk to a narrower portion of the crevasse and chimney up to the top.

In chimneying, a climber goes up a narrow part of a crevasse by jamming his back against one wall of the crevasse and jamming his cramponed boots against the opposite wall. He may let the ice axe dangle from its wrist loop and use the heels of his hands on the wall behind his back, or he may hold the pick of the axe near the adze and use the adze to dig in behind him on his right side as he works his way up. In chimneying, he jams his boots hard into the one wall and he works his back up on the other wall. Then he raises his feet, one at a time, and in the new position, works his back up higher.

As the mountaineer chimneys up out of the crevasse, the climber above should set up an ice axe belay and take in the rope as it slackens. This will provide security if the chimneying climber should slip and fall while he is on the way up.

To be doubly safe, the man in the crevasse should put his boots through his Prusik slings, just in case, and do his chimneying with his Prusik slings on.

Harnesses, Seat Slings, Belts, and Clamps

Using a climbing rope and Prusik slings, as described on the previous pages, has made glacier mountaineering a relatively safe sport. The use of Prusik slings and a climbing rope were developed early in the sport of mountaineering, and their usage has continued to the present. Most climbers today still tie into a main nylon rope and still attach their two Prusik slings, and off they go out on the glacier.

But new techniques have been developed for falling more safely into a crevasse, and for getting out more easily, and new equipment has been developed to go along with the new techniques.

For one thing, with a heavy pack on his back and a rope around his middle, a climber is top-heavy. If he falls into a crevasse, rather than hang feet down, he may find himself hanging upside down.

Mountaineers gave considerable thought to how to keep a man upright if he fell into a crevasse, and how to avoid the sudden, forceful constriction of a rope around his chest even if he did end up hanging properly, with his feet down.

The seat sling and the chest harness are the results of this thought. The development of this equipment marks a definite improvement in mountaineering safety.

CHIMNEYING

These items of equipment can be homemade or they can be purchased. They can be made from canvas or nylon webbing, or they can be made from nylon rope. Nylon webbing is the best material for slings and harnesses. The nylon is strong and durable, and the webbing does not dig into the body as much as a rope does.

Imagine the general configuration of a vest. It goes around the back, under the arms, and comes together in the front. Now imagine a very short vest that does not reach down to the waist. This is the general configuration of a chest harness. A belt of webbing goes around the back and meets in front of the chest. Two shoulder loops pass from in front over the shoulders to the rear, and are attached to the main belt permanently. The two ends of the webbing in front of the chest terminate in two loops instead of buttons. A karabiner (snap link) is used to fasten these two loops together. Karabiners are like a single link of a chain, except that they have a hinged opening which opens inward only against a spring and snaps shut if released.

If a climber uses a chest harness only, and not a seat sling, he takes the rope as it comes from the bowline knot at his waist and passes it through the karabiner which holds his chest harness linked. If he is the climber in the middle of the rope, he has two lengths of rope, one going forward and one to the rear. He passes both of these lengths of rope through the karabiner at his chest.

Using a chest harness guarantees that a climber will not end up hanging upside down if he falls in a crevasse. The rope from his waist passing through the karabiner in the chest harness will point upward, out of the crevasse, and so will the climber's head. His feet will point down. Although he still will have the job ahead of him of getting out of the crevasse, he will at least not have to start from an upside down position. A chest harness is, therefore, a desirable item of equipment as is any item of equipment which widens the margin of safety.

The trouble with chest harnesses is that they get in the way of the pack and the pack gets in the way of the harness. A chest harness made of rope is the biggest offender in this case, and a chest harness made of flat nylon webbing is the lesser offender.

Since a pack is an absolute necessity, and since a pack is already a form of chest harness, it seems obvious that the pack itself can be used for part of a rope harnessing arrangement.

I have never seen such an arrangement, but if there is none for sale anywhere (and I have not seen any for sale), a climber could easily manufacture his own. All that is needed are two loops made of canvas or nylon webbing, about an inch wide, each about seven inches long. Each one would be looped through one of the shoulder straps of the pack. After the pack is put on, simply connect the two loops at the chest with a karabiner through which the climbing rope can also be passed.

These little chest loops could be called "uprighters," since if you fell, you would fall upright if you wore them. Or they could be called "upriders," since they would ride up high on the chest. Most shoulder straps on packs are quite strong and capable of withstanding considerable strain. Also, most climbing packs have a waist strap for holding the load of the pack on the hips, close in, and centered. The main load on the rope would not be on the chest harness anyway, in whatever form it was fashioned, but on the coil of rope around the waist. The karabiner at chest level would merely serve to guide the rope and to hold the climber upright, and most pack shoulder straps should have more than enough strength to do this.

I have never seen a chest loop arrangement using the shoulder straps of the pack, but I believe I'll make one of my own one of these days when I can get around to it. To keep the upriders from sliding down, a two-inch length of nylon parachute cord could be sewn to the shoulder straps of the pack above and below where the loop of the uprider passes around the shoulder strap. The best location for these loops could be determined by trial and error after using them for a while. The more it is considered, the more appealing the idea becomes.

Some climbers, instead of making or buying a complicated shoulder harness, use a length of rope closed together to form a loop. They twist the loop once to form a figure "8" and then insert their arms into the ends of the "8." The loops are then connected at the chest with a karabiner.

One form of chest harness or another, no matter how or where made, will only hold the climber in an upright position after he has fallen. The full force of the rope will be felt at the point where it is tied to the body. If this is at the waist, this is where the climber's weight will be supported. But a very tight rope around the belly can be distracting at a time when a man should have all his wits about him. If the rope slides up from his waist to his chest, the pressure will be so great that breathing will be very difficult.

Suspended in a seat sling

One way to stop a narrow rope from digging into the body is to replace it with a wider nylon belt. Such a belt, with nylon loops sewn in at each end, or with steel rings at each end, is then connected at the waist with a karabiner. The rope, instead of being looped around the waist, is tied to the karabiner. As a matter of fact, such a belt could be made of leather up to six inches wide, and be strapped together at the front, similar to the waist belts sometimes worn by motorcycle riders. The wider the waistband, the more comfortable it will be if forced to hang from a rope while attached to it.

But no matter how wide the waistband was made, the climber would still end up hanging from a waistband if he fell into a crevasse. And so mountaineers have invented something even more comfortable. This is the seat sling.

A seat sling can be made from rope or from webbing. Webbing is better because it will be more comfortable.

The seat sling consists of two loops which are worn around the upper thighs. The thigh loops are connected to a waistband, once to the rear and once again in the front. The two front-connecting loops which come from the thigh bands may be sewn to the waistband or they may be connected by the same karabiner which joins the two ends of the waistband at the front. The climbing rope is also tied to this karabiner. A seat sling somewhat resembles the lower half of a parachute harness.

It is a bit awkward walking while strapped into a seat sling, but it is marvelous to be strapped in a seat sling if you suddenly find yourself hanging in a crevasse. There is very little constriction about the waist or chest since most of the weight of the body is supported by the thigh loops. It is almost like sitting in a chair.

All of the harnesses and slings described above make falling into a crevasse and hanging there by a rope safer and more comfortable. However, once he finds himself in a crevasse, the climber is still forced to prusik his way out with his good old Prusik knots.

But this too can be done in a different way. A rope clamp has been devised which has the same action as a Prusik knot. That is, the clamp may be slipped upward along the rope without effort, but it grabs the rope and holds it tightly if any effort is made to force it down the rope. This clamping device is called a Jumar ascender.

A Jumar ascender acts as a mechanical Prusik knot. This device has both advantages and disadvantages. On the plus side, a Jumar ascender is easy to work. If the climber's fingers are stiff from cold it is not always easy alternately to slide and loosen Prusik knots. It is easy to grasp the handle of the Jumar ascender and push it up. An upward push releases the grip of the eccentric cam on the rope and allows the rope to move downward through the device. A spring keeps pressure against the rope. As soon as there is any upward motion of rope past the cam, the device grips the rope and holds it firmly. Because the cam has a field of bluntly rounded "teeth" on it, and because these teeth grip the rope tightly, absolutely no slippage can occur, even on an icy rope. The rope can pass in one direction only through the Jumar ascender, and that is downward.

On the minus side it must be said that a Jumar ascender is a heavy and bulky substitute for a Prusik knot. Since these devices must always be used in pairs, this makes them twice as heavy and twice as bulky. In addition, a Prusik knot does not damage the main nylon climbing rope in any way. A Jumar ascender, because it has teeth, will tend to mash and chew into your good nylon rope, and will eventually destroy its usefulness as a rope.

Jumar ascenders are made in Switzerland and come in one size only. Because the gripper device in this tool is an eccentric cam, the opening it makes for the rope to pass through varies, and it can be used on any size rope from a quarter inch up to a half inch in diameter.

Another similar device is the Hiebler rope clamp, which is made in Western Germany. The Hiebler ascender works on the same principle as the Jumar ascender, but is smaller and weighs less. But the Hiebler ascender, unlike the Swiss model, has no teeth. This is an advantage in that if there are no teeth, the device cannot chew up your good nylon rope. The grip of the Hiebler ascender on the rope is nevertheless a tight one, even on an icy rope, and every bit as tight as a Prusik knot. The trick to using this kind of a device on icy and slippery rope is to give the rope a slight bend at the point where the clamp is attached before putting weight on it, and then putting weight on it gradually instead of all of a sudden. This, incidentally, should also be done with Prusik knots on icy rope.

All in all, when considering the use of chest harnesses, seat slings, and rope-clamping devices, I would say that a combination chest harness and seat sling is definitely superior to just tying the rope around your waist. On the other hand, I don't see any great advantage in rope clamps over ordinary Prusik knots. The Prusik knot works fine, weighs next to nothing, has no excess bulk, and is adequate for the purpose it has to serve.

Thoughts on the Summit

Once a climber has reached the top of a mountain, signed

Thoughts on the summit

the register book if there is one there, eaten his lunch, rested, enjoyed the view (or peered intently into the encircling fog), congratulated his fellow climbers, and exulted in his triumph, there is nothing left to do but go back down again. There are some definite techniques which are employed going downhill, and these will be covered next. But first, before we leave the lofty, snow-clad summit, it is proper to make a few observations about climbing mountains.

Why do climbers climb? Why do men want to get to the top of the mountain? Are there any lessons to be learned on the mountain which can be applied to daily living? Can anything be learned in mountaineering which is equally applicable to your job, or to life itself?

The "why" of climbing is the easiest to answer, and at the same time the hardest. Men climb (and these days women too) because mountain climbing is a healthful, outdoor sport. Climbing clears the lungs and develops them. It sharpens the eye. It develops good, healthy muscle tone not only in the legs but in every part of the body. No exercise is really exercise unless it does two things: it must get you winded and it must make you sweat. Panting and perspiration are a natural part of climbing, and fill these requirements. In an age where heart disease has become widespread, even among younger people, and where the greatest killer has turned out to be a desk or a bench, behind which a person is forced to sit quietly for eight hours a day, mountain climbing has provided the answer to how to get the violent physical exercise which the body must have to survive in a healthy condition.

In an environment of rising crime, mountaineering will develop the strength and stamina which you may need some day to defend yourself physically, not on a relatively safe mountain but on a relatively dangerous city street.

Mountaineering is the one sport where you can win without there being any loser. The mountain is an impersonal mass of rock and snow, and it doesn't care whether you climb to the top or not. Your triumph, when you reach the summit, is over yourself.

As frosting on the cake, mountaineering takes the climber

away from city grime and city noises, and brings him into the great outdoors. Climbing brings a man into intimate proximity with nature, with greenery, with solitude, with the grandeur of towering masses of rock and snow, and with the clouds and the sky. Climbing presents the climber with beautiful views, often awesome in their majestic sweep.

What about the lessons learned on the mountain? What do we learn from climbing that we can apply to daily living?

I have often stood at the foot of a mountain and thought to myself, "It is too big. I will not be able to get to the top. For me, it is impossible." But when I lowered my gaze from the summit to the ground immediately in front of me, I saw no reason why I could not proceed further, at least for a while, and so I did. By simply proceeding further, which was generally possible, I was able to go all the way to the summit, which had seemed impossible.

Confucius, in his great wisdom, noted this in a slightly different way. He said, "A journey of a thousand miles begins with the first step." And so it goes, one step at a time, until you are there.

Can you become the president of the company for which you work? Can you graduate from college? Can you go out and start your own business? Can you work hard and amass a fortune? Like the summit of a mountain, it may seem impossible to attain your goal. But can you take the first step? And the second, and the third? You answer this! You may be capable of more than you give yourself credit for.

But why try? Why subject yourself to possible failure? Isn't failure disgraceful?

Absolutely not. It is far more disgraceful to forfeit something for never having tried than to try and not succeed. Honorable failure is far preferable to never having tried at all. Indeed, if you select a very difficult mountain, it will be very difficult to succeed, and the success, if it does come, will be all the greater. If you fail, you can always try again. Or select another less difficult mountain. It is better to have lived and lost than never to have lived at all.

Man, vigorous and restless, has not survived a million years of evolutionary development just so that he can grow in a row like a cabbage. It is the nature of man to want to achieve. The highest fulfillment of man's nature is difficult achievement. This is the great lesson which the mountain teaches, and the lesson can be used on mountains, in a classroom, in an office or factory, at home—anywhere.

The Plunge Step

Eventually, after enjoying his triumph on the top of the mountain, the mountaineer begins his descent. To the uninitiated, going downhill would seem much easier than going uphill. Alas, it is not always so, or at least it is not so on bare rock or bare dirt. With each step down, the knee has to absorb the force of the full weight of the body and the pack, and it is not long before the knees begin to feel as though they were made of jelly. Under the constant pounding and jarring, the knees grow fatigued and weak as the boot steps down on hard, unyielding rock.

High climbers, fortunately, are able to get down off the mountain much more pleasantly. Or they can, at least, while they are on the upper part of the mountain where the snow covers the ground.

In descending from glaciers, or on snowfields, the plunge step is used. This is a fast and comfortable way to descend.

Plunge stepping consists of keeping the leg stiff and the knee locked in the downhill leg (the forward-moving leg). The downhill foot, as it comes down, crunches down hard, heel first into the snow. The uphill leg then swings out, the knee locks, and as it becomes the downhill leg, the heel of that foot plunges down hard into the snow. The plunge step can only be employed if the mountaineer moves right out fearlessly, in big, striding steps.

This is easy to do when going downhill, and it is not fatiguing. On the contrary, it is easier to stride downhill on snow than it is to take short, mincing steps.

Two things inhibit the beginner when he first tries the

PLUNGE STEPPING

plunge step. First, he hesitates to lock his knee, afraid that if he does this the jar of the step will be absorbed at his hip. This just does not happen. The full force of his descending weight is absorbed by the snow. The heel of his boot crunches down hard into the snow and the snow itself absorbs the force and cushions it. Once the climber realizes how soft the snow can be, he no longer hesitates in locking his knees as he descends. However, there is still the second inhibiting factor, and this is a fear of slipping, especially if the snow slopes steeply downward.

The beginning plunge stepper visualizes his foot coming down, striking the snow with his heel, the heel skidding forward, and his rear end hitting the packed snow with a resounding thump. This fear of slipping causes him to place his foot gingerly and softly on the snow, sole and heel parallel to the slope, while he retains his weight on the rear foot until he is certain the forward foot is securely placed.

But it is this very caution which is more likely to make him slip. Slow, mincing steps, and feet placed gently on the surface of the snow are just the things to avoid. If the snow is packed or compacted, or if there is any surface glaze on the snow, its upper surface will be very slippery. The only way to handle snow like this is to crunch through the surface so that the boot can get a grip on the snow beneath the surface.

The real secret in using the plunge step is always to have the weight of the body on the forward foot, and to shift the weight to the out-swinging leg as soon as the forward foot has become the rear foot.

Using the plunge step results in a vigorous, dynamic, arm-swinging stride right on down the hill.

Wearing crampons while plunge stepping just about guarantees that the climber will not slip. When in the vicinity of crevasses, or suspected crevasses, it is best to stop plunge stepping and to proceed more cautiously.

Once you are off the glacier and have removed your crampons (which you should not be in any rush to do), the plunge step may be continued on downward-sloping snow-fields with plain boots. The cleated and lugged heels on the boots will be adequate to prevent slipping if the heel is plunged down into the snow hard enough.

Downhill Skiing

If the mountaineer attached skins to his skis and walked up to the summit on his skis, his descent will be easy and rapid.

In skiing downhill from high mountains, certain differences in technique are used than in skiing down from the top of a chair lift. For one thing, a ski slope at a ski resort is usually a cleared area. The way down is clear to see if it is not marked. Indeed, it will usually be on one side or the other of the chair lift, if not directly underneath the lift itself. Also, since resort ski slopes are always at lower elevations than the elevations where high climbing mountaineers are at home, such ski slopes consist of winter snow accumulations lying on the ground. All such snow, no matter how deep it is, is gone in the summertime.

Mountaineers, on the other hand, ski on glaciers and on snowfields in the summertime, when the resort slopes consist of bare ground covered with grass or heather. Downhill skiing at these higher elevations must be done more cautiously, therefore, and more in control. It is easy to ski right into a crevasse or into a bergschrund. Crevasses and bergschrunds are most difficult to see from above, sometimes remaining invisible until almost the last few seconds. In addition, particularly in the case of a schrund, there may be a steepening of the slope just before it drops off altogether, making it difficult or impossible to stop in time.

One difficulty encountered by mountaineering skiers is that they must ski down with a heavy pack on their backs. If the pack is high on the back as it should be to minimize fatigue on the way up, this will make for an awkward weight distribution on the way down. A mere shifting of weight at the hips will not produce the same result with a high heavy pack on the back as it does without any pack at all. In addition, if the skiing is done while still on the glacier, the skiers should remain roped up. This not only detracts from the individual freedom of movement which an unroped skier would have, but the pull of the rope can easily throw a man off balance. Particularly, if one skier spurts ahead just as another slows down, he may be yanked off his feet and will probably, in turn, yank the other skier off his feet too. Usually, if skiers travel roped up, they should allow themselves more rope than sixty feet. Seventy-five feet to one hundred feet is a better rope length between members of the party if they are on skis. Once they have left the glacier, skiers may unrope and ski down the remainder of the snow as individuals.

Usually, when wearing skis, the ice axe is strapped to the pack and the skier uses ski poles. Although skis make mountaineering easier in many ways, and mountain travel speedier, they also make it more dangerous. There is no good way to arrest a fall on skis. If one skier falls and shouts the warning "falling," the best the other skiers can do is to fall themselves to one side with skis together and parallel digging into the slope at right angles to the line of the slope, and digging in downhill with their ski poles.

If a skier falls into a crevasse, chances are there will be enough slack in the rope to give him a good, powerful "hit" when the rope goes tight. This punishing blow will knock all the wind out of him and leave him dazed as he hangs by the rope. In this winded and dazed condition, he will have to lift his skis, one at a time, and release the bindings, allowing each ski to drop to the bottom of the crevasse. This will be necessary so that he can get his boots into his Prusik slings. For a dazed skier, this may be more than he can do, and his entire rescue may have to be performed by others, without his aid and cooperation. Whether or not he ever gets his skis back will depend on the depth and configuration of the crevasse.

Despite the dangers which mountain skiing presents, many climbers prefer skis to snowshoes or to cramponed boots just because skiing is so quick and easy and convenient. Skiing is pleasurable too, as any skier will quickly tell you. It is fun to ski on down a slope instead of walking down. In some ways it is even safer than walking. Small and narrow crevasses may be

jumped in perfect safety on skis, and in less time than it takes to think about it. Also, a man walking on a snow bridge exerts all his weight on the bridge. A skier can shoot over the bridge and exert very little downward force. Such force as he does exert is distributed over a greater area, and for a shorter period of time. If he flexes his knees and springs slightly just before he arrives at the snow bridge, he will cross the bridge in an almost weightless condition, and what little force he exerts will be of extremely short duration. This certainly is safer than walking over the bridge.

The very speed of skiing is a safety feature. In case of an impending blizzard, a man on skis can quickly descend from the mountain while a man without skis may be caught there and forced to suffer through the storm.

Glissading

Using skis is not the only way to slide down a snow slope. A climber may slide down standing in his boots, or he may sit down and slide on the seat of his pants. He may even lie down and slide in a body glissade. Sliding downhill is a safe and acceptable way of getting down a mountain slope. Sliding down on snow is called glissading or skooming or shooming. There are two basic types of glissades: sitting and standing. A body glissade is a variation of the sitting glissade.

While up high on the glacier and wearing crampons, the sitting glissade is usually used. It is possible to glissade with crampons on in a standing position if the slope is very steep and if the snow is not compacted, but it is difficult and tiring. A standing glissade should usually be attempted only without crampons.

In a sitting glissade, the mountaineer simply sits down on the snow, his legs pointed downhill, and he slides on down. He holds his ice axe ready for self-arrest and he is ready to arrest himself if his slide becomes too rapid, or if he loses control. He maintains control with his legs and with the ice axe. The left hand, holding the shaft of the axe near the ferrule, is lowered whenever the climber wants to steer or to slow down. The spike of the axe is dragged along the snow on the left side, either lightly or deeply, or it is raised from the snow if no braking or steering action is required. The head of the axe is held up, in front of the right shoulder, and if self-arrest becomes necessary, the climber rolls to his right and plunges the pick into the snow.

The legs are also used to maintain control in a sitting glissade. If the legs are kept close together and the heels of the boots are raised, this will speed up the slide. If the legs are spread out, a mound of snow gradually accumulates between the legs, and this slows down the glissade. By shifting weight to one cheek and raising the other, the climber may be able to slide right over this snow pile. If it grows too big, it will stop the slide. The climber then shuffles over it and starts to slide again. Another way to slow down is to raise the knees somewhat and dig down with the heels of the crampons.

A sitting glissade is the easiest, most comfortable, most restful, and most convenient way to descend from a mountain. The descent, coming at the end of the climb, comes at a time when the climber is tired from all his uphill efforts. It is absolutely delightful to be able to sit down and slide downhill.

The only trouble with the sitting glissade is that it can get the seat of the pants all wet. If the climber has had the foresight to reinforce the seat of his pants with several layers, one of which is waterproof neoprene-coated nylon, he will not only retain a dry rear end, but he will, in addition, have one that is warm.

After the climbing party has descended from the glacier, the members may unrope, remove their crampons, and proceed further downhill as individuals.

Isolated snowfields can and do exist on mountains below glaciers.

Without crampons, it is possible to do the standing glissade. This is somewhat a misnomer since the stance taken could more correctly be described as a "crouching" glissade. It is a real "standing" glissade only if the snow slope is not too steep.

Doing a standing glissade is something like skiing without

skis. The mountaineer slides down a snow slope with his feet close together and parallel, pointed downhill. The knees are bent well forward and the body leans well forward. The ice axe is held at the left side. The right hand crosses the body and holds the head of the ice axe at the narrow part of the adze. The pick is pointed forward, or downhill. The left hand holds the shaft up high, but not too close to the head, and the spike of the axe is dragged in the snow on the left side. The climber is ready, as always, to go into self-arrest if the slide should get out of control. On very steep slopes the knees are bent sharply and the body is brought down low, close to the snow. On gentler slopes, the knees can be straightened somewhat, and the climber rises closer to a standing position.

Sometimes, in descending, a snow slope is encountered which, although short, is extremely steep. Such a slope is best negotiated by a body glissade. In the body glissade, the climber sits down at the top of the slope, as though he were going to go down in a sitting glissade. Then he rolls to his right, puts his weight on his right hip, extends his feet forward, and he sinks the pick of the axe into the snow, as in self-arrest. He then wiggles his body over the edge and begins a slow slide being careful to keep it under complete control. He controls the slide by pulling the pick partially out of the snow, but not completely out. Withdrawing the pick from the snow lessens the friction it provides, and down goes the climber, scraping snow with the pick. If he starts to move too fast, he digs the pick in deeper and digs in with his boots. This slows him down. If necessary, he goes into complete self-arrest before loosening the pick again and proceeding further down.

The pick must never be removed completely in a body glissade, or the climber will plummet down immediately.

I once saw a girl climber on Mount Rainier coming down a very steep snow slope about twenty feet high. There were rocks at the bottom of the slope protruding through the snow. She made the mistake, half-way down, of pulling her pick completely out of the snow. She dropped the last ten feet like a sack of potatoes and landed among the rocks. Fortunately, there was enough snow around to cushion her fall, and she was not hurt.

But she had the wind knocked out of her enough to scare the rest of us in the party. We thought we had a casualty, and we almost did.

Rarified Atmosphere

When a high-climbing mountaineer leaves the lowlands behind him and travels up to where the glaciers and snowfields are, he enters a different world from the one he left behind him.

Two environmental factors change drastically as he goes up the mountain. These are temperature and air pressure. We have already considered how temperature drops with increased elevation in Chapter 1. It is this temperature drop at higher elevations that makes it possible to sit down on the cool snow on a glacier in the summertime while the general population swelters in the summer heat down in the lowlands.

What about air pressure? What difference can air pressure make? As we shall see, it can make a very great difference in several ways.

The atmosphere is a sphere of air which surrounds the earth, like an ocean. We all live near the bottom of this ocean of air. This ocean is composed of matter in a gaseous state, and it is the weight of this matter reacting to the earth's gravitational force which keeps the atmosphere in place. Air is composed of 78 per cent nitrogen and 21 per cent oxygen, which together make up 99 per cent of the total. The other 1 per cent consists of argon, carbon dioxide, and other gases, and also some water vapor and dust. The weight of this ocean of air may vary according to certain conditions, but it averages 14.7 pounds per square inch at sea level. If we go upward from sea level, we rise above a part of the atmosphere. The remainder, which is still above us, weighs less and therefore exerts less pressure. At 18,500 feet elevation, the weight of the air is 7.35 pounds per square inch, or half of what it was at sea level. At an altitude of 53,000 feet, the weight of the air is only 1.5 pounds per square inch, or 10 per cent of what is was at sea level. In other words, at 53,000 feet, 90 per cent of the mass of the atmosphere is below us and only 10 per cent is above. Eventually and gradually the atmosphere fades away to a vacuum as we rise higher above sea level. At 100,000 feet altitude the air is quite thin even though aircraft and balloons have exceeded this altitude. At about 200 miles above sea level there is no more air as such, although some ionized particles of matter may exist in what is otherwise a vacuum.

If we plotted air pressure from zero to 14.7 pounds per square inch on the Y axis of a chart, and elevation above sea level on the X axis, the pressure line would fall very steeply at the beginning and then taper off to a very gradual slope to the right, almost parallel to the X axis. The slope would be so gradual that the pressure line would not reach zero until the chart read about one million feet of elevation above sea level (about 200 miles).

The significant thing about this pressure line is not that it is very gradual on its right end. This fact is only of interest to astronauts, or to scientists studying the aurora borealis. The significant thing is that the line falls very steeply at the left end. The left end of the chart contains the elevations found on mountains.

At about 7,500 feet, for example, atmospheric pressure is only 75 per cent of what it is at sea level. At 20,000 feet, atmospheric pressure is less than 50 per cent of that at sea level. These are elevations where a man can stand with two feet on the ground.

Because the air is so thin at higher elevations, a climber gets less oxygen than he would get at sea level. He still breathes air containing 21 per cent oxygen. The percentage does not decrease. The amount of air itself decreases.

At higher elevations the lower air pressure makes it difficult to breathe. Even when he is not exerting himself, the climber finds that he cannot always breathe normally. Normal

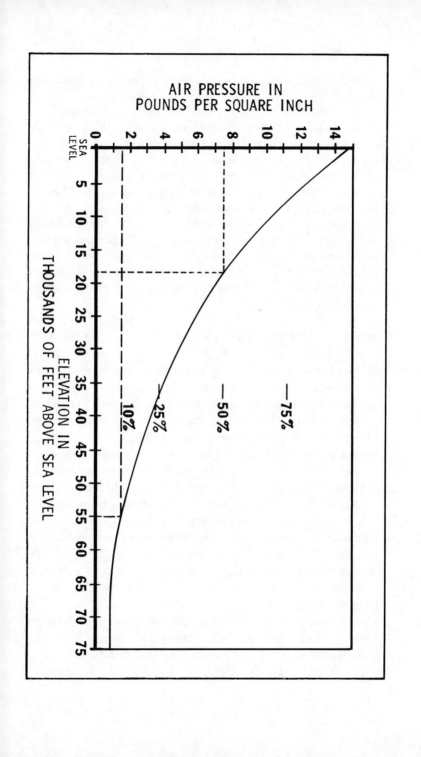

breathing will not give him enough oxygen at reduced air pressure. The higher a climber goes, the more this will be true.

Breathlessness at high elevations may be countered by consciously breathing more often and more deeply than would be normal at sea level. If the climber is winded, he will gasp for air without thinking about it. But if he sits and rests for a while, if he has made camp, for example, unless he makes a conscious effort he will begin to breathe normally. When he does this, he deprives his body of necessary oxygen.

Conscious control of breathing is called hyperventilating, and a high climber should hyperventilate all the time. Hyperventilating is breathing as though you were out of breath even if you think you are not out of breath. Unless a high climber hyperventilates, he will gradually succumb to anoxia, a term meaning oxygen deficiency.

All climbers who are at 10,000 feet or higher suffer from anoxia to varying degrees. The only way to avoid this is to bring oxygen bottles along on climbs on high mountains. Without this oxygen, anoxia sets in and continues until the climber descends into thicker air.

Some of the symptoms of anoxia are obvious. These are chronic fatigue, chronic laziness, and chronic breathlessness. Sometimes anoxia will cause nausea in climbers. Other symptoms are not obvious at all, but insidious instead. When the lungs cannot deliver enough oxygen to the blood, not only do the muscle tissues feel this lack, but so does the brain. When the brain becomes anoxic, the mind wanders, it becomes difficult to remember things, concentration becomes difficult, and judgment becomes fuzzy. Very often anoxia will produce a languid feeling of well-being, similar to being slightly drunk. The feeling may last for days, or until the climber gets back down to where there is more air. Fortunately, there is no hangover from anoxia.

It is necessary to know what anoxia is, and to be able to recognize its symptoms. If the climber finds himself becoming lackadaisical in the face of potential danger, or listless at a time when he should act decisively, he should make a strong conscious effort to gather his wits together. First hyperventilate, then concentrate.

Sun Goggles and Sun Cream

Another effect of the atmosphere is that it filters sunlight. When sunlight reaches down to the earth, we see it from the bottom of our ocean of air. The light we get at sea level is soft and diffused because of this filtration. At higher elevations, where less filtration has taken place, sunlight is harsher and has more glare.

But light is a form of radiant energy. The electromagnetic spectrum is far wider than that part of it which we can see with our eyes. Starting with the shortest wave lengths and increasing in wave length, there are the following: very short gamma rays, X-rays, and ultraviolet rays; then, the visible spectrum from violet, blue, and green through yellow, orange, and red; back to invisible radiation as long infrared waves, and finally radio waves, which are the longest waves of all.

The atmosphere filters all wave lengths, but it filters the shortest wave lengths the most. It is fortunate for us that this is the case, because if this were not so we would be mercilessly bombarded by ultraviolet radiation, by X-rays, and by gamma rays. High irradiation from gamma rays and X-rays would be fatal. Excessive radiation from ultraviolet rays can kill cells in the epidermis. And even infrared rays, on the other end of the spectrum, can kill skin cells by burning them. Everybody has experienced peeling skin caused by sunburn.

Since the atmosphere filters light and other radiation, as we go up on a mountain and rise above some of this atmosphere, the rays that reach us are less filtered and more potent. Also more radiation is present at higher elevations. As we have already noted, at an elevation of 18,500 feet fully half of the mass of the atmosphere is below us. So, too, is 50 per cent of the filtrating power of the atmosphere. At this elevation, and higher, the sun glares unmercifully on the landscape and its harsh rays, visible and invisible, become very powerful.

There are two dangers present in this environment to the mountaineer. The most important danger is to his eyes. The other danger is to any exposed skin.

Excessively bright light can be injurious to delicate eye tissues. At high elevations, not only is the glare of the sun very strong but, in addition, it is reflected from the snow and ice below eye level so that the light comes from above and below—from all directions.

To protect the eyes from this strong light, which sometimes is so strong it imparts an unreal quality to the landscape, goggles must be worn.

Sun goggles should have very dark glass lenses, and there should be shielding on all sides of the lenses so that light may not reach the eyes except through the lenses. Goggles should be attached by means of an elastic band worn around the head. They should be secure in place so that if the mountaineer goes through violent maneuvers such as jumping or falling or self-arrest, the goggles will remain in place. The best color for the lenses is neutral dark which transmits colors in their true values—not in green, or blue, or amber tones. Such true-color lenses are available. An ideal lens would have additional features such as glass which filters ultraviolet and infrared rays, and which is shatterproof.

Ordinary sunglasses are not sun goggles, and should not be used in snow mountaineering. One-piece goggles with a plastic lens, such as used in winter skiing, should also not be used in high mountaineering in the summer. The direct overhead sunlight experienced in the summer in the thin air at high elevations is much more powerful than the oblique rays of sunlight which illuminate ski slopes at lower elevations in the winter.

As a matter of fact, if sunglasses are worn as protection against snow blindness in the wintertime at low elevations, it is not so important what kind of glasses are worn. Ordinary sunglasses will be adequate for this kind of use in most circumstances. However, even for low-elevation use in the wintertime, it is best to get goggles or sunglasses that have shielding on the sides and below the lens so that glare off the snow will not be able to reach the eyes by bypassing the lenses. Snow blindness can be a painful and disabling malady.

If it is possible to get a painful sunburn in just a few hours in the summertime at the beach, at sea level, imagine how much more of a sunburn it is possible to get at a high elevation where thinner air makes for less filtered sunlight. And not only are the sun's rays stronger up on a mountainside, but they are reflected up from the snow so that the sun's rays attack from all directions. High up in the snow, it is possible to get severe sunburn under the arms, under the ears, under the chin, and at the nostrils.

The best defense against sunburn is, of course, clothing. When you are high on a mountain, you will be wearing enough clothing usually so that only your hands and head will be exposed. If you are wearing gloves, a parka, and sun goggles, only a part of the face will be exposed. Small as this skin area may be, it must nevertheless be protected, or it will be severely burned.

Protection against sunburn is achieved by using sun cream. Sun cream should be smeared on liberally, on all exposed skin surfaces, and it should be replaced periodically, if it becomes washed off by perspiration.

Sun tan oils and sun tan lotions of the type used at the beach in the summer are not as effective as a good sun cream or glacier cream. Cosmetics which darken the skin are useless. Only a good sun cream will give adequate protection, and only if it is used generously and often enough.

In addition to sun cream, zinc ointments may be used. Desitin is an excellent brand. Zinc ointments are opaque white substances which do not wash off with perspiration as easily as sun cream. Zinc ointments give total and long-lasting protection. One smearing is usually enough for all day.

In my own case, I use Sea and Ski sun cream on my face, neck, ears, chin, and cheeks. In addition, I use Desitin on my nose and on my upper lip and nostrils. I have found this combination to be very effective. Usually I replace the Sea and Ski several times during the day, after I have sweated it off. If my nose gets runny, which sometimes happens if it is extremely cold, I also replace the Desitin on my upper lip and nostrils, once or twice, or as required.

In using sun cream it is important to rub it in the areas where you might not ordinarily think you would get sunburned. Rub it all over the ears and inside the ears too. Rub plenty of it under your chin. Don't forget to put some on the back of your neck.

In addition, keep your body completely covered with clothing. A friend of mine was wearing knickers and long wool stockings when we climbed Mount Olympus in the heart of Olympic National Park. Although it was cold up there in the snow, the exertion of climbing had both of us perspiring aplenty. In an effort to cool off, he pulled his wool stockings down and exposed his bare legs from knee to ankle to the sun. He should have known better, and probably he did know better, but he left his bare skin exposed for several hours. By the time his legs were visibly red it was already too late. He pulled his stockings up then, but all that did was prevent additional burning. The sunburn which he did acquire was so severe that several water blisters formed eventually, some of them the size of a quarter. He probably had to sleep for several nights with his feet stuck up in the air.

I have seen others, strangers to me, hiking at fairly respectable elevations over snow, naked from the waist up in an effort to get a sun tan. In each case I have tactfully mentioned the danger involved, sometimes already obvious from a deep red skin. In some cases, these people put their shirts or jackets back on. In others, they chose to continue their exposure to the sun. I know from having observed the results on friends what the sun can do at high elevations, and I pitied those people whose worship of the sun reached the point where they offered themselves up as a burning sacrifice.

Climbing Safety

Mountaineering safety should be more than just an abstract phrase or a dry set of rules. Just as there are always dangers present in the middle of a city, there are always dangers present up on a mountain. To make the mountain environment less dangerous, the climber should always be aware that dangers are present and he should make himself deliberately safety conscious. Good safety habits are developed more from having the correct attitude than they are from following any set of rules. The correct attitude may be summed up as follows:

Safety first; the summit second.

If you climb with this philosophy in mind at all times, there will definitely be times when you turn back before reaching the summit of some mountain. Just remember that this is not the worst thing in the world, even though at times it may seem that it is. The worst thing in the world is to get killed. Also in the worst category is to become crippled or maimed or disfigured.

Acts that are obviously reckless are easy to avoid by just not being reckless. Avoiding dumb acts is a matter of using your intelligence and experience and thinking ahead a little bit. Intelligence is the capability of seeing that which is not obvious or that which is not there at all to be seen. Intelligence is the capacity to see consequences, especially more distant or less obvious consequences. How will the same route be hours from now when you return? How will it be when you are tired, when it is dark, when it appears different?

Climbing safety, more than anything else, is a matter of doing the safe thing rather than the daring thing.

In going out to climb a mountain, the safe mountaineer should follow two rules in their proper sequence. These are:

Rule 1. Climb in such a way as to be able to return from the climb enriched from having had the experience.

Rule 2. Climb all the way to the top.

As long as these rules are followed in their proper sequence, there will be a safe climb. As soon as a climber reverses the sequence and makes the summit his number one aim, he becomes a dangerous climber, both to himself and to all his fellow climbers. Rule 2 must always remain subordinate to Rule 1.

You don't have to get to the top. You do have to return safely.

Remember that there are always better and higher mountains to climb than the one you are on. To climb them, you have to return safely from the one you are on at the moment.

6] Snow and Ice Travel

WHETHER TRAVELLING uphill and downhill or cross-country, walking on snow and ice is different from walking on dry ground in several respects. The most important respect is that snow and ice are cold. Even thawing slush, encountered in the warming days of spring, is ice-cold. Since no way has been invented yet of walking on air, the feet have to be in constant contact with this icy surface. If the camper is abroad in late fall, at a time when many hunting seasons are open, he may be out in new-fallen powder snow.

Although cleated and lugged soles and heels are always a good feature on any boot to be used in the snow, the kind of low boots sold for climbing are not the best boots for general travel over a snow-covered landscape. These boots are usually manufactured by the same concerns which manufacture ski boots, and the so-called "climbing" boots are first cousins of ski boots with their stiff, straight soles, their very thick insulation, and their stiff and rigid uppers. Some kind of gaiters or leggings must always be worn with such boots or else they quickly take in powder snow at the ankle. A so-called "climbing" boot is not much more designed for hiking than is a ski boot.

The best boots for being generally outdoors in the snow are somewhat higher than most climbing boots. Ten inches high is just about ideal. Such an ideal boot will have cleated and lugged soles and heels, a moderate amount of insulating material, and soft, pliable uppers, particularly the part of the boot that goes around the ankle. A plain toe is preferable to a moccasin toe because the stitching at the moccasin seam will catch snow and hold it until it melts. An excellent brand for general winter camping is Bone Dry. Bone Dry boots are not insulated. This is no big disadvantage, however, if they are bought in a size large enough so that several pairs of wool socks can be comfortably worn inside the boot.

In my opinion, the best all-around winter boot is the Danner insulated boot with Montagna soles and heels. This boot is eight inches high and is warm and comfortable. It is made to withstand rugged use. Danner boots are excellent for hiking long distances over snow and ice because they are not excessively heavy. Yet they are also ideal for high mountaineering because of their excellent construction and rugged dependability.

Although I have never personally owned double boots such as the ones made by Loewa and by Hochland, I don't think I would like them because of their excessive stiffness and their excessive weight. I have no doubt that double boots must be warm enough, but on the other hand I know that the Danner boots are plenty warm too.

In an extreme cold-dry condition where not too much hiking will be involved, mukluks or mucklicks make excellent footwear. Mukluks are boots made of thick felt material which reach almost up to the knee. For additional warmth, and to make the interiors of the mukluks last longer, wool socks should be worn. Although mukluks are warm and comfortable, they wear quickly at the sole unless the bottom of the boot is protected. An outer, moccasin type of fitting made of leather can be worn outside of the mukluk at the foot part of it. This will lengthen the life of the mukluk considerably if much walking around is to be done.

Cross-Country Skiing

If you will be travelling over the snow on skis, your choice

NATURAL LAY OF HAIR

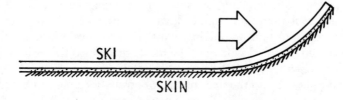

SKI

SKIN

MOVING FORWARD HAIR LAYS DOWN
NO RESISTANCE

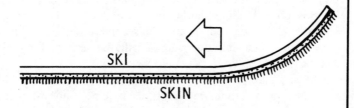

SKI

SKIN

MOVING BACKWARD HAIR STANDS OUT
RESISTING MOVEMENT

USE OF SKINS

Seal skins on skis

of boots will be influenced by the fact that you must be able to fit your boots to the bindings on the skis.

There are boots on the market which are combined climbing boots and ski boots. Such boots are made by Henke, Raichle, and by others. They are qualified to be called climbing boots in every way, being of rugged construction and having Montagna soles and heels (with cleats and lugs), but in addition, they have a square sole at the toe and a grooved slot at the heel so that they can be held in ski bindings.

The steady forward shuffle which is the gait used in moving along on level snow on skis is a different action entirely from the steep forward lean used in most downhill skiing. The binding on skis for this kind of use must be different therefore from a downhill binding. A cross-country binding, or touring binding, must allow the heel of the boot to rise up off the ski. Because the toe of the boot is the main point of contact, the binding should hold the toe firmly forward, and should grip the sides of the toe strongly enough to prevent a sideward motion of the heel of the boot.

Although inflation has plagued this country as well as others for a long time, I don't know of any item that has risen so steeply in price as skis. Each year skis seem to cost more than they did the year before. When skis alone, without bindings, cost more than a complete outfit used to cost, including skis, poles, bindings, and boots, I wonder how far it can go, and how much the youngsters who ski today will be willing to pay before they call things to a halt. Sometimes I wonder. Maybe there is no limit.

At any rate, these expensive skis, with supple forebodies, stiff tails, epoxy-aluminum-wood "sandwiches" and promises of the ultimate in high-speed performance while "blasting" the hill straight down, are not required by the cross-country skier.

As a matter of fact, if skis are going to be used for extensive cross-country touring, they will be subjected to considerable abuse, and the last thing in the world you will want is an expensive pair of skis. Fortunately, there are still skis available with moderate price tags which are completely adequate to every skiing requirement except perhaps "bombing" down 55 degree slopes of ice.

In selecting skis, stand with your heels on the floor and raise your arm. The ski should be long enough to reach the tip of your extended fingers. A good, long ski is necessary because you will not only have to support your own weight, but also the weight of your pack. Be sure, when the binding is mounted on the ski that the hold-down for the heel cable is well forward of the heel so that you can raise the heel of the boot somewhat off the ski.

The time to buy skins is when you buy your skis. It is false economy to try to do without skins if you will be out in terrain which is the least bit hilly. To travel uphill without skins means using the herringbone step or worse still, taking parallel steps sideways up the slope. With skins you can point your skis uphill and shuffle directly up the slope with a minimum of effort. Skins work everywhere except on a glazed and icy surface.

Unfortunately, not many Americans have used skins or are familiar with them. Many chair lift skiers have never even seen skins, although they have been skiing for years.

Skins are made in the same width as the bottom of the ski. Hardware is attached to the skins so that they can be attached at the tail end of the ski and then stretched tight and clamped at the forward end. Usually there are two additional clamping points which go right over the top of the ski, one in front of the boot, and one behind the boot. A good set of skins is so light that it weighs next to nothing. Yet what a difference skins make!

Skins are made from the hides of seals and other animals, and include the animal hair. If the skin is arranged along the longitudinal axis of the ski in such a way that the hairs point backward as they point down (and this is the way ski skins are made) then moving the ski forward tends to fold the hairs up along the skin while moving the ski backward makes the hairs move out perpendicular to the skin and to catch snow. This action, by thousands of hairs, prevents the ski from sliding backward. Consequently, when skins are mounted on the bottom of skis, the skis can only move forward. With skins, uphill walking becomes not only possible, but relatively easy and simple.

As advantageous as skins are, I have no doubt more Americans would use them if they knew about them. Certainly more mountaineers would switch from snowshoes to skis if they realized how much less fatiguing it is to go uphill wearing skis with skins rather than snowshoes.

Genuine sealskins cost about $30. However, there are so-called mouton skins available which are synthetic. Good-grade synthetic skins cost about $15, and I have seen some available for as low as $8.

When skiing downhill, the skins should be removed from the skis. The most convenient place to carry skins is wrapped loosely around the waist and tied into a loose knot there.

It is not possible to ski under all conditions and on all terrain, and because of this, if you are abroad in the winter with skis, it is a great convenience to have a pack which has the capability for carrying skis.

I have seen two types of packs organically designed for carrying skis, and there are probably more. One of these was a tubular canvas pack, shaped somewhat like a duffle bag and equipped with shoulder straps. The main portion of the pack is for carrying clothes and equipment. Two side pockets, one on each side, running the full length of the pack, are for skis. The tails of the skis are inserted into these slots and the skis are slid in until they touch the bottom. The pack I saw was of Swiss manufacture, and unfortunately I don't remember the brand name. You may see one like it around, however, in your sporting goods store.

The other pack I saw was manufactured in Boulder, Colorado. It was made of heavy, waterproof, nylon duck material, with leather straps and a reinforced leather bottom. The nylon was of high-visibility orange. Side pockets were attached to the pack on each side in such a way that a ski could be slid down between the main part of the pack and the side pocket.

There is a potential inconvenience in a pack like this in

which the skis are carried low in that the butt end of the skis will poke into the legs as you walk. This can be overcome by tying the forward ends of the skis together, above the back. Bringing the forward ends closer together will spread the bottom ends apart so that they can clear your legs.

Some packs are very simply designed for carrying skis. They have a pair of loop straps on each side of the pack.

Because skis are as long as they are, there is no way to carry them which is not awkward to some extent. Because of this awkwardness, you will constantly, despite your best intentions, bang the skis into trees, rocks, etc., along the way. This is one reason why skis used in cross-country travel get much more abuse than skis used for downhill skiing only and only at resort ski slopes. For this reason skis should not be brought along unless you intend to wear them most of the time, and to carry them only on minimal occasions.

In addition to the knocks which skis receive while being carried, they experience other abuse right on the trail. The woods, or a high mountainside, are not the same as a well-tended ski slope at a ski resort. There is much more likelihood

that you will hit hidden rocks, slightly submerged below the surface of the snow, while touring across the countryside than you will on a carefully-tended ski slope. In areas where snow has blown and drifted, it is easily possible to ski over deep snow one minute and the next minute to move out over a frozen, gritty, sandpaper-like ground just barely covered with an eighth of an inch of snow.

However, despite all the wear and tear on your skis, and despite the fact that for each hill where you slide down you must first walk up, cross-country skiing can be a lot of fun. From a practical standpoint, cross-country skiing is a feasible way of moving about over a snow-covered landscape. The skis enable you to stay on top of the snow and to cover a lot of ground with a minimum of effort.

Snowshoeing

Snowshoes are made in two basic configurations: those with tails and those without tails.

Snowshoes that do not have tails are called "cabin" models, since they are most conveniently used at or near a cabin in the snow.

Snowshoes with tails are touring models. Only touring model snowshoes should be used in cross-country hiking with any kind of a load and for any real distance.

The models without tails include the bearpaw and the Green Mountain snowshoes. The bearpaw is the shortest and broadest model, the most difficult to walk with for any length of time, and the easiest to use in turning and maneuvering. A bearpaw, because it is so short, is absolutely flat. The Green Mountain snowshoe is a modified bearpaw and is somewhat longer and narrower than a bearpaw. The Green Mountain model is therefore a bit more difficult to maneuver in, but a bit less fatiguing for straight walking. Both the bearpaw and the Green Mountain models are rounded in the front and rounded in the back, and are "cabin" models.

If you have a cabin in the woods or in the mountains where

BEAR PAW

GREEN MT. BEAR PAW

MICHIGAN

CROSS COUNTRY

TRAIL

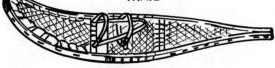

SNOW SHOES

you spend time in the winter, either one of these models is convenient to have around for making short trips over deep snow. Without snowshoes you are likely to be up to your crotch in snow, or deeper, every time you venture out of the cabin. Since this is not conducive to travel, you will find that you are a voluntary prisoner in the cabin itself, unable to move about at all, except perhaps to a cleared spot where your car is, or out on a snow-cleared roadway. All the beauty of the snow-covered woods will be closed to you, even short, exploratory trips, unless you become able to walk on the snow. This is the kind of situation for which the short, rounded snowshoes have been developed.

For more extensive travel, and for cross-country touring, a snowshoe should be used which has a tail. Models with tails include the Michigan snowshoe, the cross-country snowshoe, and the trail snowshoe. These models all turn up at the front like a ski, and are all longer and narrower than the tailless models. Unfortunately, like skis, they are difficult to turn in.

The Michigan model is the widest of the touring snowshoes. In some respects it resembles a bearpaw except that it has a long, trailing tail and is turned up at the front. The cross-country and the trail models are narrower. The trail model has the most pronounced upsweep at the front, and is the longest, being five feet long.

The long tails on these snowshoes may seem like a disadvantage at first, but they are good features. In walking, the tail drags in the snow to the rear, and this keeps the front of the snowshoe pointed automatically forward.

Snowshoe harnesses only hold the toe of the boot to the snowshoe itself. A thong goes around the heel, but this is only to keep the boot from slipping out of the harness. The heel of the boot rises up off the snowshoe as you shuffle forward, and the tail of the snowshoe drags in the snow. The upswept forward part of the snowshoe is useful in that the leading edge will not slice into the snow below the surface. The upsweep compacts the snow and keeps the snowshoe on top of the snow at all times.

Almost all snowshoes are made with leather thongs laced

and crisscrossed together, then varnished or shellacked, or otherwise finished. This leather slowly and gradually stretches. Also it very quickly wears out if you do any walking at all on rocks or on bare ground. A better material for snowshoe webbing is nylon rope. A lighter nylon cord is used in the forward and rear sections of the snowshoe and a quarter inch nylon rope is used in the center section. Snowshoes made with nylon instead of leather are much more durable. Indeed, nylon netting will probably outlast the wooden frame itself. Also, rodents, insects, etc., are not likely to nibble away on nylon the way they may on leather thongs while the snowshoes are being stored. And nylon is very durable in the presence of bacterial action. Leather thongs will eventually rot away.

The standard designs of snowshoes, while awkward to use, are nevertheless usable. The best touring ski is a five-foot-long, or longer, trail model with a pronounced upsweep for the first twelve inches. This is a rather narrow snowshoe, and reasonably comfortable to use for travelling a long distance while carrying a heavy pack.

From time to time, manufacturers have come out with die-molded plastic snowshoes. I have never yet seen one that was any good. The ones I have seen were weak. They had holes spaced throughout the area of the snowshoe for getting rid of powder snow which accumulated on the upper surface. But such snow could not fall through these holes, which were too small to do their job, and large snow accumulations quickly resulted, making the snowshoe heavy to lift. Also, without an upsweep at the toe, it was possible to slice into the snow below the surface when moving the foot forward, thus making it almost impossible to lift the foot up any more.

In travelling uphill on snowshoes, just as travelling uphill on skis, or with boots and crampons, whenever the going gets to be too strenuous, the rest step should be used. Just shuffle ahead, one step at a time, and count breaths between steps. Use the rest step just as often as necessary.

Whenever camp is made, the snowshoes can be stored out of the way by poking the tails into the snow. Be careful not to put the snowshoes where they will receive too much heat from the campfire. When using snowshoes to travel uphill on a mountain over deep snow drifts, the snowshoes may be left behind after you have climbed above the softer, drifted snow. Most precipitation on mountains is between 5,000 feet and 10,000 feet high. At the higher elevations (above 10,000 feet) there will tend to be less snow, and it will tend to be more compacted. If the snowhsoes are left behind, be sure to leave them in a spot where you will be able to find them again on the way down. Stick them into the snow so that they stand on their tails. For added ease in finding the snowshoes again on the way down, tie a piece of orange or red crepe paper or plastic ribbon to the tops of the snowshoes.

White-outs

A wilderness traveller is often in the same situation as the navigator on a ship out of sight of land. Just as the waves stretch out in all directions toward the distant horizon, so also the undulating hills may stretch out in all directions without giving any clue about which way to go. And just as a ship may have to sail through fog, so, too, the wilderness hiker may have to travel through fog. Indeed, a common phenomenon in the wintertime is the white-out. A white-out can occur in the summertime on a mountain if you are high enough to be in snow.

A white-out is a distinctly white fog or haze which blanks out all landmarks, near or distant, and leaves the traveller with the impression that he is swimming in a sea of milk. If the fog is heavy, persons or objects become lost in it, and invisible, if they are only twenty or thirty feet away. But even with a lighter haze condition, the gradual blending of the landscape into the white soup takes place at fifty feet, or at most, at not much farther than one hundred feet away.

Being in a white-out for the first time may be a curiously pleasant experience or it may be terrifying, depending on the outlook of the person involved. As a white-out develops and the haze closes in, the traveller finds himself gradually cut off from the rest of his environment until suddenly it seems that he is completely alone—the only person left in the whole world. If the white-out becomes thick, it may even be difficult to tell which way the grade lies on a mountain slope, and the traveller finds himself jarring his foot because it hit the snow before he thought it would, or else he may fall, or almost fall, because as he steps forward, the snow is six inches or a foot lower than where he thought it would be, and where he had psychologically prepared himself to step on the ground.

I have experienced such a white-out on a rather steep snow slope, and after a while I was convinced that I didn't even know which way was up.

If the human eye is confused by a white-out, the camera eye sees even less. I have snapshots that were taken in a light white-out in which I could see certain landmarks and terrain features that were not too far away. None of these landmarks or terrain features are visible in the photographs.

If someone wants to get away from the noise, the hustle and bustle of everyday life, the sight of other people, and from civilization in general, a white-out is the place to do this. Wrapped in the silent haze, you feel as if you are hidden from everybody, and that nobody can find you. The sense of isolation can be very pleasant, bringing with it a sense of peace the like of which would be hard to duplicate in any other way.

By the same token, to a people-oriented individual, suddenly finding himself in a white-out may cause feelings of anxiety, or even of terror or panic. There are people who just can't be alone, and there is no greater way of being alone than to be alone in the winter in a white-out.

Route Finding and Navigation

On a map it is easy to draw a line from one point to another. On the ground, it is usually impossible to travel in a straight line. Routes have to be chosen which are compatible with the terrain. Rivers have to be crossed at bridges or where they may be ferried over. Streams have to be crossed where they are the narrowest, or forded where they are the shallowest. Thick, windblown areas in the woods have to be skirted. Cliffs and other very steep grades have to be detoured.

In travelling any great distance on foot, it is not of any great importance to have your exact location pinpointed at all times. Being lost is a matter of definition. You are not necessarily lost if you do not know precisely where you are. In the woods it doesn't always matter. If you know approximately where you are, and can locate yourself on a map as being in a general area, then you are not lost.

One of the worst things about really being lost is that the mere recognition of the fact creates a restless tension which does not allow the hiker to relax, or to think calmly and rationally. Prodded on by a vague but driving fear, he feels he must keep moving onward, and if he continues to do this without rest, he will sooner or later drop from sheer exhaustion.

If you think you are lost, the first thing to do is to sit down and relax. Force yourself to stay in one place for a while, while you try to think things out. Remember, you are not entirely lost. You know what country you are in, and you know what state you are in, so you know approximately where you are. There aren't many places where you can walk fifty miles without crossing some kind of a road, so you can rest assured that locating yourself will just be a matter of time, one way or another. If it is within a few hours of darkness, better make a camp and stay put until the morning.

In the morning, if you have no map or compass (and shame on you if you are without these necessities!), walk until you find a stream and then follow the stream downhill. One stream always leads to another, and streams join other streams until they become rivers. Almost any place in the world, if you follow a river downstream long enough you will come to a human settlement. You may come to a bridge before you come to a human habitation if the area is at all civilized and settled. A bridge always means there is a road. Switch from following the river to following the road. Sooner or later you

COMPASS

will meet somebody and he will tell you exactly where you are.

If you do have a compass and a map of the area where you are (and you should always have these things with you), you may be able to locate yourself on the map by comparing the terrain around you, including streams, with likely areas on the map. If there are mountains in the vicinity, these can be seen at longer distances, and make excellent reference points.

It is preferable not to get lost in the first place, of course, and not getting lost means either that you know the terrain well enough to get where you want to go without ever using a map, or knowing, in strange terrain, where you are on your map.

Winter navigation is both easier and more difficult than it is in the summer. It is more difficult because in the winter, particularly under a blanket of snow, the ground tends to have a uniformity of appearance, a sameness in all directions, and distinct features may be difficult to locate. On the other hand, because the leaves are off all the deciduous trees, you can often get more distant views in winter than are possible in the summertime. This will enable you to see distant landmarks which would not otherwise be visible.

To locate yourself on your map, you have to relate features shown on the map to features on the ground. In order to do this you have to orient your map. This means you have to hold your map so that north on the map points to the north. This is easily done with the compass. Your map should indicate somewhere what the magnetic declination is in the area depicted by the map. It is necessary to know this because your compass needle will point to the magnetic north pole while the vertical lines on your map point to the geographic north pole. To orient your map, place it on some flat surface and put the compass on top of it. When the compass needle has stopped swinging, it will be pointing toward magnetic north. Now turn the compass slowly until north on the compass is the required degrees left or right of the needle to adjust for declination. Then turn the map beneath the compass so that north on the map coincides with true north as shown by your compass. In doing this, be sure you place your rifle, ice axe, or any other steel equipment at some distance from the compass so that the compass needle is not deflected by these masses of steel.

U.S. Geological Survey maps show magnetic north in the margin as an angle to the left or right of true north. With this kind of map, simply line up the map so that this line (magnetic north) is in line with the direction in which the compass needle points.

To pinpoint your exact location on the map you get a three-point "fix." A fix is obtained by first establishing what is called an LOP, or "line of position." To get an LOP, you aim your compass at some distinguishing landmark such as the peak of an identified mountain, and note the compass reading. Correct this reading for magnetic declination. Then add or subtract 180° from this compass sighting to get what is called a reciprocal reading. For example, if it is 90° (or due east) from where you stand to the landmark, then it must be 270° (the reciprocal reading) from the landmark to you, or due west. This means that if you draw a line on the map from the peak in a direction of 270°, your position will be some place along this line. This is why the line is called an LOP, or line of position.

Since a full circle adds up to only 360°, if your addition of 180° to your compass reading gives you a number greater than 360°, simply subtract 360° from your total. An easier way to do this, however, and one which will give you the exact same answer, is to subtract 180° from your reading if the addition will produce a number greater than 360°.

For example, supposing your compass sighting gives you a reading of 225° (which is southwest).

THEN

Either: 225°   Or: 225°
        +180°   −180°
        ─────   ─────
        405°   45°
        −360°
        ─────
        45°

As can be seen from the above example, it is easier to simply subtract 180° in this case rather than add it and then subtract 360° from the total. The answer is the same in either case, and the LOP which results from this sighting tells us we are on a line going 45° from the identified landmark.

Getting one LOP does not tell us where we are. It merely tells us that we are somewhere along this line. The next step is to establish at what point on the LOP we are. This is done by obtaining a second LOP from a different compass sighting, made, for example, from a second identified mountain, or other landmark.

Theoretically, two LOPs should make a fix, since if we are some place along one line and some place along a second line, the only place where we can be is at the point where the two lines cross.

But compass readings are subject to error, and to obtain a reliable fix, *three* LOPs should be used. Ideally, when a three-point fix is drawn on the map, the three LOPs should converge at one and the same point, and this is our location on the map.

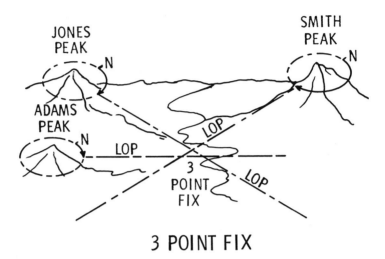

3 POINT FIX

In practice however, because of imperfections in compasses and in the people who read them, the three LOPs almost never meet at one point. Instead, they miss each other and form a triangle. Since it is not possible to know which LOP is the least accurate and which is the most accurate, the safest way to use the three-point fix is to assume that you are located in the center of the triangle.

Such a triangle should be fairly small, and once you have located yourself as being within the triangle, you can try to refine your position further by comparing the map to local landmarks such as streams, hills, etc.

If the triangle obtained from a three-point fix is excessively large, and you are reasonably sure of your compass sightings and of your arithmetic, then you must assume that you have incorrectly identified one or more of your landmarks.

An LOP may be obtained in other ways than from compass sightings. A road or a river or the shore of a lake may serve as an excellent LOP. Sight off to a landmark, and where your LOP crosses the river or the road, you have your position.

Trust your compass. It is far less likely that your compass will get confused than that you will. If you don't trust your compass, throw it away when you get home and get one that you will have faith in. Then have faith in it. Your compass, unaffected by your own confusion, or other states of mind, will continue to point to magnetic north, even when you are convinced it should be some place else. If you are not sure of what the magnetic declination is in the locality where you are, you can check it at night by taking a sighting at Polaris, the north star.

Always carry a short pencil along with you, with an eraser, and a short, six-inch ruler or other straight edge for drawing LOPs on your map. Draw the lines lightly and erase them after you have established your position.

In buying a compass, buy one that is filled with liquid. The liquid dampens the movement of the needle, minimizes oscillation, and makes readings quicker, easier, and more accurate. Such a compass is called an "aperiodic" compass, since there is no periodic swing of the needle back and forth until it finally comes to rest.

Also, buy a compass which will give you readings in degrees from 0° at the north, clockwise to 360° at the north again. General directions, such as NNW or SSW, are of little value on a compass for accurate navigation.

In choosing routes, whether on level snow in the winter or on a mountain in the winter or summer, always take advantage of the long view and the distant view. Very often, it is easy to see where and how you should travel from a distance. Try to memorize the landmarks and their relationships to each other before you get close to them. Glance at the map and see how these landmarks look on a flat piece of paper. Later on, when you are in among them, the nearer ones may block the view to the more distant ones, but you will have a better knowledge of what lies before you, and of what the best route will be, and what your alternate routes, if any, may be.

There are advantages to travelling in the winter. One inch of rain averages ten inches of snow. Six inches of rain averages five feet of snow. Because of snow cover over the ground, it is often very easy to travel right over the top of bushes and undergrowth. In the summer you might not be able to travel at all in the exact same locality because of thickly impenetrable underbrush. In the winter you can walk right over it all, on the snow, with the tangled growth several inches or several feet beneath the soles of your boots.

Wands

Most garden supply stores sell slender bamboo rods about three feet long and about a quarter inch thick for use in tying plants upright, or for use as trellises. These rods are usually painted green, to blend with garden decor, but they may be any color. They are light and they are strong. A bunch of them, about six inches in diameter, does not make a heavy load. One of these, held in the hand alone, looks like a conductor's baton, or a magician's wand. These rods are used by mountaineers, and they are called, strangely enough, wands.

Wands are gathered together into a bunch or *fascine* or "fask," and stuck into the pack down along one side, with the upper lengths protruding above, out of the pack. They may be used as they are, or they may be split at the top and a length of colored crepe paper or plastic ribbon inserted into the split. The crepe paper or plastic should be of some highly visible color such as bright red or orange.

I suppose mountaineers can be called "fascists" because they use fasks of wands; however, you would have to spell the word with a small "F," since their use of wands is in no way political. Mountaineers get used to being called all kinds of things anyway, and one more epithet, more or less, will not make any difference to them.

Wands are used to mark a route when travelling over snow or on a glacier. They are usually used for short trips, lasting one day or not much longer than that, and they are used to mark a return route when there is a likelihood that weather may close in and obliterate distant views.

On a completely white snowfield, it is amazing how far away a wand can be seen, particularly considering its slim dimensions. But wands should not be spaced very far apart. If the weather does close in, visibility will be diminished, and wands should be spaced at such distances that when the party arrives at one wand, it will be able to see the next one.

It is not necessary to place wands all along the entire route. Parts of the route will be obvious just from the general lay of the land. As a general rule, wands should be spaced farther apart where the route continues in a straight line, and closer together where the route changes direction.

On the return trip, this is kept in mind, and if the next wand is not visible, you continue in a straight line until you see it.

As already mentioned, the wands are kept upright in one side of the pack, and they protrude from the pack like arrows from a quiver. Usually one wand carrier will be able to carry enough wands to mark a route. However, if it is expected that the route will be long and tricky, several members of the party should carry wands so that there will be enough of them. On the return trip, the wands are retrieved and returned to the pack. The most convenient way to do this is not to try to jam each wand back into the pack as it is recovered, but simply to pick it up and carry it until several have been thus recovered, and then return the bunch to the pack all at once.

Snacks While Travelling

In freezing cold weather, an outdoorsman should make every effort to have two hot meals every day. These meals should be breakfast and supper.

It is too inconvenient, however, to try to have a third hot meal. Even when in camp, it is usually possible to get by without a hot lunch. If in a camp, the midday meal may be enhanced by a hot drink such as coffee, cocoa, or tea. This is easy enough to do if there is already a fire going anyhow.

But as a general rule for outdoor travel in the winter, lunch should consist of cold food. If travelling, in fact, it is almost an absolute necessity to dispense with a hot lunch.

Travel imposes certain conditions on the cold-weather outdoorsman. A good, hot meal takes time and effort to prepare. After it has been consumed, the traveller should rest for a while so that he may digest his food properly. With so much time devoted to food preparation and to digestion, the traveller will not travel very far.

The best way to handle the midday meal when travelling over the winter landscape is to eliminate it entirely. This does not mean going without food from breakfast until supper. On the contrary, in expending a considerable amount of energy to keep moving through the snow, and indeed, just to keep warm when standing still, more food is required than would otherwise be normal. But this food should be eaten in the form of snacks throughout the entire day. Start snacking an hour after breakfast and keep it up all day long.

Highly concentrated foods should be used for this kind of snacking. Nuts are always good, as well as being tasty. Raisins are also excellent. Beef jerky is delicious, and consists of almost pure protein. Small sticks of pepperoni are excellent too. Pepperoni has the added advantage of containing fats, and fats are necessary food elements for winter sustenance. A hard-boiled egg, brought along from home, can make a delicious snack. All of these items can be conveniently carried in the pockets in small plastic bags or other wrappers or containers.

An obvious snacking item is candy. Small candy bars are easy to stuff into the pack and into the pockets and the fats and sugars they contain are good sources of energy for the cold-weather traveller.

Getting a drink in freezing weather is more of a problem than eating. Water freezes at 32 degrees Fahrenheit, and below that temperature you have ice instead of water. One would think that at very cold temperatures the body does not perspire, but it does. Water or other liquids are necessary. Unfortunately, there is no easy way to get water when it is very cold. The most practical way to handle this problem is to consume all the liquids you will need at breakfast time, and at supper, when a fire or a stove is going, and do without liquids during the day.

Sometimes it is possible to scoop water from a stream which has not completely frozen over. Also, if you feel very thirsty, try carrying your canteen inside of your jacket. This will sometimes work, although I know that water can freeze in a canteen held under several layers of clothing, almost right next to the skin.

If the weather is not excessively cold, and it is possible to drink water from the canteen, stuff some snow into the canteen after you have had your drink, and you will have more water to drink at the next rest stop.

I have noticed also, that even when it is quite cold, if the sun is shining brightly, solar heat will be absorbed by the pack, and this will somewhat warm a canteen in one of the outside pockets. If you are marching with the sun on your left, put your canteen in one of the pockets on the left side of the pack. Sometimes, also, enough solar heat is absorbed this way to thaw frozen pepperoni, or a frozen candy bar. Using the heat of the sun, when it is available, you can not only get a drink of liquid water, you can also save wear and tear on your jaw muscles by having unfrozen food to snack on.

One thing to remember about water, summer or winter, is never to drink from mountain streams if the water is milky in color, or gray, or chocolate-colored. This opaqueness is due to suspended glacial silt, and this silt consists of microscopic particles of mineral matter as sharp as ground glass. Several good swallows of this kind of water and you will end up flat on your back for days at a time, not so much sick as internally wounded.

On the subject of water, many mountaineers prefer plastic water bottles to the old fashioned aluminum canteens. The plastic bottles are light, strong, and easy to keep clean. I have found, however, that aluminum canteens have advantages of their own. They are not really heavy and they are stronger than plastic. But the best thing of all about an aluminum canteen is that it can be set near a fire, or, if necessary, stood right on a stove. Needless to say, plastic water bottles should never be exposed to direct heat in this manner. Heating an aluminum canteen will quickly melt the ice in it. In addition, it will warm the water in the canteen so that you do not have to douse your teeth with ice water every time you take a drink.

Effects of Low Temperatures

Life is not the same outdoors in the winter as it is in the summer. This is obvious. But what are some of the specific effects of very low temperatures? As a general rule, everything slows down as it gets colder, or stops completely. Running water freezes and becomes standing ice. Soft butter becomes hard and unyielding. Food freezes and must be thawed in the mouth first, before it can be chewed. For this reason it is a good idea to break candy bars into bite-size pieces before leaving home for the frozen wilderness.

Chemical reactions are slowed down as temperatures decrease. A perfectly good battery becomes weak when it gets cold, and it may act completely dead if it is frozen. Flashlight batteries should be tried after being warmed by the fire before they are thrown away as dead. They may merely be in hibernation and still have lots of life left in them.

The human body reacts strongly to low temperatures. The metabolic rate increases, and the body works at a quicker tempo to maintain its temperature at 98.6 degrees Fahrenheit. Food fuels and body fat are consumed in greater amounts when it is cold. The liver becomes more active, and works harder.

One immediate by-product of cold is fatigue. Since the body must work at a heightened rate just to maintain a normal body temperature, even a so-called relaxed state is a state of higher body metabolism when it is cold. Cold is, therefore, enervating. Constant exposure to extremely low temperatures chill the body despite its best efforts to maintain 98.6 degrees. Among outdoorsmen, there is an expression: "getting cold-soaked." Getting "cold-soaked" describes what happens to you sooner or later when you are out in temperatures below 32 degrees Fahrenheit, and particularly when you are out in tempera-

A cornice

tures below zero. For some men, it may take several days in the woods to become cold-soaked. For others, it may happen in the first hour or two after being outdoors.

One symptom of being cold-soaked is fatigue. This is not a sudden, overpowering weariness, but a chronic, just-below-the-level-of-awareness, lower level of energy. Your strength and your endurance seem somewhat less than what they should be, but you are not sure. You are aware of cold, but hardly. Your nose and ears are cold. Your hands and feet are cold, or so it seems. You are able to perform all work normally, and you can work for prolonged stretches of time, but at a somewhat reduced level, or so it seems. All the muscles in your body are tense, but not overly so, and you are really relaxed, but not for sure.

One sure way to know when you have become cold-soaked is to go into a heated cabin or other warm building. If you are cold-soaked, your eyes will smart and you will quickly become sleepy. In addition, even though the room is warm, you may suddenly feel cold, and begin to shiver. The reason for these reactions is the following: When you do go into a warm room, your body senses the heat and your muscles actually do begin to relax. It is this overall relaxation which produces the almost instant sleepiness and the feeling of being chilled.

Cornices and Stream Tunnels

It is customary to think of cornices only in connection with high mountaineering, and it is true that very long cornices or cornices with extensive overhangs do usually occur only along mountain ridges. However, a cornice may occur anywhere where snow has blown and drifted and smaller, less extensive cornices may be just as dangerous as large ones.

A cornice is an overhanging area of snow that extends out past the cliff over which it lies, or over the edge of a crevasse. But a cornice may also exist, and often does exist, over a running stream, and this can be in the lowland just as well as in the mountains.

Most mountaineers know better than to approach close to the edge of a snow-covered cliff unless they are belayed by someone. They will usually take this same precaution if they approach close to the lip of a large crevasse. But I have seen otherwise cautious mountaineers hike up along a snow-covered stream bed with scarcely a thought about what was under their feet.

A swiftly running stream will carve out a tunnel for itself far larger than the stream itself. Deep snow may cover the stream, but the tunnel of air will thin out the snow directly above it. Walking over such a stream, on the snow, is about the same as walking over a snow-covered crevasse up on a mountain. It may be worse. Almost for sure, winter lowland travellers will not be roped together as they hike along the gully where the stream is running. Even if they were roped up, this would be of help only in getting a man out of the stream; it would not prevent him from hitting the rocks in the stream bed with full force. It is quite possible that even if lowland travellers were roped up (which is not likely to be the case), there might well be ten or fifteen feet of slack in the rope. Since it is possible for the snow to be less than ten or fifteen feet deep, if a man fell through the snow into a stream, he would fall without being stopped by the rope. It should be kept in mind that even a ten-foot fall onto rocks can be very damaging. If you don't believe ten feet is very high, go and measure a place which is ten feet high and jump off.

A ten-foot fall into a running stream (running over rocks) would be bad enough on a warm summer day. Such a fall in freezing weather into ice water is mortally dangerous. An arm or a leg may be broken in the fall. A head injury might result. Added to these pleasantries, the man who falls into the ice water will have his clothing quickly soaked, down to his underwear and his socks. Needless to say, such exposure in freezing weather will result in a man's freezing to death in very little time unless vigorous and decisive action is taken immediately. Such action should include, after bringing the victim out of the stream, a quick and complete change of clothing right down to the skin. If there are enough people in the party, someone should begin immediately to make a fire. But the clothing change, out of wet clothes and into dry, should be done first, before anything else.

Since a man who has fallen into a stream in winter will begin to suffer from exposure almost immediately, he will be numb and dazed and unable to help himself to any great extent, and it will be up to his friends to remove his clothes for him and put his dry things on him.

Next, and only after the victim is in dry clothing, he should be brought to a fire so that he may warm himself. Hot drinks may then be made over the same fire.

Stream tunnels are no joke, and they should be treated with

A stream tunnel

all the respect one gives to crevasses. Open streams should be approached cautiously, with the idea in mind that a cornice may overhang the stream from either side. Even if you are not injured when you drop through the snow, it is no fun to stand ankle-deep or knee-deep in ice water in the dark and wonder how you will climb up that ten-foot interval and get back out through the hole through which you fell, or up the overhanging and slippery ten-foot bank of snow on one side of the stream or the other.

Unfortunately, a stream running through a stream tunnel makes very little noise. Sometimes, in the spring, when parts of the stream tunnel have melted away and the course of the stream is marked by a line of open holes, the stream may be heard from some distance. But more often than not, you have to be directly over the hole to hear the running water. The safest course of action, if you suspect a stream tunnel exists, is to walk along one side of the gully, the higher side if the two sides are not of equal height, and to keep your eyes and ears open.

Needless to say, river banks of large rivers should be approached with the same care, if they are snow covered, as would be used in approaching any suspected cornice.

Avalanches

"Cannonballs" are rocks which one way or another become thawed and loosened from their original locations and start rolling and bouncing downhill. A cannonball may be as big as a garbage can or as small as a bowling ball, or even smaller. Except for good luck, there is no defense against cannonballs. Some climbers wear helmets on certain kinds of climbs as head protection, but these helmets are only effective against pebbles. The kinetic energy in cannonballs is so great that if a climber were to be hit by one of them, the chances are excellent that he would be dismembered. A cannonball careening down a mountainside probably has more energy than a real cannonball shot out of a cannon. I have seen a mountain

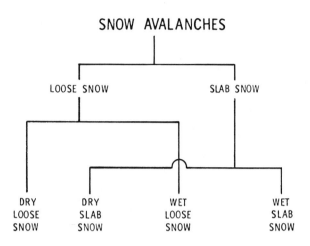

cannonball strike the trunk of a pine tree almost a foot thick and splinter the trunk like a toothpick. The tree hardly slowed the cannonball down.

Cannonballs usually travel too fast for someone to get out of their way. All that you can do if one seems to be heading your way is to get down prone so as to present as small a target as possible. These missiles often bounce quite high in their trip downhill, and one may bounce high over you as it passes.

Mathematically, the probability of your being hit by a cannonball is quite remote, standing or prone, and it is comforting to know this. But mountaineers have been struck by them now and then. If it is a thawing type of day and there is more cannonading going on than usual, the best thing to do is to leave the area as soon as possible.

Besides rocks, snow may avalanche down from mountains.

Snow avalanches are considerably more dangerous than cannonballs. Snow avalanches begin at some point, but they widen as they go downhill and they may cover an extensive area before they stop.

Only two conditions are necessary for an avalanche to occur: sufficient snow and a steep enough slope. If you are on open (that is, not forested) terrain, and if there is snow on the slopes above you, an avalanche is possible. If you are among trees, this fact alone is usually assurance enough that an avalanche has not occurred and probably will not occur in that area.

There are two basic types of avalanches. These are loose snow avalanches and slab avalanches. Sometimes the two may occur in combination.

All avalanches are dangerous. But of the two types, the loose snow avalanche usually is the less dangerous. A loose snow avalanche is very impressive to look at. Great billows of smoke-like snow dust are churned up. The avalanche is very rapid and it is not possible to outrun it, nor even to get out of its way. Except at its bottom, where the avalanche stops, a loose snow avalanche does not involve a deep thickness of snow. If the loose snow avalanche takes place in a very large and open area and involves a large amount of snow, it may develop considerable speed. High speed avalanches create hurricane-like winds sometimes, and when they do, these winds may blast objects down which stand in their way. The winds may be effective even off to the sides of the avalanche, out of the slide path, and they may continue in front of the avalanche even after the avalanche itself has stopped.

In addition to the loose snow avalanche, there is the slab avalanche. A slab avalanche occurs when one stratum of snow (or several strata) lets go of the mountain and starts to slide down. Considerably more snow mass is involved in slab avalanches than in loose snow avalanches and, in addition, if the slab is deep enough, slab avalanches may also consist of rocks and boulders mixed in with the snow. Although slab avalanches generally have less velocity than loose snow avalanches, the speed of a slab avalanche depends on the steepness of the slope. Slab avalanches generally begin on high, steep slopes and have considerable velocity when they first start. But as they grow massive, and as the slope becomes less steep, they slow down until they move quite slowly before coming to a stop.

Whereas a loose snow avalanche usually begins at one point, a slab avalanche may begin along a wide front. All of a sudden the snow loses its grip on the mountain, lets go, and almost instantly it is falling at a very high velocity. Since a large mass of snow is involved, and since it moves at great speed, a slab avalanche has tremendous force and immense destructive power. Particularly when slab avalanches consist of wet and heavy snow, they will sweep everything before them and can only be stopped by a decrease in the steepness of the slope. Wet slab avalanches can uproot large trees and carry them for a considerable distance. They can carry huge boulders as cargo.

The power of a slab avalanche is dependent on its mass, and the mass of snow involved depends on the depth of the fracture. If the fracture goes down only one foot, let us say, to a second compacted layer of snow, the avalanche will have less mass than if the fracture were ten feet deep and included all the snow down to the bare ground. Another factor which will affect mass is water. Water is heavy. If it has been raining into the snow, the weight of the rain water will add to the mass of the snow slab. Sometimes rain will trigger a slab avalanche by adding so much weight to the slab that the friction which holds the slab to the mountain is overcome. A wet slab avalanche has the same tumbling, churning, rushing effect as a wall of water escaping from a burst dam, and it can be stopped just as easily!

Late winter and early spring are the seasons for avalanches. This is the time to avoid steep snow slopes. This is especially the time to avoid steep snow in chutes, gullies, and habitual avalanche paths, and it is the time to be very careful about walking near the bases of snow-covered cliffs.

If you are caught up in an avalanche, the best thing to do is kick the legs and move the arms in a swimming motion and try to remain at the surface of the snow. Continue kicking and "swimming" until the avalanche itself stops moving. Then, if you are below the surface, move the arms about and punch away as much snow as possible from the area around the face, so as to be able to form as large an air pocket as possible. If buried, the next thing to do is to relax long enough to make a decision about which way is up. Then, tamping the snow be-

SLAB
AVALANCHE

DEPTH
OF FRACTURE

FRACTURE
LINE

BARE DIRT OR NEXT
COMPACTED LAYER OF
SNOW

hind you with your feet, you dig with your hands in the direction of up. Moving in wet slab snow is almost impossible. Movement is somewhat easier, but still difficult, in wet loose snow and in dry slab snow, and the least difficult is in loose dry snow.

After an avalanche has stopped, those members of the party who are on the surface of the snow must begin immediately to search for members of the party who are buried.

Avalanche cord helps searchers find buried victims, and if there is any possibility of an avalanche occurring in the terrain where you plan to be, it is an excellent idea to use avalanche cord.

Avalanche cord is brightly colored nylon line (usually red). It is tied around the waist and dragged along behind the hiker on the surface of the snow. Avalanche cord should be at least seventy-five feet long. A hundred feet make a better length. Nylon is very strong and the cord need not be thick. A diameter of one eighth of an inch is adequate. Even three thirty-seconds of an inch will do. The important thing is to have an easily visible color. In an avalanche, the avalanche cord will tend to remain at or near the surface of the snow. Even if the man wearing the cord is buried, searchers can locate him by finding any part of the cord on the snow and following the cord until they come to the man around whose waist it is tied. Following the cord, they will know where to dig.

Nylon avalanche cord should be burned at each end to melt the fibers together and prevent fraying. In addition, knots should be tied along the length of the cord at twenty-five feet, fifty feet, and at seventy-five feet (when using a hundred-foot cord). A single knot is tied at twenty-five feet. Two knots are tied about a half-inch apart at fifty feet (which is the middle of the cord). Three knots are tied at seventy-five feet, again about a half inch apart. That end of the cord which is closest to the three knots is the end which is tied around the waist. Using knots in this manner saves rescuers time if both ends of the cord are buried after an avalanche. The people involved in the rescue know they must go along the cord in the direction of more knots, that is, from one to two to three, to find the victim.

If a seventy-five-foot avalanche cord is used, the knots should be spaced approximately nineteen feet apart, again at one half-inch intervals for two or more knots.

Snowmobiles

Snowmobiles are a controversial subject. I am on the side of the conservationists who believe that our wilderness areas should be preserved and protected not only from unsightly eyesores but also from noisy earsores. Many of us go into the wilderness not only for the natural beauty, but for the peace and quiet to be found there.

In many areas, there is no more peace and quiet in the summertime. Power saws snore angrily in the woods and can be heard for miles. In recent years, the so-called "trail bikes" have invaded the forests, and in some places, the Hondas and the Toyotas and the Hodakas and the Suzukis and the Yamahas and the Sears and the Harley-Davidsons roar along the back roads and the trails until you wish you had brought ear plugs along.

Things used to be different in the winter, however. Once the snow covered the trails and the power squadrons were forced to stay home, it was possible to enjoy the splendors of the snow-covered landscape and to bathe in the very special silence that only a noise-absorbing blanket of snow could provide.

Today, this is no longer true. Snowmobiles snort out into the wilderness these days just as easily over the snow as motorcycles went out in the summer over dry ground. The majestic silence of winter is fractured by unmuffled snowmobile engines.

I can't understand why these people don't go out on their feet. After all, walking keeps you warm, and you can really freeze sitting still on a snowmobile while the motor does all the work for you and a frigid breeze whips past your face.

But it looks like snowmobiles are here to stay. Snowmobiles are used around ski resorts for various chores, and they are

A snowmobile

being used in logging operations in the wintertime. There are more of them being manufactured and sold every year for use in recreation.

The state of Minnesota has many miles of public snowmobile trails and is developing hundreds of miles more in the state parks there. In fact, snowmobile trails exist in every state cold enough to have snow, and it is only in our national parks and in the "wilderness areas" of our national forests that snowmobiles are forbidden, as are also trail bikes in the summertime.

Call it progress, or call it whatever else you will, it seems certain we will be seeing more snowmobiles in the years to come than we used to see.

Snowmobiles have definite utilitarian value. Trappers can make a quick round of their trap lines in no time at all on a snowmobile where such a trip might take a week travelling on snowshoes. Farmers and other people living on the edge of forests use snowmobiles to haul lumber quickly and effortlessly. Winter fishermen use snowmobiles to get to their fishing spots and they may even haul along their huts. Hunters use snowmobiles to get quickly into remote areas where they can then dismount and look for their game. Even more convenient, hunters use snowmobiles to haul their game out of the woods, back to the car. Under the category of "sports," there are snowmobile races held around the northern edge of the United States and some such racing competitions have even included snowmobile jumping. Racing usually takes place near urban centers, and these activities do not disturb the quiet of the back woods. To the credit of the Evinrude people, they advertise "quiet" snowmobiles.

For the benefit of those people who are interested in snow-mobiling, the following information is offered.

Safety should be always kept in mind when operating a snowmobile. One of the most basic things is to dress warmly. You can't act safely if your body and mind become numb from the frost. The lack of physical activity involved in sitting on a vehicle and whipping along in a speed-made wind makes the use of warm clothing absolutely mandatory. Special attention should be given to keeping the hands, face, and feet warm.

If racing, a crash helmet should always be worn.

Whether racing or just trail riding, goggles should always be worn to protect the eyes. The eyes need protection from the cold wind, from whipping branches as the snowmobile drives past trees or bushy growth, from bits of snow or ice which may be flung back from a vehicle to the front, and from the glare of the sun on a bright day.

Since snowmobiles do not have supercharged engines, they will not operate efficiently at high elevations. Since you will be operating in the lowlands only, ordinary ski goggles should provide adequate eye protection. It is best to have three interchangeable plastic (or safety glass) lenses for these goggles: a dark green or dark smoked lens for use in bright sunlight, an amber lens for dull, misty days, and a clear, colorless lens for night-time use on those beautiful moonlit nights when the snow is almost as bright as in the daytime, and for catching a glimpse of the aurora borealis.

Needless to say, you should never ride alone at night. Always take a passenger or ride as a member of a party. Make sure your lights work, and that the headlight and taillight are not covered with snow. Avoid river and lake crossings at night, or you may disappear completely, never to be heard from again.

Additional safety suggestions for snowmobiling are as follows:

Do *not* hot rod along trails! Join a racing club if you want to race.

Always carry a survival kit including first aid supplies, emergency food, flashlight, basic tools for minor repairs, and a spare rubber belt drive. And know how to change the rubber belt drive.

When the drive track becomes clogged with snow and ice, do not have one person lift the rear of the snowmobile from directly behind. He may be struck by flying chunks of ice, or by rocks. Always have two people lift the snowmobile, one standing on each side so that the rear is clear. Also, be careful to do this in a place where innocent bystanders will not be struck by flying debris.

The throttle should always be set at a low idle when starting the motor, otherwise you may end up in a comical (or dangerous) situation in which you find yourself running after your riderless snowmobile as it takes off for the distant countryside. Of course, if you have a snowmobile with a self-starter, you will not have this problem.

Driving the snowmobile should be done with the same care used in driving an automobile. There are open places where you can go faster, and there are other places where you should proceed cautiously. Driving over frozen rivers and lakes should always be done with care, and only during the daylight hours. The driver should keep a wary eye out for slushy spots, especially in the thawing weather of spring. Going through slush in a snowmobile is like going through mud in a car. Stop and go around the slush if possible. If it is not possible to stop, or to get off the trail, accelerate and keep moving until you are on solid snow again. If you slow down or stop in the slush, you will be stuck and you will have to wrestle the vehicle out by hand or be towed out.

All kinds of accessories are now available for snowmobiles, including fishing huts (pulled horizontally, then set up vertically), trailer tents, and side cars. The best accessories are trailer sleds.

Although most snowmobiles are powered by motors developing 25 horsepower or less, this power is enough to pull very heavy loads over snow trails because of the lack of friction from snow. A snowmobile can pull the weight of many adults on a trailer sled. A snowmobile can pull five or more trailer sleds in tandem on a packed trail. Trailers are used for hauling wood, supplies, game, people, or anything else you might want to haul. Because trailer sleds do not have brakes, they should always be pulled with tow bars, never with a rope.

Skiers can be towed with a rope either up a slope so they can ski down or just along the countryside, on level ground. After adjustments have been made in the bindings so as to hold boots, water skis may be towed by a snowmobile.

The following is a partial list of brand names and/or manufacturers of snowmobiles:

Arctic Cat	Sno-Dart
Mercury	Sno-Flite
Polaris	Snowcruiser (Sears)
Skee-Horse (Johnson)	Viking
Skeeter (Evinrude)	Yamaha
Ski-Bird	Yukon King
Ski-Doo (Bombardier, Ltd.)	

Snowmobiles are used quite a bit in Canada. When I was up to Banff and Jasper, I saw them parked around here and there and everywhere. But in that region they are used more for utilitarian reasons, just to get around over the snow, than for sporting reasons, although they are used for that too.

7] Winter Camp Cooking

THINK OF those young, slender, attractive secretaries you have seen in one office or another in your business dealings. Well-groomed, chic, and charming, these personable young ladies are a pleasure for the eye to behold. One of the most pleasing things about them is their trim, slender figures. But if you think this slenderness is accidental, you are probably mistaken. Young girls are all clothes conscious, and being clothes conscious, they are figure conscious. Being figure conscious, they are all on diets. If you don't believe this, wander past two of them when you see them engaged in deep, low-voiced conversation. The chances are that they will be talking about their respective diets. Or, better still, watch what they eat at lunch time. Some of their meals would keep a healthy canary hungry.

Ask any one of these good-looking girls how many calories a certain item of food has and the chances are either: (1) that she will know, and can tell you immediately; or, (2) that she will be able to pull a little booklet out of her purse and read the correct answer off to you from the tables in the booklet.

Girls are wonderful. Their ways are often mysterious to men, but they are wonderful.

Now, what are calories? And what has all this to do with winter camp cooking?

Calories are units of measurement of food energy. Food is

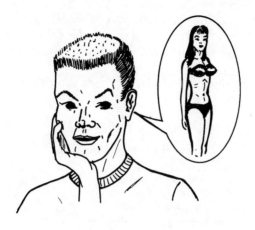

fuel for the human body. To be energetic, in fact to be able to move at all, we need fuel in the form of calories.

In the wintertime, when considerable fuel must be used just to maintain body temperature at its normal level, and when, in addition, strenuous outdoor work will consume considerably more fuel, the caloric intake must be high.

Normally, a child about six years old needs 2,000 calories daily. At fifteen years of age this rises to 3,000 calories daily. After the age of fifteen, the caloric requirements change, depending on sex. At the age of twenty, girls need 2,500 calories per day, or less, whereas boys continue to need 3,000 calories or more per day. With increasing age, the caloric requirement diminishes, and by the age of sixty-five, a woman's daily requirement drops below 2,000 calories a day and a man's to 2,500 calories.

These are average figures and depend on such factors as height and weight, upon the season of the year, and upon how active an individual is.

In this book, we are concerned with active males in a freezing or frozen environment. Regardless of age, from sixteen to sixty-five, the daily caloric requirement under these conditions is high. It will vary from one individual to the next, but it will remain very high.

For winter camping, winter sports, winter mountaineering, and for other cold weather activities, *the daily calorie intake should be about 5,000 calories.*

Here is a short list of certain foods showing their caloric content:

FOOD ITEM   CALORIES

Food Item	Calories
Asparagus, cooked	20
Beets, cooked	27
Cabbage, cooked	14
Cauliflower, cooked	25
Cucumbers, raw	12
Lettuce, raw	15
Mushrooms, canned	11
Pickles, dill	11
Radishes, raw	20
Tomato juice, canned	21

The number of calories in the foods shown is for 100 grams of the edible portion of the food. The source for this data is the U.S. Department of Agriculture.*

A hundred grams is about 3.5 ounces, or about .22 pounds. In other words, 100 grams is almost a quarter of a pound.

These are obviously the kinds of food that slender young secretaries should eat while on their diets. These foods would not give an active man much energy for doing strenuous work, especially in very cold weather. They are listed here only so that they can be contrasted with the list which follows.

The following is a list of high-calorie foods. These are the food items which are suitable for winter in the outdoors.

* Watt and Merrill, *Composition of Foods—Raw, Processed, Prepared,* Agricultural Handbook No. 8. Bureau of Human Nutrition and Home Economics.

FOOD ITEM CALORIES

Bacon	630
Barley	349
Beef, cooked rump	378
Butter	716
Butterscotch	410
Cake, dark fruit cake	354
Cake, pound cake	434
Candy, hard	383
Candy, caramels	415
Cheese, cheddar	398
Cheese, Swiss	370
Chocolate, sweet, milk	503
Chocolate, unsweetened	501
Cookies	436
Fat, cooking, vegetable	884
Frankfurters	248
Fudge	411
Ham, cooked	400
Hamburger, cooked	364
Honey	294
Jam	278
Jelly	252
Lard	902
Liverwurst	263
Macaroni, cooked	149
Nuts, Brazil	646
Nuts, cashew	578
Nuts, peanuts	559
Nuts, pecans	696
Nuts, walnuts	654
Oils, cooking	884
Oleomargarine	720
Pork, link sausage	450
Peas, split	344
Potatoes, boiled	83
Potatoes, French fried	393
Raisins	268
Rice, cooked	119

Sardines (in oil)	214
Sirloin, cooked	297
Spaghetti, cooked	149
Sugar	385
Tuna, canned	198

As can be seen from these tables, if you eat a quarter of a pound of mushrooms or pickles, you will take on 11 calories. If you eat a quarter of pound of walnuts, you will take on 654 calories. That's quite a difference!

Obviously, your winter menus should be planned with those foods that are in the high-calorie list.

A study of this list is revealing. Many people think of macaroni and spaghetti as being high in calories, and therefore fattening. But these foods contain only 149 calories, and will not provide as much energy as one might expect. Even more surprising is that boiled potatoes only provide 83 calories, or about half the calories of macaroni and spaghetti.

With this in mind, you should add plenty of butter or oleomargarine to your potatoes. In fact, if you mash them, you should add so much butter or oleomargarine that your mashed potatoes look yellow instead of white.

Don't worry about getting fat while eating all these calories. An active outdoor life in the snow will consume so many calories that you not only won't get fat, you may even lose weight. It isn't only calorie intake that counts, but also output. Intake minus output may equal zero, or it may even be a negative number.

Food energy, that is caloric content, is not the only element in food to consider. Foods also contain proteins, fats, minerals (such as calcium, sodium, phosphorus, iron, sulphur, etc.), and vitamins. A balanced diet should include all of these elements. If you are going on a lengthy winter expedition, your dietary requirements should be carefully considered when making out a list for food supplies. However, if you will only be out in the woods for the week-end, don't worry about a balanced diet. You can balance your diet on Monday after you return. But even on the shortest winter hike, your food should provide you with an adequate amount of calories. If you don't get your calories, like an automobile without gasoline, you will slow down and stop.

Remember also, that your so-called "warm" sleeping bag and "warm" clothing do not generate any heat whatever. Whatever heat you feel comes from yourself, from the food you have eaten. All that these insulating items do is keep your own heat in the immediate vicinity of your body. Warmth does not come from clothes, but from the calories in food.

Another consideration to keep in mind is that sugar will ruin your teeth. In all food planning, and on all your menus, try to minimize the use of sugar. Instead use fats, oils, butter, and oleomargarine as much as possible.

One more thing to consider is alcohol. All fatty foods and oils are processed through the liver. On a winter diet, your liver will have a full-time job handling your high-calorie foods. Alcohol prevents the liver from doing its job properly. You should therefore avoid using alcohol altogether while out in the woods in the winter. Give your liver a break. Wait until you have been back home for a day or two and then you can have your whiskey in whatever quantity suits you, but avoid it in the woods or you will be cold or fatigued or both.

Polar bears, incidentally, which live on a diet consisting almost exclusively of seal fat, have such active and rich livers that they cannot be eaten by human beings. Even Eskimos, who waste absolutely nothing, will not eat a polar bear's liver.

In planning a winter camping trip, the menu should be worked out in detail. Write down each meal, including every item of food in that meal. A written menu is a help in several ways. First, it becomes the basis for a shopping list to be used in your local supermarket or grocery store. If your shopping list is complete, you will not forget or omit any food items. Next, if you have a menu written down on paper, you can go over it item by item and visualize how you will prepare this food in camp. In doing this, you can establish which pots and pans and bowls and plates and utensils you will need, and the order in which they will be used. Lastly, while in the woods, you can use your menu as a calendar. On longer backpacking trips I usually lose all sense of time after a day or two in the woods. But as I have each meal, I cross it out on the menu with a large, pencilled "X." By glancing at the day and date for the column where the meal I have just eaten is listed, I can ascertain what the date is.

The second item listed above is important. You do not want to bring along any equipment that you will not use. By looking at the menu, and visualizing how you will prepare each meal, you will be able to decide on your exact equipment requirements. Some of this business can be trickier than it sounds.

For example, in preparing a Wilson's packaged breakfast for two, available in many sporting goods stores, the following must be considered: The meal consists of dehydrated potatoes, diced dehydrated ham, and powdered eggs. As soon as we know we will have powdered eggs, we know we will need: (1) a frying pan; (2) some kind of frying grease; (3) some kind of a mixing bowl for mixing the powdered eggs with water; (4) a spatula for frying and scrambling the eggs. Next, we will need a second frying pan for the potatoes, or else, if we want to carry only one frying pan, we will need a plastic dish or bowl (not metal, this will cool the food off too fast) for holding the hot potatoes after we have fried them and while we are frying the eggs. Another reason for choosing only one frying pan is that if we will cook over a gasoline stove, and not over a fire, the single stove can only handle one frying pan at a time. It is impractical to try to backpack anything heavier than a one-burner stove into the woods. In the Wilson packaged breakfast, the potatoes come in a plastic bag, but the diced ham comes in a can. Therefore, last, but never least, we know we will need a can opener.

Let us now mentally prepare this breakfast in the woods over a one-burner stove. We light the stove and put a pot of water on it. The pot can be heating while we get dressed or do other early morning chores in camp. If we have Tang on the menu, we either put the powder in a cup and add ice-cold water and stir, or we can wait until the chill has gone out of the water in the pot on the stove, and use cool, but not ice-

cold, water. After the water in the pot is boiling, we can have
a cup of cocoa or coffee. Swiss Miss powder makes delicious
cocoa and Nescafé makes excellent coffee. If you take your
coffee with sugar and cream, you should have had sugar and
powdered coffee lightener on your menu and on your food
shopping list.

Now, fully dressed, and with a hot drink in our bellies and
with perhaps another hot cup filled and ready, we take the pot
of water off the stove and set it aside on a sweater or on the
empty pack (but never on the snow) and get down to the
business of making breakfast.

The little can of diced ham is opened and filled with warm
water and allowed to stand so that the dehydrated ham can
soak up the water.

The potatoes are emptied into the frying pan and water is

added so that the dehydrated pieces of potato can soak up the water which they require. The potatoes are heated over the stove and stirred occasionally so that they get to be cooked at the same time they are soaking up their water. The stirring may be done with a spoon or with a spatula.

At the same time as the potatoes are cooking, the powdered eggs are slowly mixed with water. This can be done in one of the soup bowls, using a spoon. The second camper can mix the eggs while the first camper heats the potatoes.

When the potatoes have soaked up all the water in the frying pan, they are reconstituted. Now butter or oleomargarine must be added to the pan to prevent the potatoes from burning. In the summer, you would add just enough butter to insure proper frying. But in the winter, you add great big gobs of butter because this will add calories to the meal.

When the potatoes are nicely browned, you scoop these out and fill the other camper's bowl or eating dish. Remember, one bowl is fully occupied now holding the powdered egg mix.

After the potatoes have been emptied from the frying pan, more butter is added to the empty pan and melted over the stove. Now the egg mix is poured into the frying pan and the bowl is scraped out with a spoon into the frying pan to make sure you've got all the egg mix there is.

If there is any remaining water in the can of diced ham, this is now either thrown away or else added to the eggs in the pan, depending on how hungry and how thrifty you feel at the moment. The diced ham itself is dumped into the eggs. Using a spatula, the ham-egg mixture is stirred constantly in the frying pan until it is done. This does not take very long.

In the meanwhile, the second camper now takes half of the potatoes from the one bowl and puts them in his own bowl. The ham-egg mixture is divided from the frying pan into the two bowls equally. The pan is removed from the stove and the pot of water is returned to the stove. At any point along the meal there is always hot water available for more coffee, cocoa, tea, or what have you.

As hot water is used from the pot, more cold water is

added so that there is always a good supply of hot water.

A breakfast such as the one just described is ineffably delicious, and it turns a cold, half-awake, bumbling camper into a lively and spirited human being, full of energy and good cheer.

In going through the meal in this manner, we have seen what equipment we will need. From the description above, it is obvious one camper alone could not prepare this meal with only his own equipment. If he wanted to have this meal alone, he would require one extra bowl, either for holding the potatoes after they are done or for mixing the egg powder. However, since this breakfast is packaged for *two* people, and states this on the label, it is not likely that one man alone would have it on his menu unless he were a very hungry man.

All planned menus should be visualized this way, one step at a time, in order to determine equipment requirements. If possible, type your menu, as this makes it easier to read and to use.

Use tempting, attractive words to describe what you put on the menu, as this makes using it more enjoyable. Try to copy the language you've seen on menus in a restaurant. Use words like "steaming" and "creamy" and "hot." Remember it's all a matter of outlook. You wouldn't be interested in eating "bug spit" but you would enjoy "honey." Eating a "dead animal" or a "cow corpse" might repel you, so use "steak" or even "T-bone steak," "sirloin steak," or whatever it is. You wouldn't care for "curdled animal secretion," but you would enjoy "cheese."

At the end of this chapter there is a sample menu for a backpacking trip for a four-day week-end.

Included in this menu is a Thermos of coffee for lunch. If you are in a fixed base camp, taking along a Thermos of coffee for lunch is no trouble at all, and certainly worth the slight effort involved. However, if you are travelling cross-country with a heavy pack and making camp in a different place every night, it will probably be best to eliminate the Thermos and save time and weight.

If you will be backpacking, you can get freeze-dried pork

chops and freeze-dried hamburgers in cans. Freeze-dried foods are extremely light. Some of them come in cans not because the can is needed for the preservation of the food, but because freeze-dried foods are so fragile they would be quickly crushed into a nondescript powder if they were squeezed into a tight pack unprotected. Actually, you could bring fresh pork chops along in real cold weather if you set your pack outdoors as soon as you packed it. One of the great conveniences of winter camping is that food is kept fresh in your pack for a very long time just because it is so cold.

Beef stew can be bought in cans right off the shelf in the supermarket. However, these cans are heavy. If you will be backpacking you'll be better off to get dehydrated or freeze-dried beef stew. This usually comes in plastic bags, and it weighs very little.

Pound cake, chocolate cake, and other cake is sold in cans, either as army surplus or right in neighborhood supermarkets. Needless to say, you should not try to backpack with cake unless it is protected by a can for freshness and from crushing.

Soup can also be bought in cans, but even though one more can of water has to be added per can when it is being cooked, such cans are heavy. For backpacking it is best to get the dehydrated soups which come in plastic envelopes.

If you camp in a trailer, or in a large tent in a fixed location, near the car, you have a very wide latitude in your selection of meals. In fact, weight does not even enter the picture as a problem. On the other hand, you are limited this way to a half day's journey away from a camp which will be the same each night. If you backpack through the snow, the weight of your pack is an immediate and primary problem. Despite this, backpacking through the snow in the wintertime, or even in the summer at snow levels in the mountains, gives you a marvelous sense of freedom. You just come and go as you please.

There is one general difference between cooking when on a climbing expedition in the summer snows and cooking at lower elevations in the winter. This is the matter of consumption of liquids and of salt. Although perspiration takes place at all seasons of the year at all elevations, considerably more perspiration takes place in the strenuous work of climbing. Water and salt are lost in perspiration and must be replaced. High mountain recipes must therefore be such that much water and salt is included in each meal. Stews are excellent for high mountain meals and so are soups. Plenty of salt should be added to these meals. In low elevation meals in very cold weather, the stews should be less watery and less salty. These somewhat thicker stews can be thinned out by adding butter or oleomargarine to the pot.

As a matter of fact, excessive use of salt should be avoided in the winter as this tends to make a person thirsty, and there just may not be that much drinking water around. An excellent way to take on some salt, incidentally, in summer or winter, is to use leftover bacon fat like butter. Smear it on bread and eat it. This not only gives you some salt, but also gives you the calories in the bacon fat.

If the weather is cold enough, you can bring along frozen foods in your pack and they will stay frozen until you heat them up. Remember that frozen foods should not be thawed and then refrozen. Remember also that unless you use a hacksaw, it is impossible to cut frozen foods. Frozen foods should, therefore, be bought in usable sizes, or cut to usable sizes before freezing. Once they are frozen, and once you've packed them in your pack, that's the size you've got and that's the amount you'll have to cook.

Last, but not least, a few words about a chore that none of us like, but which is necessary and important—washing dishes and pots and pans.

There are lots of ways of getting this done. The main thing is to get it done with a minimum of fuss and bother, and with the least time wasted.

I always count the number of hot meals which will be cooked on any given trip and pack in one Brillo pad for each meal. Brillo pads are very convenient because each pad contains its own soap.

MENU
FOUR-DAY HUNTING TRIP TO _____
NOVEMBER 28 THROUGH DECEMBER 1, 197__

197__ DATE	BREAKFAST	LUNCH	SUPPER
WEDNESDAY NOV. 27, 197__	At Home	At Work	At a Roadside Restaurant
THURSDAY NOV. 28, 197__	Tang Soft-Boiled Eggs Bread, Butter, Jam Nescafé	Nuts and Cheese Slices of Salami (Thermos of hot coffee)	Olives Beef Stew with Potatoes Ry-Krisp and Butter Hot Swiss Miss
FRIDAY NOV. 29, 197__	Tang Wilson's Breakfast Poundcake and Butter Nescafé	Nuts and Raisins Beef Jerky (Thermos of hot coffee)	Pork Chops Steaming Rice and Butter Pound Cake & Butter Hot Swiss Miss
SATURDAY NOV. 30, 197__	Tang Tomato-Rice Mulligan Nescafé	Nuts and Candy Pepperoni (Thermos of hot coffee)	Beef-Vegetable Stew with Noodles Pound Cake and Butter Hot Swiss Miss
SUNDAY DEC. 1, 197__	Tang Beef and Barley Soup Pound cake & Butter Nescafé	Nuts and Candy Pepperoni (Thermos of hot coffee)	At a Roadside Restaurant

During each meal, keep a pot of hot water going at all times. This is not only for coffee or cocoa, but so that you will have warm dishwashing water at the end of the meal.

After you have finished eating, use a combination of pine needles and snow or just plain snow to scrape out all the excess food and fat from dishes, bowls, utensils, etc., and then use the Brillo pad to scrub everything down with hot water.

If you clean out your frying pan first, you can use the frying pan as your kitchen sink, cleaning everything and scrubbing it down in the pan. Save some clean hot water for a final rinse for everything. Then rinse out the frying pan and you are all finished.

8] Hunting in Snow and Ice

MANY EXCELLENT books have been written on *how* to hunt.*

In this chapter we will not attempt to go into general discussion about *how* to hunt, but rather assume that the reader knows something about this already, from personal experience or otherwise, and cover those aspects of hunting which relate to cold weather. Since many open seasons in hunting come in the fall or winter, it will be useful to relate these activities to a cold weather environment. The later in the season you hunt, the more this should be pertinent.

Not all animals can be hunted in the winter, since some animals hibernate. Among these are squirrels, chipmunks, and bears. The polar bear does not hibernate, but all other bears do, including the black bear and the grizzly bear. (Of course, bears do not hibernate in tropical climates.) A hibernating bear makes no sound, does not move, and gives off very little odor, and the chances are slim that you will see a bear in the dead of winter. Be grateful for this, for a bear awakened from his winter's sleep will undoubtedly greet you in a very bad humor. But even while the grizzly sleeps, other animals may be hunted, sometimes in extremely cold weather. Hunting in the winter is obviously different from hunting in the summer or fall.

* One of the best books I have seen on hunting is *The Art of Hunting Big Game in North America* by J. O'Connor.

First and foremost, the big difference between a summer landscape and a winter landscape is that in the winter the leaves are gone from the deciduous trees and snow lies on the ground. A deer does not have foliage (except evergreens) for concealment in the winter, and he may often be seen from a considerable distance if he is there to be seen at all. Furthermore, a deer leaves few tracks in soft, springy moss and none on leaf-covered ground and on rocks. But he leaves tracks all over the place when there is snow on the ground. In addition, tracks do not last as long in snow as they do in mud, for example, especially if more snow continues to fall, and so not only are tracks more visible in snow, but they tend to be fresher. In fact, if it is snowing at the time when you see tracks, you are guaranteed that the tracks are almost brand new.

Unfortunately, the very things that make the deer more exposed to your observation and detection, make you more exposed to the deer.

In some ways a deer's eyesight is not as good as that of a man's, but in other ways it is better. A deer cannot distinguish colors. Red, green, blue, and brown all appear to the deer as varying shades of gray. The deer sees the world just as you see it in a black and white snapshot. Time after time I have had a deer look at me while I wore a bright red jacket and then look away again and go about his business. But a deer will detect movement, even the smallest, seemingly insignificant movement, immediately; and he will be off and running. This inability to distinguish visual details, but to spot any kind of movement applies not only to deer, but to most animals. Notable exceptions are pronghorn antelopes and hawks, eagles, vultures, and buzzards. These creatures can see anything in their direct line of sight, apparently, no matter how far away it is, and apparently even if it is still.

Binoculars

To equalize an animal's ability to spot movement at a great distance, the hunter turns to binoculars. Binoculars enable a

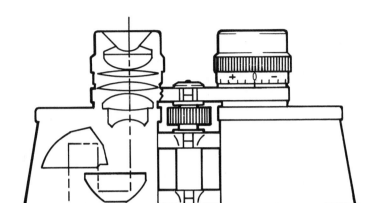

Binoculars

hunter to advance visually before he advances physically. In the open terrain which winter makes of many landscapes, binoculars become an absolute necessity for the hunter.

Binoculars are designated by two numbers, with an "X" between them. The first number indicates the magnifying power of the glasses. Thus a six means that you see an object at six hundred feet with the glasses about the same way you would see it at one hundred feet without the glasses. At sixty feet, you see an object approximately the way it would look if you stood ten feet away from it. The number which follows the "X" tells you the size of the objective lens in millimeters.* Thus, a pair of binoculars designated 6 × 30 means the binoculars magnify six times and have an objective lens 30 millimeters in diameter. The objective lens, incidentally, is the one farthest from your eye.

If you divide the size of the objective lens (expressed in millimeters) by the magnifying power of the binoculars, you

* One millimeter = 0.03937 inches
One inch = 25.4 millimeters

get the size of the exit pupil in millimeters. 6 × 30 glasses have an exit pupil of 5 mm. From this it can be seen that 6 × 30, 7 × 35, 8 × 40, and 10 × 50 binoculars all have the same size exit pupil. 8 × 30 glasses have an exit pupil of 3.75 mm.

The exit pupil is the little circle of light which you see in the center of the rear lens when you hold your binoculars out at arms' length.

Light goes through your binoculars, comes out of the exit pupil, and then enters through the pupil of your own eye. The pupil of your eye changes size automatically depending on how much light there is. On a bright day, the pupils of your eyes shrink down to mere dots. On a dull day, and at night, your pupils enlarge, to let more light in. When you enter a dark theater after coming out of the bright daylight, you can't see anything until your pupils enlarge.

Your eyes, when using binoculars, can only take in as much light as your pupils allow in. On a bright day, all binoculars will seem equally bright. This is because the pupils of your eyes will be smaller than the exit pupil of the binoculars, and therefore unable to receive all the light delivered to them by the binoculars. But in the evening, after your pupils have expanded, they may be the same size as the exit pupil on binoculars, or larger. In this situation glasses with an exit pupil of 5 mm. will give you a brighter image than glasses with a 3.75 mm. exit pupil, because your own pupils will be larger than 3.75 mm. and thus able to take in more light. In dim light, the larger the exit pupil is, the brighter the image will appear.

This light-gathering quality of glasses used to be called "relative brightness," and was obtained by squaring the size of the exit pupil. Using this formula, 8 × 30 glasses had a relative brightness of 14, and 8 × 40 glasses a relative brightness of 25. This made sense since, if the power of the binoculars remained the same, the larger the objective lens became, the more light the glasses were able to allow to pass through.

But using this formula, all binoculars which had an exit pupil of the same size (6 × 30, 7 × 35, 8 × 40, 10 × 50, etc.) should theoretically have had the same "relative brightness."

Actually, the larger glasses were able to gather more light

than the smaller ones, and so a newer formula was developed which resulted in a numerical rating called "twilight performance." This is obtained by multiplying the magnification by the size of the objective lens and taking the square root of the product. Thus, $6 \times 30 = 180$; $\sqrt{180} = 13$. To the nearest whole number, the following standard binoculars have the following twilight performance:

MAGNIFICATION × DIAMETER	TWILIGHT PERFORMANCE
6×30	13
7×35	16
8×40	18
10×50	22
15×60	30

From the above it can be seen that the greater the magnification and the greater the size of the objective lens, the brighter the image will be in dim light. This is important in winter viewing when there are so many dull and gloomy days and when twilight lasts such a long time both mornings and evenings. Your game can see movement in dim light and you should be able to also.

Just in case I've given the impression here that it doesn't matter what kind of binoculars you buy except for differences in magnification and size of objective lens, let me set the record straight immediately.

The most important thing glasses should do is focus properly and resolve images clearly. It is better image resolution which makes the main difference in glasses and in their prices. You can buy 6×30 binoculars for $15 and also for $150. Each pair is worth the price you pay for it. Precision lens polishing and lens positioning are expensive processes, but they make for better binoculars. The difference between excellent and poor binoculars can be easily seen by looking at some distant object first with the one pair, then with the other. Good binoculars give sharp and clear resolution to all images.

For a long time I hunted with a pair of Zeiss 10×50 binoculars. They were excellent glasses, particularly for hunting from high stands at twilight in Europe. I shot so many deer there over a period of several years that I lost count of them. But these glasses were best of all for those night boar hunts when the moonlit snow made large patches of ground white as daylight and the boar had to be seen over a considerable distance in the moonlight in the thickets where they hid. Brrr! Those were cold nights!

The 10 × 50s were bulky and heavy and I replaced them eventually with the 7 × 35s which I use now. I think if I changed again, I might go to a pair of 6 × 30s, or even try out a pair of those pocket-sized binoculars which I've seen advertised.

For pronghorn hunting in the wide open hills of Montana you would need good 10 × 50 glasses. These glasses are also necessary for mountain goats and sheep. But for hunting deer in woods, or in semi-wooded country, a lesser magnification is adequate, and 6 × 30 binoculars are more than enough.

Still Hunting for Deer

A good way to hunt in frigid weather, if you can stand the cold, is to still hunt. The advantage of still hunting is that it only takes a few hours. If you live some place where you can jump into your car and be at the place where you will hunt within an hour or so, you can get your hunting in and then go home again and get warm.

In still hunting, you go out and scout an area to determine if deer (or other game) are present. You check tracks, the lay of the land, and you look for a good shooting location. Then you leave.

The still hunt begins when you return in the darkness before dawn. Bundled up to protect yourself from the bitter cold, you take up your shooting position and you sit absolutely still and observe the terrain within your field of fire. Daylight gradually suffuses the landscape with light and when it becomes light your deer hopefully will come cautiously (and absolutely silently) along and you will get your shot.

MULE DEER

If the terrain is completely covered with snow, it will be relatively easy to spot the movement of your deer, as he will appear to be black against the white background. But if the snow is laying in patches and there are patches of bare ground, you will have to use your binoculars constantly and observe the dark areas between the snow patches. Deer do make noise sometimes, and I've heard them coming in wooded areas long before I've seen them. But at other times deer have moved so silently that I've been suddenly surprised to look up and see one close by without ever having heard a sound.

In still hunting, once you spot your deer you still have the chore ahead of you of shooting him. This means you must lower your binoculars, raise your rifle, aim, and squeeze the trigger, all without any sudden or jerky movements, and all in total silence. All of the live deer I've known were completely uncurious, and had absolutely no desire to investigate strange noises. One sound from you, and that deer will be off and running, and your still hunt will be over for that morning. For this reason, when I still hunt, I always have a round in the chamber, ready to go, and I always have the safety off.

In this kind of a situation, for noise control, move very slowly and exaggerate your slowness. Be careful not to let the binoculars clink against the rifle. Control your breathing. Don't sigh out loud as you settle into your shooting stance just before holding your breath when you squeeze the trigger.

I shot a tender spike buck in the very first season in which I hunted in the state of Washington less than an hour's drive from Seattle, and this was on a still hunt as described above.

Incidentally, I was wearing a bright red hunting jacket over all my other clothes when I shot this buck. Shortly before I shot him, he looked at me for a while but I remained absolutely still. He obviously could not distinguish the red color. He apparently was satisfied that there was no danger where I was and he looked at other areas of the woods and proceeded slowly on his way.

Still hunting can be done anytime during the day, but is best done early in the morning or late in the day as these are the times when deer are more likely to be moving from one location to another.

Stalking Deer

It is possible to stalk a mountain goat. It is possible to stalk other game. It may even be possible to stalk a deer in open country, or in semiopen country, from a very long distance.

I am convinced, however, that it is impossible to stalk a deer in the woods. A mountain lion may be able to do this, but it cannot be done by a human being.

A relaxed deer is always sufficiently alert to see, smell, or hear a human being long before the human being can get close to him in the woods. The deer will simply move quietly off.

Drive hunts are expressly forbidden by law in many states (and maybe in all states for all I know). But if one hunter takes up a shooting position at the head of a ravine and another hunter walks quietly up the ravine, if there are any deer in the ravine they will walk ahead of the moving hunter and may be shot by the stationary hunter who is waiting for them. This is really a form of drive hunting even though most states would allow this to pass as legal. It is not necessary to shout or to beat drums to have a drive hunt. Just having a man walk silently through the woods will do the trick just as well. This illustrates just how impossible it is to stalk a deer because apparently no matter how quietly the hunter moves through the woods, the deer know he is there and they move even more quietly ahead of him.

If you are hunting with a partner or in a group, stalk-driving is a good way to hunt. Split the group into two. Station one or more hunters at the head of a ravine, downwind from the ravine, and then have the other hunter or hunters make a great circle and come up the ravine toward the stationary hunters. It can be determined if an area is likely to have deer by either seeing one at a distance with binoculars or by seeing fresh deer tracks in the snow.

Another way to hunt deer is to use what I call a semistalk. In hunting this way, the hunter simply walks along slowly and as quietly as possible. He uses his binoculars constantly to scan in a downwind direction. He travels either downwind or crosswind, but never upwind. He watches the snow and the open ground for fresh tracks. In a semistalk, the hunter is looking for any deer, not for one particular deer. But once he sees a deer, or sees fresh tracks, then the semistalk turns into a real stalk as the hunter attempts to get into a shooting situation with that one particular deer.

As mentioned above, the odds are very much against the hunter and very much in favor of the deer in a stalk. But luck might play a part in the hunt and good luck combined with good skill will result in getting that deer after all.

Wind plays an important part in stalking. A strong wind will blow away the scent of the hunter and also some of the noise he makes. Deer are aware of this and they constantly watch in their downwind direction, and listen. The crunch of a boot into icy snow, the snap of a frozen twig as it breaks, the cough of a hunter, all these things will send them off and running. But if the wind is loud enough and strong enough, the hunter may still make out.

Mountain Goats

More than anything else, a successful mountain goat hunt is a matter of doing a lot of preliminary work.

Goats are creatures of habit, and they range over a specific and limited area.

If you have a goat tag, the thing to do is to get out into the mountains before the season starts and climb around mountains in several areas until you locate a good goat area, or several good goat areas. This is usually strenuous work, but this will get you in shape for the hunt itself, and for the even greater work of getting your goat down off the mountain after you have shot it.

The climbing ability of goats is amazing, even to those who have seen them time and time again. They will go almost anywhere—on the steepest slopes and on the narrowest ledges. In late summer and early fall, when most mountain goat seasons are open, the goats are usually very high, up where the snow is. In the winter and early spring, when there is snow in the valleys, goats will come down to lower elevations. I have seen a goat browsing in green woods in early spring, at an elevation about a thousand feet lower than the nearest snow, his white coloring making him stand out in sharp contrast to the green all around him.

Mountain goats live in such a high environment that this alone usually is enough to protect them from their enemies. But in addition, they have wide and open views, and so it is not the easiest thing to get close to a goat, even close enough to shoot him.

But just because their habitat provides them with so much security, goats tend to be less alert than other game, and more open and smug in their movements. Also, because they live at such high elevations, they tend to confine their watchfulness to areas below themselves. If you can climb up higher than where the goats are (not always an easy trick) and observe them from above, there is every likelihood that the goats will not see you and you can take your time in picking one out as your target.

MOUNTAIN GOAT

Billy goats and nanny goats both have horns and look alike. Because of this, hunting restrictions do not apply to sex. However, the billy goats tend to remain by themselves so if you see a lone goat, the chances are that it is a male. The nanny goats and the kids stay together in small groups.

Take your time when you have spotted a goat. Look his horns over and if they don't look big enough, let him go and find another one. Distances can be deceiving and if you quickly shoot the first goat you see, you may shoot a small nanny goat or even a kid. If you see several goats together, some larger and some smaller, there probably isn't a male among them except among the kids. Let them all go and look further until you can find a solitary male.

Goats will tend to stay in one place for a long time and when they browse, they move very slowly along. This gives you plenty of time to look them over in your binoculars, and you should not be in any rush to shoot.

Goat hunting is one circumstance when you will appreciate having really good binoculars, and a mountain goat is one of the game animals which will make you appreciate having a powerful pair of 10 × 50s.

In shooting, try not to shoot a goat while he is on a ledge which is situated over a steep slope or over a cliff. The goat will fall and his horns will break off, and there goes your trophy. In addition, you may have a difficult time in locating and recovering your kill. There are more level spots, even in the mountains, and this is where you should shoot your goat.

Elk

Whereas mountain goats live up in snow country and have to be hunted up where they live, elk come down from the high country in the fall and spend the winter in the wooded lowlands. But most elk seasons are so late in the year that there is every chance you will be hunting elk in the snow, or, if not in snow, in some pretty cold weather anyway.

Unlike nanny goats, elk cows do not have antlers. If you see an antlered elk, it is always a bull. Unlike deer, elk do not travel alone, but in herds, sometimes in quite large herds. Occasionally, bull elk can be seen alone.

Elk begin to rut in the fall and after several weeks of bugling, fighting with other bulls, herding cows into their harems, and staying awake nights to worry about their cows and to defend them, the bulls have meat which is strongly flavored and pretty tough. Later in the season, the bulls recover from all these strenuous activities and their meat becomes blander, more tender and more flavorful, and they put on some fat for the winter. The later in the season you shoot your elk, the better the meat will be. A strong, healthy bull with an adequate harem is a contented bull, and this contentment is reflected in better tasting, prime elk meat.

Many people think of elk as forest animals, and they are right. But elk spend a good deal of time in high elevations and in many ways they are mountain animals. They spend every

ELK

summer just as high as they can get, cooling off in the snow patches where you might only expect mountain goats to live. Even in early fall they are still at the highest elevations. Eventually the icy mountain winds and the snow forces them down into the low country.

An elk, also called wapiti, is a great and beautiful animal. There is no more impressive trophy than a magnificent rack of elk antlers. The animals themselves are huge and a single elk provides a huge quantity of meat. An elk once crossed the road in front of my car in early morning twilight. Since there were farms in the area, I thought at first that the animal was a horse, he was so huge. Then, in the headlights, I made out his great antlers, and I knew. In a matter of seconds he had crossed the road, entered the woods on the other side, and was gone.

Elk have very large lungs. When it is cold but there is no snow on the ground, their breath can be seen from a long distance away as it condenses into large white clouds. Sometimes it is possible to see the elk's breath, a periodic exhalation, but not see the elk itself. When looking ahead with binoculars, it is a good idea to look for the white steam clouds formed by an elk breathing. The clouds are large and unmistakable in their regularity. However, when the ground is white with snow, elk breath cannot be seen easily, if at all.

Elk travel for longer distances than deer. Where a deer will live out his entire life in a comparatively small area, elk will range for miles. This should be kept in mind when you find fresh elk tracks. Don't bother tiptoeing along to follow the tracks. The elk are probably far away. Instead, look at the lay of the land and look at your map, and circle around to a likely area a mile or two ahead of where you saw the tracks. This is where the elk are more likely to be. Even if you find very fresh tracks in snow, it is better not to try to follow them, but to circle around and try to intercept the elk some place ahead. An elk can easily outwalk and outrun a man, but he may walk into shooting range if you are situated in the right spot.

Elk are such large and massive animals, and they have such warmly insulating skin and hair, that the meat will spoil unless it is cooled off as quickly as possible. This is true in even the very coldest weather. For this reason an elk should be cleaned, skinned, and quartered just as soon as he is killed. Have a sharp knife along, a whetstone, and a hatchet for the bones.

Wild Boar

There are no wild boar native to the United States. The closest thing we have is a small wild pig called the peccary. Peccaries live throughout South and Central America and in Mexico, where they are called *javelina*. In the United States,

WILD BOAR

peccaries live only in the states adjoining Mexico: Texas, New Mexico, and Arizona. When fully grown, a peccary weighs from forty to sixty pounds.

Real wild boars are native to Europe and Asia. They range throughout the woods and forests of France, Germany, Czechoslovakia, Poland, Russia, and on to Siberia. These huge animals, frequently weighing four hundred or five hundred pounds, are a great source of annoyance to the European farmers because they come out of the woods and root up the crops that the farmers have planted.

If they are intensely hunted, they will leave an area and go some place else. For this reason, farmers in Europe are glad to see them hunted and lose no tears when some are killed. But the wild boar has been hunted for at least four thousand years, or since before the storied Calydonian Boar Hunt of Homer, and he is still around. Even pre-historic Cro-Magnan man knew him, hunted him, and drew pictures of him in his caves. During World War II, when millions of European men were out hunting each other instead of the boars, there was a huge increase in the boar population everywhere, and their crop ravages were extensive.

European wild boar are large and strong animals. Despite their huge bulk, they are capable of running very fast and they are quite agile. They become fierce animals when cornered, or when wounded. They have large, curved, sharp tusks, and they have great strength. A cornered or wounded boar will charge out suddenly and attack any hunter in sight.

The safest thing to do if charged by a boar, if there is time, is to climb a tree. But you better get up fast because the boar will rear up and try to bite you or slash you with his tusks. A grown boar can reach up about six feet so you've got to get up high and fast. Even a sow without tusks has immensely strong jaws and teeth and could probably take on a two-by-four in one bite.

I know of one American Army colonel in Germany who was hunting in his off hours, several years after the end of the war. He wounded a boar and went after the trail of blood on foot. Suddenly the boar charged from out of a thicket from so close that the colonel in backing off from the boar tripped and fell backward over a log and dropped his rifle. The colonel had a .45 caliber army pistol and he drew that from his holster and blasted away at the boar while struggling to his feet. The boar charged him and sliced about five pounds of meat from his rear, upper thigh. Bleeding profusely, and down on his hands and knees, the colonel continued to fire at the pig with his .45 automatic. By them, another member of the party ran up and killed the boar with several shots from his M-1 (Garand) rifle, using .30-06 ball point ammunition. I don't remember how many .30-06 and .45 bullets they counted in that boar, but there were quite a few. As I remember, the colonel spent the next few months in an army hospital flat on his belly.

Boar hunting can be, and usually is, very exciting. In Imperial India, boar hunting was considered a fitting sport for British officers in the Royal Bengal Lancers. They hunted them there with lances, but always on horseback.

In Europe, boar are hunted in three ways. High stands are built on the edge of woods, especially in areas near farms. The hunter goes to the high stand, climbs up the improvised ladder, takes his binoculars out, and he sits quietly and waits. High stands are used at dawn and at dusk. At dawn the hunter arrives while it is still dark so that he will have been in position for some time when it starts to get light. For evening hunting, the hunter arrives in late afternoon and remains in the high stand until it is too dark to see.

A second method used in hunting boar is to drive hunt. In drive hunting, a group of hunters take up positions along the edge of a wood, or along a forest road. The drivers circle around and then walk directly toward the hunters. They do not shout or make unusually loud noises. On the other hand, they make no attempt to be stealthy or quiet. Just their presence, moving through the woods, is enough to move the game ahead of them. In a boar hunt, other game such as deer, rabbits, foxes, badgers, etc., are allowed to pass through the line. But if any boar come by, the shooting begins. Since boar almost always travel in groups, there will be either no boar at all produced by the drive or there will be a number of them—perhaps ten or twenty or more.

If there is snow on the ground, a drive hunt can take place at night. Any kind of a moon at all will light up a snowy landscape. A full moon on a snowy landscape will make it so bright that it seems like daylight.

A third method for hunting wild boar is to use dogs. Not many people are aware of this, but Great Danes were originally bred to be boar fighters. Normally, when hunting with dogs, the dogs do not fight with the boars but get quickly out of their way. They track the boar, bark, make noise, and let the hunters know where the boar are. In snow in daylight it is possible to follow boar tracks without using dogs, but the pigs are so wary that they may be difficult to find. They are smart. They travel in great circles and they come in again on their own tracks, which they made earlier. They may detour from their first trail only to return to it. There is no way of knowing when tracks taking off in a new direction mean that the boar have really gone there. Should you waste time and investigate, or should you move on quickly ahead? One guess is as good as another. It adds to the excitement of the hunt. The only thing you can be sure of on a boar hunt is that when you do see one, you better shoot straight. A wounded boar is a mean and ugly customer. If you wound the animal you are obligated to follow the red trail through the snow until you can find him and finish him off.

Boar meat does not look or taste like pork. It is dark and lean. The boar meat that I ate tasted more like beef than anything else. But then I'm not sure I taste things as they really are. Once, when I was in Oslo, on my way up to Trondheim, I ate whale meat with potatoes and brown gravy in a restaurant in the Oslo railroad station, and the whale meat tasted to me like veal. Cooked moose always tastes like beef to me too.

Hunting weapons are a matter of personal taste, and every hunter will swear by his own rifle. I have always hunted with a bolt action .30-06 caliber rifle. I like it because a .30-06 can be used on almost any big game and because .30-06 ammunition is available everywhere. I prefer the bolt action because I think this action is the simplest, most reliable, and least likely to be jammed up by snow or affected by very low temperatures.

9] Arctic Climate Survival

W H Y a chapter on "survival"? Particularly, why a chapter on survival in arctic climate?

You may say you never expect to visit the Northwest Territories of Canada, or the Yukon, or Alaska, where arctic climate can be expected. You may be right, but you can never tell for sure.

Also, keep in mind that you can have arctic weather conditions right in the "lower forty-eight." It may be 40 degrees Fahrenheit above zero in Anchorage and Ketchikan and 40 degrees Fahrenheit below zero on the same day in Butte, Bismarck, Duluth, and Milwaukee. Actually, if you find yourself in the wilderness in any temperatures below 32 degrees Fahrenheit, you are more or less experiencing arctic weather. As I mentioned in the preface, I once nearly froze to death in a temperature of 20 degrees Fahrenheit above zero. Nowadays, I don't even think of a temperature like that in the woods as being excessively cold.

There are good and valid reasons for learning survival techniques for cold weather conditions. First of all, and most important, it is always possible to get lost in the wilderness on a hunting trip or on a cross-country skiing trip. Once lost, you still must survive long enough to find your way out again, or until you can be rescued. Also, it is always possible to get caught in the wilderness, or up on a mountain, by a raging blizzard. Once you are snowed in, you must continue to survive until you can get back to civilization, or until civilization can come to your rescue.

The reasons listed above are the main reasons why it is to your advantage to study and learn cold weather survival techniques, but there are other reasons. Knowing how to keep yourself alive with a minimum of equipment and supplies in a wintry environment, and knowing that you know, will give you a wonderful sense of confidence and independence.

In addition to the above, there are long-shot reasons for learning winter survival. These are the things which just never will happen to you—or will they? Could your automobile ever get caught in a blizzard far from any town or city? It has happened to lots of people. It could just happen to you. Airlines now fly the "great circle" routes between the United States and other places. These are sometimes called the polar routes. The great circle route is the straight line which a rubber band will make over a globe when you stretch the rubber band between two cities. A flight between Chicago and London passes over Goose Bay in Labrador. A flight between Seattle and Copenhagen passes over Greenland, not too far from the North Pole, as well as over the Northwest Territories of Canada and over Baffin Island. A flight between San Francisco and Tokyo passes over the Aleutian Islands. You could conceivably be a passenger on such a flight, and the plane could conceivably be forced down in a northern wilderness. It has happened before and will undoubtedly happen again. If you are lucky enough to survive the crash, you should be skillful and willful enough to survive the wait until you are rescued. Also, under the category of long shots, there could be a nuclear war. In the grim aftermath of such a catastrophic event, if you were lucky enough to survive intact, you could be faced with long winters without coal, oil, or electricity, and with a completely disrupted food distribution system. Once the finely woven fabric of civilization is torn, we are reduced to elemental things such as survival itself.

Hopefully, you will never be on a plane which crashes in the arctic and, hopefully, there will never be a nuclear war. The survival techniques and information in this chapter are therefore written from the viewpoint of being most useful to someone lost in the wilderness in cold weather.

General Preparation

You should not go into the woods with the intention of getting lost. Quite the contrary, you should make every effort to navigate accurately and not to get lost. But it is something which nevertheless can happen, and it is possible to prepare for it.

Always carry a few more items of food than you think you will need. A few candy bars can be a great comfort to a lost hunter. A small can of tuna can be tucked away in the pack. Small cans of pemmican are sometimes sold in sporting goods stores for use as emergency rations.

Always carry at least one knife. Even if you don't like to carry a sheath knife, be sure to have a small folding knife in your pocket. Survival is always somehow possible with a knife. Without it, it is improbable.

Always carry a length of nylon fishing line (braided nylon —not monofilament). This can be used not only for fishing, but for making snares, tying things, etc. And don't carry just a short length of nylon line. Take along a ball of it fifty yards long. Then you know you will have enough. To keep the ball from unraveling, put some pieces of plastic tape around it. A fifty-yard ball of line is not large. It is quite small.

Always have enough matches, and always have some of your matches in a waterproof container. A good waterproof container is an excellent long-term investment. I've got a Marbles waterproof match container which I bought so long ago that it seems I've had it always. I've even used matches from it on several occasions, and I've been very glad to have dry matches on those occasions.

On page 38 of this book is a list of ten essentials for mountaineers. These are items of equipment which should always be brought along on winter expeditions even at lower elevations.

The Will to Live

Having equipment and supplies along will assist you in the grim task of survival. But the most important element required to survive is the will to live. Courage in the face of adversity, determination never to surrender yourself to circumstances, and just plain guts, are the things that will bring you through from there to here.

Sitting in a warm and comfortable room as you read this, you may belittle the psychological aspects of survival. You may say that everybody has the will to live. Under comfortable circumstances, this is true, but in the harsh environment of zero weather, low or absent food supplies, and fatigue and hopelessness derived from panic, confusion, and disorganization, it becomes easy to say, "What's the use?" Loneliness may also be a depressant, although this varies very much with the individual.

Yes, it is possible to be gradually defeated, gradually and imperceptibly, until the point is reached where there is no more will to live, until there does not seem to be any great difference between surrendering and not surrendering, until indeed, in one form or another, the thought occurs: "To be or not to be: that is the question."

Unfortunately, there is no way to intellectualize on living in such a way as to make it everlastingly attractive. A groom about to go to bed with his bride on the first night of his honeymoon has an absolute will to live. He has much to live for, and it is immediately there. It is something else altogether to be freezing painfully to death and starving at the same time, alone, with no hope for bettering the situation. Under such circumstances, no matter how much one may have philosophized on the attractiveness of living, death begins to have attractions of its own, and like a tired man desiring sleep, a suffering man may welcome any end to his suffering, even a permanent end.

One of the ways to try to prepare in advance for survival is to know that it is possible for the will to live to fade away. Just being aware of this possibility may help in keeping it alive. Accept that you may be defeated, but refuse to accept surrender. Try to avoid panic first by acting slowly and deliberately in all that you do and, second, by establishing a daily routine. Then, to avoid resignation, make plans for what you will do after you have been rescued, or after you find your own way out. Visualize the first meal you will have when you can get home or to a good restaurant. Think of your wife or your girl friend (or of both, if both you have) and visualize yourself back together with her. Think of someone who hates you and would like to see you dead, if there is such a person, and visualize how disappointed he will be to see you alive again. Try to create strong emotions that will keep the will to live alive within you.

And remember, no matter how much bad luck you run into, there has to be an end. Sooner or later your luck will change for the better. The following is a "survival" type of poem which I wrote when I was in my profound teens, which tries to say this.

> Circumstances weighed me down.
> I sagged down on one knee.
> But I stood up erect again.
> No crawling gait for me!
>
> Then Fate struck hard and smashed me down,
> And I was still and prone.
> But I arose and travelled on.
> My will was still my own!
>
> Then Circumstance and Fate combined,
> And savage lightning struck at me.
> Bruised and burned, but still alive,
> I wondered what the worst would be.
>
> But Fate and Circumstance now left,
> To elsewhere find more willing prey,
> And I am still upon my feet,
> And I am still upon my way!

SUN GOGGLES

Snow Blindness, Frostbite, and Freezing

The three most obvious hazards to reckon with in an arctic environment are snow blindness, frostbite, and cold exhaustion, or freezing.*

Snow blindness is caused by glare from snow. If the ground is completely covered with snow and the sun is shining, the danger of snow blindness is very great, but snow

---

* I have been out in some very cold weather and I have experienced mild degrees of snow blindness, frostbite, and cold exhaustion, and so I am familiar with these things from personal experience. But not being a medical doctor, I sought out authoritative information which had been approved by doctors. My sources of information for this section are the following: *The Ship's Medicine Chest and First Aid at Sea* published by the U.S. Public Health Service; and *Field Manual 21–76*, titled *Survival*, published by the U.S. Department of the Army.

blindness may be caused by glare from snow even on a cloudy or foggy day.

Snow blindness is prevented by wearing sun goggles at all times during daylight hours. If you do not have sun goggles, you can make a pair by cutting narrow slits in wood, leather, plastic, or whatever you happen to have around. Darken the makeshift goggles by rubbing charcoal on them. It also helps to darken your nose and cheeks with charcoal, soot, or dark-colored mud.

An obvious symptom of snow blindness is a burning feeling in the eyes combined with a "grainy" or "sandy" feeling. Also, along with this, there may be difficulty in discerning high and low spots in the snow. If you think you are in a white-out, be sure to protect your eyes. When everything appears uniformly white, and the ground appears uniformly level, it may be a genuine white-out, or it may be an early symptom of snow blindness.

The only cure for snow blindness is absence of light. Being up and about only at night is one way to accomplish this. If there is more than one person involved, it may be possible to blindfold the victim of snow blindness during the daylight hours.

There is no such thing as getting used to the glare from snow. Rather than help ward off a second attack of snow blindness, the first attack makes the victim more susceptible than he was before his first attack. Each succeeding attack of snow blindness makes the next one easier and more likely to happen. The best way to handle snow blindness is to know what causes it and never to let it happen.

Frostbite occurs when the temperature in some body area is lowered so much that blood circulation and lymph circulation slow down and stop. Once circulation stops in that area, not only is there no more warming effect from the blood, but there is also no more nourishment. The cells in that area die.

Wind, combined with very low temperatures, usually causes frostbite. The likeliest places for frostbite to occur are the fingers and toes. Next likeliest are the ears, cheeks, and the heel of the foot.

Frostbite may sometimes cause pain, but more often than not, it occurs without any special pain. A sure symptom is coldness plus lack of feeling. Also, if you can see the area, it looks white or gray.

Frostbite should be treated with warmth. *Never rub snow or ice on any frostbitten area!* Frozen flesh bruises very easily. Rather, try to warm it gradually and steadily. A sure sign of frostbite is severe pain in the area once it has been warmed and once feeling begins to return to it. If warmth causes only a tingling feeling, then the area was cold, but not frostbitten.

Activity will help to prevent frostbite. If you run around, jump up and down, do knee bends, or any other kind of physical exercise, this will warm the body and increase blood circulation. If you are too fatigued to do this, wiggle your toes within your boots and your fingers within your gloves. If you have a fire going, use heat from the fire to warm your feet and hands.

The danger from extreme frostbite is gangrene. But even mild frostbite will kill outer layers of the skin. After the frostbite has been warmed and treated, the skin may blister and peel in a day or two. Do not break open any blisters. Do not peel any skin away. Let these things happen in their own time. Keep these areas as warm and clean as possible until the new skin can grow in.

In addition to frostbite, there may be general freezing of the entire body. This is sometimes called "cold exhaustion," sometimes called "exposure," and sometimes called just plain "freezing to death."

Prolonged exposure to very low temperatures, especially combined with a chilling wind, will eventually work to reduce the body temperature to below 98.6 degrees. An inadequate diet and fatigue will work to accelerate this process. Early symptoms of freezing are shivering and stiffness. The body feels painfully cold and most movement requires an effort of will. As the freezing continues, the sight becomes dim, the shivering stops, movement becomes almost impossible, even with the will to do so, and a general numbness and stiffness overcome the body. The body no longer feels cold, but feels

GROUND TO AIR EMERGENCY CODE

I	REQUIRE DOCTOR, SERIOUS INJURIES	K	INDICATE DIRECTION TO PROCEED
II	REQUIRE MEDICAL SUPPLIES	↑	AM PROCEEDING IN THIS DIRECTION
X	UNABLE TO PROCEED	LL	ALL WELL
F	REQUIRE FOOD AND WATER	N	NO
≫	REQUIRE FIREARMS AND AMMUNITION	Y	YES
□	REQUIRE MAP AND COMPASS	⌐	NOT UNDERSTOOD

actually warm. An irresistible drowsiness and numbness permeate the victim, despite his stiffness, and he goes comfortably to sleep, never to awaken.

The only defense against freezing is heat. This means, first of all, having an adequate diet, if possible, with adequate calories. It also means getting sufficient rest and sleep so that body metabolism may function normally. Next it means being dressed warmly so that body heat is not lost at too rapid a rate. In addition to clothing, it means having shelter from the wind and weather. Redundant though it may sound, the way not to freeze is to keep as warm as possible; the way to treat someone who is suffering from cold exhaustion is to warm him up. A person who has been frozen should be warmed gradually and steadily until he is warm enough to shiver and to feel cold again. Then, all such cold victims should be treated for shock.

Signaling for Help

Modern life being what it is, if you get lost in the wilderness someone will know you are missing and a search will be organized. But one man, or even several men, may be very hard to see and to find.

Since aircraft are used so much these days in search and rescue operations, you should keep in mind that whatever you can do to make yourself more visible from the air should be done as soon as possible.

If you are in an area where large expanses of open snow are visible to the air, you can make letters and words in the snow by tramping them out. Make your letters as large as space permits. What may ordinarily seem large to you may be too small to be visible from an aircraft. Make your letters thirty feet high, even fifty feet high if you have the space, and leave ten-foot spaces between the letters. Tramp out either HELP or SOS.

The following ground-to-air signals are included in the U.S. Army Field Manual on *Survival:*

In addition to the ground-to-air signals tramped out in the

MORSE CODE

A	•—		**N**	—•
B	—•••		**O**	———
C	—•—•		**P**	•——•
D	—••		**Q**	——•—
E	•		**R**	•—•
F	••—•		**S**	•••
G	——•		**T**	—
H	••••		**U**	••—
I	••		**V**	•••—
J	•———		**W**	•——
K	—•—		**X**	—••—
L	•—••		**Y**	—•——
M	——		**Z**	——••

snow, lay brightly colored pieces of cloth on the ground where they can be seen from above. If you see an aircraft flying by and it seems low enough to see you, wave the brightly colored cloth like a flag. Also, wear conspicuous clothing. If you have a bright-colored garment, wear it outside your other clothing if you can.

If you have a fire going, keep some damp wood or damp leaves near it. If an aircraft looks as if it may pass reasonably close to your position, put the damp materials on the fire so that they can produce smoke. Smoke coming from an uninhabited area in the wilderness will attract the pilot's attention. If you are in a location for several days and you notice a scheduled airliner passing you at the same time each day, prepare your fire in advance so that it is already smoking when the airliner goes by the next day.

A mirror, or even the polished surfaces of an empty tin can, can reflect sunlight and be seen from a very great distance. Try to reflect sunlight on passing aircraft.

At night, use your flashlight. Flash three dots (quick flashes), then three dashes (long flashes), and then three dots again. This is SOS in international Morse code, and it is a universally recognized distress signal. If an aircraft flies close by at night, or in twilight, you may even be able to give the pilot a message. On page 247 is international Morse code.

It is a great help if you can memorize the international Morse code. Learning it can be made into a game in which two people practice at the same time by sending signals to each other with flashlights. But even if you do not memorize this code, it is a good idea to have a copy of it along with you in the woods.

Get a 3 × 5 inch piece of file card, or any other reasonably heavy or durable piece of paper and copy the international Morse code down with laundry ink, indelible pencil, or other durable means of writing which will not be obliterated or smeared if it gets wet. Then put the code in one of the side pockets of your pack and keep it there. If you ever need it, you'll have it with you.

Just to be doubly safe, copy down the ground-to-air signals on the back of the same piece of paper.

Shelters, Igloos, and Ice Caves

Cold kills. In order to survive in an arctic climate, it is necessary to keep warm. In still air, your clothing alone may be able to keep your body heat in the immediate vicinity of your body. But still air is something you cannot depend on. The wind may blow. It usually does. A combination of low temperatures and high wind will chill you quickly. It is absolutely necessary to be able to get out of the wind when the temperature is low. The obvious way to do this is to build a shelter. A shelter will not only protect you from the wind, but it may, if it is properly constructed and utilized, provide you with a considerably warmer environment than the outside air. Heat loss through your clothing may be retained in an enclosed shelter. If there is less of a temperature differential between your body and the air next to your outer clothing, your clothing will retain more of your body heat, and you will be warmer.

Various types of shelters can be constructed, depending on the circumstances, the terrain, the amount of the snow cover, and the amount of other materials (such as wood) which are available.

If you have a hatchet along, or a small saw, and if there is wood around, it is not difficult to build a shelter made of wood. If you don't have these tools, use your knife.

Much has been written about using a lean-to as a temporary shelter, but I fail to see what kind of shelter a lean-to provides. It is not shelter from the wind since it has one wall only and every wind changes direction sooner or later. A lean-to will not hold warm air, since it has no roof and no side walls. Also, since it has no roof or walls, it is not a shelter against falling snow. A lean-to is made by setting a horizontal pole (limb) between two closely-located trees among sup-

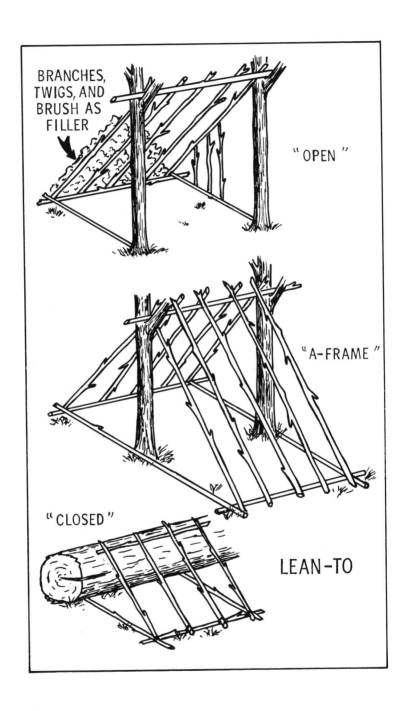

BRANCHES, TWIGS, AND BRUSH AS FILLER

"OPEN"

"A-FRAME"

"CLOSED"

LEAN-TO

porting branches in the two trees at a height of five, six, or seven feet from the ground. Straight or near-straight poles (or limbs) are then leaned from the ground against the horizontal pole at an angle of about 45 degrees from the ground. The spaces between the leaning poles are then filled in with branches holding dead leaves, with twigs, or with any other available material.

A lean-to may be constructed without too much trouble, but on the other hand, it may not be worth the trouble to construct it.

A far better shelter can be made by building a double lean-to, and then building a closed-in wall on one or both ends.

To do this, build a lean-to as already described. Then, using the same horizontal pole, build another lean-to in the opposite direction. When this is complete, you will have a type of A-frame construction, but each end will be open. Close in one end completely by leaning several poles from the ground up to the tree at one end of the shelter and then by covering these poles in the same manner in which the side walls were covered. If evergreen trees are in the area, all the walls can be "shingled" from the ground up to the roof. Lay the branches so that the needles point downward. Work from the ground up, and not vice versa, so that as the layers of evergreen branches overlap, the upper ones always cover the lower ones.

The other end, or open end, of the shelter can be left open, partially closed in, or closed in fairly completely, depending on how and where you will make a fire.

If the terrain is wooded, but hilly or rocky, it may be possible to build a lean-to type of shelter against a steep embankment, or against a large boulder, or between two large boulders. Imagination and ingenuity have to be put to work to take advantage of whatever resources are at hand. But no matter how or where the wooden shelter is built, it should be more than just a crude structure, suitable perhaps for a Neanderthal man. It should be closed in enough to do the job for which it was intended. That is, it should be a shelter.

In the heavily-forested areas of the northwest, where trees grow to quite large diameters, it is not uncommon to find very long logs on the ground which at their stump end may be six, seven, or more feet in diameter. These logs decay very slowly, and it is decades before they are absorbed into the forest floor. A lean-to can be made against one of these fallen giants, and then closed in at one or both ends. If there is sufficient depth of snow, and there usually is in the mountains of the northwest, a snow cave can be made by tunneling down next to one of these logs and using the log itself as one of the walls of the cave.

Snow caves, more usually, are dug in glaciers, on the higher slopes of mountains. A snow cave may be dug anywhere, however. A snow cave is a temporary shelter. When a blizzard threatens, or is already there, digging a snow cave may save your life. You pick a snowdrift, or a place on the glacier, if that's where you are, and you start digging.

I have long been an advocate of bringing along a garden trowel on winter trips. A hand trowel is light but strong. Digging snow with the hands soon makes for wet gloves and frozen fingers. Sometimes, in packed snow, it is not even possible to dig with the hands. But with a hand trowel you can chop away and dig away as deeply as you please. If you do not have a hand trowel, a stick may be used to loosen the snow, or a knife, after which it can be kicked away with the boots.

In digging a snow cave, you select a drift and dig into the bottom of it. If on a glacier, select the base of a short but steep snow pitch. Dig horizontally until you have a hole about three feet in diameter. When you have tunneled in several feet, change direction and dig upward at a 45-degree angle. Then, when the bottom of your tunnel is high enough to be higher than the top of the tunnel at the entrance level, stop digging upward and enlarge the area by either tunneling straight ahead further, or off to both sides. Level off a platform where you can stretch out and rest. Tamp down the area on the entrance side of the platform so that you are able to sit on the platform and put your feet down. In doing all this digging, you will have left the cave several times to get rid of the snow you had to remove. You should therefore have some kind of idea as to where the inner room in the cave is in relation to the surface

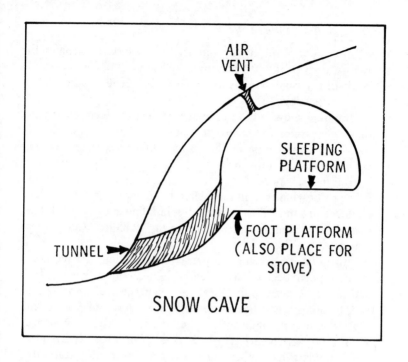

AIR
VENT

SLEEPING
PLATFORM

FOOT PLATFORM
(ALSO PLACE FOR
STOVE)

TUNNEL

SNOW CAVE

of the snow slope above it. It is necessary now to poke a hole in the roof for ventilation. This can be done with the shaft of the ice axe, with a stick, or with the hand trowel. A one-inch hole is all that is necessary. The hole should not be poked through the highest part of the roof, but somewhat lower, and on the side toward the entrance. In getting rid of the last amounts of excess snow, these can be built up around the entrance to close most of it off. An opening should be left, however, for ventilation.

Once the cave is dug, lay out your equipment on the sleeping platform. You can sleep on your skis, snowshoes, or whatever else you have. Put your waterproof plastic ground cloth down so that it is between you and the snow.

When you make a fire, keep your stove down on the lower level where you have tamped out a place for your feet. You can cook over the stove, heat water for coffee, cocoa, or whatever you want, or just burn it for warmth. It is somewhat awkward to cook with the stove below you, but it makes the inside of the cave much warmer if you keep the stove at as low a level as possible.

Building snow caves and living in them for several days at a time is a part of the standard training received by soldiers in the Swiss army. Snug in their alpine bivouacs, they wait out whatever storms come their way.

But it is not necessary to be on a mountain or among snow-drifts to be able to build a shelter from snow. It can be done on level ground. This is done by building an igloo. "Igloo" comes from the Eskimo word *igdlu*, which means "snow house."

An igloo is a strong and permanent dwelling. I have heard about a polar bear climbing on an igloo without caving it in, and polar bears are quite heavy. When the seal hunting gets bad, Eskimos leave their igloo settlements and move on to find a place where the hunting will be better. There are reports of such igloo settlements remaining erect for several years after their builders have abandoned them. This demonstrates the durability of igloos. Inside, igloos are cozy and warm. Eskimos may live in them for weeks or months at a time during which time the temperatures outside may reach as low as 60 degrees below zero Fahrenheit.

An igloo provides warmth because snow is a good insulator. The thicker the walls of the igloo, the warmer the igloo will be. Ice should not be used for constructing an igloo, nor even snow which is very compact. It is the air trapped in snow which does the insulating, and the looser the snow, the better the igloo. An inhabited igloo melts on the inside from heat generated from people and from fires. This melted snow soaks into the dry snow around it and refreezes. It is this snow and ice mixture which gives igloos so much of their strength.

If additional snow falls after the igloo is built, this thickens the igloo walls and makes them stronger and warmer.

There are many ways to build an igloo, just as there are many ways to build a house out of wood. Igloos may be large or small, thick or thin, and high or low. Basically, an igloo is a

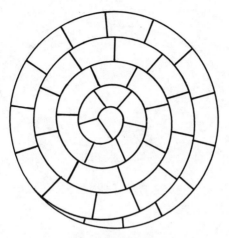

SINGLE SPIRAL

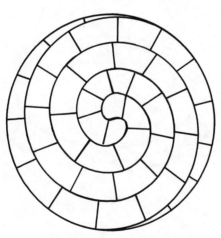

DOUBLE SPIRAL

IGLOO (TOP VIEW)

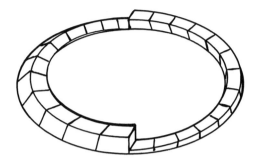

START OF DOUBLE SPIRAL

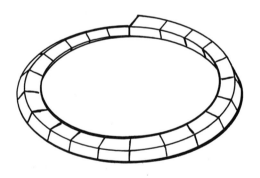

START OF SINGLE SPIRAL

hemisphere, or a dome. Outdoorsmen have experimented with A-frame type igloos, with pyramid shaped igloos, and with other configurations, but the dome still remains the best, strongest, warmest, and most durable design.

One man alone can build an igloo, but it is much easier if there are two or more people to do the work.

A common mistake is to make the igloo too small. If you are travelling, and will spend only one or two nights in the igloo, a small one will do. But if you know you will be staying in one place for some length of time, it is worth the extra work to build a more spacious igloo.

A six-foot inside diameter may be adequate for two men for one night. A ten-foot inside diameter will make a far more comfortable snow home.

Unfortunately, tools are required to build an igloo and without these tools it is difficult. A machete, really a tropical tool, is excellent for igloo building. A long carving knife and a saw are also excellent for this purpose. But these are not likely to be items included in a hunting trip, or even in a backpacking trip. Also excellent would be one of the older type bayonets having a length of twelve to eighteen inches. In an

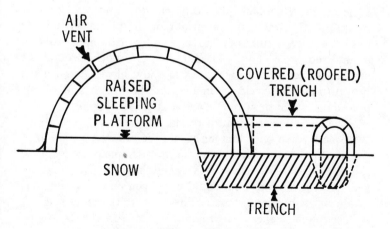

Side view of igloo and door tunnel

emergency, an ordinary short knife can be used, and a stick about two feet long. Where life and death hang in the balance, use whatever is available including a hand trowel, the tail end of a ski, a ski pole with the disk removed, an ice axe, an unrolled empty tin can, or whatever you can think of that is handy. A small, crudely built igloo is better than no igloo at all.

Construction of the igloo can be done at ground level, but you will have a warmer igloo if you raise the floor above the ground. This is done by making a circular pile of snow at the site where you will build your igloo. Not only can this snow be used to raise the floor level for greater interior warmth, but you can stand on this snow when you place your upper level snow blocks.

Decide on an interior (not exterior) diameter, and start laying snow blocks in a complete circle around your interior diameter line. Do not leave an opening for the door. The door should be cut out later.

Let us say we will build a small igloo, and we want an inside diameter of seven feet. Draw a seven-foot circle in the snow. Now place a circle of snow blocks next to each other so that their inner edges are on the line. Use snow blocks about a foot square to a foot and a half square. At two opposite points on the circle, the blocks should be cut down until they are at ground level. Gradually the height of the blocks should rise until they are a full foot or foot and a half high, halfway around the circle. This is like building two ramps around the circle. As each of the two rows of snow blocks completes a half turn of the circle, it encounters the lowest end of the preceding row of snow blocks and it builds right up on it.

The basic construction of the igloo, in other words, is like two spirals, each one climbing up on the other. A variation of this is to use one spiral only for the complete circle. Two spirals, however, are better than a single spiral because you can get a steeper pitch to your spiral when you raise it to the same height in half the distance. This is better engineering. A steeper pitch makes construction easier for the following reason: As you build the igloo up, you also lean the wall inward to achieve your eventual dome shape. A block of snow placed on top of another block of snow only has contact along its bottom edge. If it is leaned in too steeply, it will simply fall off the block below it unless it has some other support. This other support comes from the snow block making contact with the block on its side. It is lateral contact with the preceding block in the row which permits a snow block to lean in towards the center without falling down.

There is an additional advantage to using a double spiral rather than a single spiral. A single spiral ends at the center of the dome. To close the hole in the roof, and to give support to the entire structure a "king block" or "key block" is required. A double structure, on the other hand, runs into itself and the need for a key block is eliminated.

When blocks of snow are placed, the thin spots between blocks are mortared in with soft snow. This should be done on both the inner and outer surfaces. Cutting and trimming is done with each block to make sure it fits properly with the block below it and with the block next to it. Don't be afraid to let loose snow fall inside the circle. This helps to build up the floor level.

When the wall height is about half-way up, select an area for cutting out the door. This should be in a place where it is 90 degrees to the direction of the prevailing wind. Reinforce the area where the door will be by mortaring loose snow into all the chinks, and reinforce the area above it. Then cut out the door area.

If the floor is at a higher level than the snow outside, continue cutting snow away beyond the door until you have a semicircular clearing inside the igloo just inside the door. Later on, when the igloo is complete, you can sit on the raised platform and put your feet down into this lowered area. This area can also be used for storage.

Once the igloo is completely closed in, you can see from the inside where all the thin spots are because daylight will shine brightly through these thin spots. Use snow, and mortar these thin spots from the inside and from the outside to thicken them.

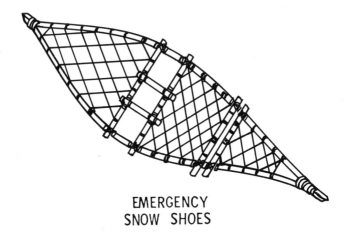

EMERGENCY
SNOW SHOES

You may or may not want to build a snow tunnel. If the weather is severe, it is a good idea to build one. Build it around the door opening and extend it out several feet. You will have a warmer igloo if you build a longer snow tunnel from the door, and build a curve into it so that the wind cannot blast directly into the igloo through the door. A good way to build a tunnel is to dig a trench first, leading away from the door of the igloo. Use the snow removed from the trench to build up the sides of the trench, and to roof the tunnel (trench) over. If your entrance tunnel is at least partly below the ground level, and the inside igloo floor is at least partly above the ground level, you will have a warmer igloo.

Last, but not least, make a ventilation hole in your igloo. Use your ice axe or a stick, and with a screwing motion, drill a hole through the roof somewhat below the center, and on the side away from the door.

After you have lived in your igloo the first night, it will already be stronger than when you built it because of melting from heat in the igloo and subsequent refreezing. On the second day you can add snow to the outside wherever you think this will do some good, and to the top blocks, which you probably placed very gingerly and with a minimum of mortaring. Each day you live in it, the igloo grows stronger and after several days it is quite a sturdy structure. Pile loose snow as deeply as you please right over your ventilation hole in the roof and redrill your hole all the way through to the outside.

It is true you will lose some heat through the ventilation hole, but you will lose less than you think. When there is any kind of a fire in them, igloos are amazingly warm. If you do use a stove, or burn anything at all in the igloo, you will need the ventilation hole to make sure you are not overcome by noxious gasses.

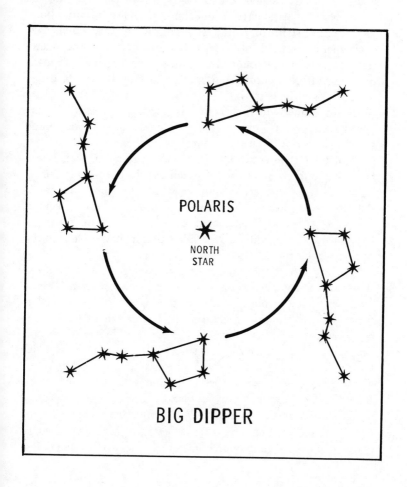

POLARIS

★

NORTH
STAR

BIG DIPPER

Emergency Travel

It is impossible to travel over deep, powdered snow in plain boots. If you already have skis or snowshoes with you, your travel problem is solved. If you do not have snowshoes, you can make a pair if you have enough cord of some kind. Cut two four- or five-foot lengths of willow, alder, or other green wood. Tie them together at each end. Pull them about a foot apart and tie in one-foot long separator rods where your toe and heel will go, which is forward of the center. Webbing can be made from parachute shroud lines, if there are any about, from tearing strips of cloth, from empty tin cans which have been opened and cut into one-inch strips, or from other material you may have around. In a pinch, webbing may be made by tying in more short lengths of willow or alder in a crosswise or crisscross pattern.

Determining which direction is north is necessary if you plan to travel with any degree of accuracy, but determining which way is north without a compass is difficult.

North of the Arctic Circle, Polaris, the north star, is too far directly overhead to be of much use. In the "lower forty-eight," Polaris is a perfect indicator. Keep in mind that while Polaris remains in one place, the big dipper does not; it rotates completely around Polaris once every twenty-four hours. In looking for the big dipper remember that it may be low in the northern sky or it may be directly overhead.

In the daytime the sun can be used to determine directions. If you have a watch, point your hour hand at the sun. Halfway between the hour hand and the twelve on your dial is south. Do not use this method shortly after sunrise or shortly before sunset. At these times of the day use the sun itself and simply remember that the sun rises in the east and sets in the west.

As you travel, remember that one of the contributing factors to cold exhaustion is fatigue. Do not put off sleep until you are exhausted. Stop to rest. Take a short nap while you are resting. Take frequent naps. It is better to wake up from a short nap chilled and cold but rested, than to keep moving

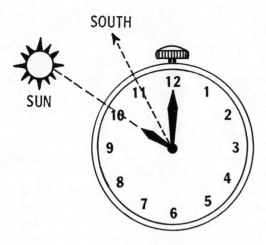

Finding south with a watch and the sun

until you are so tired that when you do go to sleep you never wake up at all.

Animals and Survival

If you are lost in the wilderness in the winter, there are two potential relationships you can have with animals. They can eat you, or you can eat them. Almost universally, animals are afraid of men, and very likely you will not have to defend yourself from an animal. Even the largest animals will smell you and try to avoid you. However, in the woods you can never be positive about anything. Human beings have been attacked by bears, wolves, mountain lions, wolverines, and other animals, including moose, and such occurences may well happen again.

Bears hibernate in the wintertime. But they are awake and at large in the northland in the fall and in the spring. Also, in summer mountaineering, it may be necessary to pass through lower forest growths before getting up the mountain to where the snow is.

The possibility of meeting a bear in the woods is always an exciting one. Seeing a bear, as I have done several times (each time unarmed), when there are no steel bars between you and the bear is thrilling, to say the least. In such a situation the thought invariably occurs: What would happen if the bear decided to attack?

The mere fact that you and the bear have suddenly confronted each other without warning means the bear must be just as surprised as you are. Surprise is an emotion. Rational and intelligent human beings will do unpredictable things when they act emotionally. What about a bear?

The dyed-in-the-wool conservationist who believes that bears should never be harmed under any circumstances has probably never had to stand his ground in the woods and stare a bear down. In my own mind I've already decided that even though I may have no chance to win, I'm going to fight to prevent becoming a meal. A seven-hundred-pound grizzly and a two-hundred-pound man are an uneven match. But, by George, I figure I'll at least let that bear taste the spike end of my ice axe just as hard as I can push it down his throat before he gets a taste of me.

Indians have killed bears with nothing more than a spear. They have worn the grizzly's claws as a necklace with great pride, as well they might. My fellow Latvian Alex Siemel has killed many jaguars in South America with a spear. When I asked him how difficult this was, he said it was easy, the most difficult part being to bring yourself to face a charging jaguar with only a spear.

A spear is an excellent defensive weapon. A spear is easy to make. All you need is a reasonably straight sapling seven to nine feet long. Sharpen the thicker end with your knife, cut away the side branches, and you have a genuine spear in your hand. The way to use a spear defensively is to keep it in your hands and thrust with it. Do not throw it.

The knife itself is a defensive weapon. A hatchet is an even better defensive weapon. But the best defense is the one maintained farthest from you. Because of this, a spear is ideal for defense.

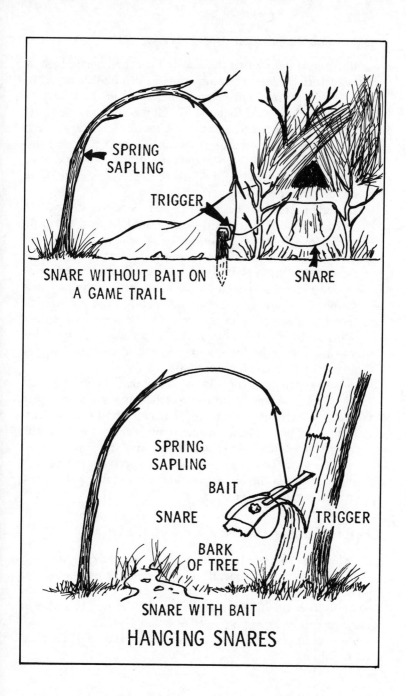

SPRING
SAPLING

TRIGGER

SNARE WITHOUT BAIT ON
A GAME TRAIL

SNARE

SPRING
SAPLING

BAIT

SNARE

TRIGGER

BARK
OF TREE

SNARE WITH BAIT

HANGING SNARES

But man is more often the hunter than the hunted. Lost in the wilderness without firearms, how can you find an animal to eat? Bears, squirrels, and marmots hibernate in the winter in the north, and can't be found at all. However, many northern animals do not hibernate, and may be found right through the winter. These include rabbits, porcupines, wolves, foxes, and ptarmigans, which are a northern variety of grouse and have feathers on their legs. Most of these northern animals have white fur or white feathers in the winter.

Porcupines feed on bark and if you see wood stripped of bark it is a good sign that a porcupine may be in the area. If there is snow, follow his footprints and when you find him, spear him. Do not pick up a porcupine or any other animal unless you are sure it is dead. Even a wounded rabbit can give you quite a bite if it suddenly comes alive after you thought it was dead. All mammals are good to eat, but avoid getting sick from eating diseased animals. Always cook them thoroughly.

Do not throw away any part of an animal. Save the skins for warmth. Save the entrails for use as bait in a snare, or for fishing. Save the bones for use as tools.

Snares are an excellent way to catch animals. Once they are set, you need not remain in the area but may go about other business. A snare may be set along an animal trail without bait. If a bird, rabbit, or other animal comes along the trail, the snare may catch him just because he is passing through.

If snares use bait, they may be set anywhere where it is possible or likely that an animal may be caught, and do not have to be set along game trails.

Winter Fishing

The lakes and ponds of the northern United States and of Canada and Alaska frequently hold grayling, trout, whitefish, pike, and ling. Northern rivers may contain salmon and sturgeon. River snails and fresh water periwinkles may be found in the lakes and streams of northern forests.

Snails and periwinkles may be simply picked up where they are found.

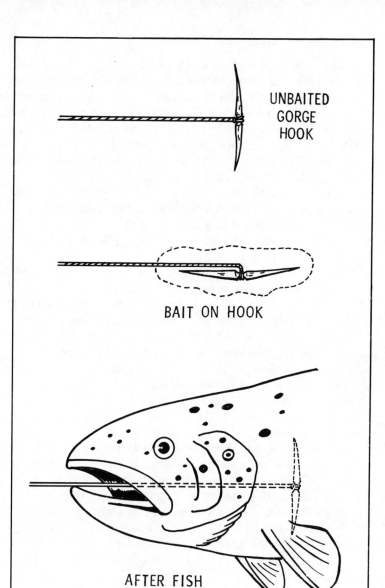

UNBAITED
GORGE
HOOK

BAIT ON HOOK

AFTER FISH
SWALLOWS BAIT

Fish may be speared, shot, caught by hand, or stunned with a rock or a club. Before spearing for fish, lower your spear into the water slowly and note how refraction causes the spear to seem to be bent at the point where it enters the water. Memorize the extent of the angle of the bend. Then when you do see a fish and are ready to thrust your spear at him, correct for the refraction error, and thrust quickly and suddenly at where the fish actually is and not at where he seems to be.

The best fishing hooks are, of course, factory-made steel hooks with barbs. These hooks are small, light, and strong, and they do the job for which they were designed. They catch fish. If you have fishhooks along, your fishhook problem is solved. Just use them.

If you do not have a fishhook, you can improvise one by making a stomach hook, or gorge hook. This may be made from a piece of steel, fresh green wood, bone, or any other suitable material at hand. Make it about an inch long (two inches long for large fish), and sharpen both ends. Tie the line to the center of this hook, then turn it parallel to the line and insert a large enough piece of bait onto it to cover it completely. Once a fish has eaten the bait, the hook swings crosswise in the fish's stomach and holds the fish tight.

Deciding on what to use for bait can be a problem. Use animal entrails if you can't get anything else. Once you have caught your first fish, cut open his stomach and see if you can determine what he has been feeding on. If you can get this, use it as bait. If you can't determine anything from examining the fish's stomach, try using the entrails of the fish, or a cut piece of the fish itself. Sometimes northern fish will strike at anything that shines which they see moving in the water. Cut out a small piece of tin can and fasten it near the hook so that it can reflect light. If you have nothing else, try using a small piece of cloth for bait.

On a frozen lake, chop a hole in the ice and try fishing right through the ice. Since the fish will probably congregate in the deepest part of the lake, chop your hole near the middle of the lake.

You can construct a so-called "lazy fisherman" to do your

LAZY FISHERMAN

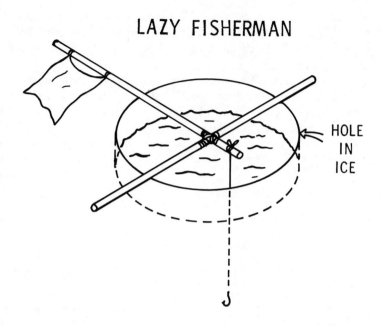

HOLE
IN
ICE

fishing for you while you tend to other business or keep warm by a fire on the shore. To construct a lazy fisherman, you need a flagpole and a hinge pole. The hinge pole should be at least twice as long as the size of your hole in the ice. The flagpole can be somewhat shorter. The two poles are tied together at the exact center of the hinge pole in such a manner that the two poles are at an angle of 90 degrees from each other, and so that the lower end of the flagpole extends past the hinge pole for a distance which is less than the radius of the hole in the ice. The fishing line is tied to the lower end of the flagpole and lowered into the water. The hinge pole is then laid across the center of the hole in the ice. The flagpole lies on the ice at right angles to the hinge pole. If a fish takes the bait and pulls on the line, this pivots the flagpole, causing it to rise to a vertical position. When you see the flagpole of the lazy fisherman in a vertical position, you simply go out on the ice, remove the fish, rebait the hook, and lower it into the water again.

The flagpole can be seen when it is in a vertical position even if it has no "flag" on it. But for easier visibility, you can fasten a bright-colored cloth or ribbon to the flagpole, if you have one available.

If the weather is extremely cold, any hole you make in the ice will tend to freeze over again if left alone. To prevent this, cover the hole with twigs and brush and then cover the twigs and brush with loose, powder snow.

Index